Pension Systems

Pension Systems
Beyond Mandatory Retirement

Edited by

Elsa Fornero

Professor of Economics, Faculty of Economics and Director, Center for Research on Pensions and Welfare Policies (CeRP), University of Turin

Paolo Sestito

Ministry of Labour and Social Policies, Government of Italy

Edward Elgar
Cheltenham, UK • Northampton, MA, USA

Published by
Edward Elgar Publishing Limited
Glensanda House
Montpellier Parade
Cheltenham
Glos GL50 1UA
UK

Edward Elgar Publishing, Inc.
136 West Street
Suite 202
Northampton
Massachusetts 01060
USA

A catalogue record for this book
is available from the British Library

Library of Congress Cataloguing in Publication Data

Pension systems : beyond mandatory retirement / edited by Elsa Fornero and Paolo Sestito.
     p. cm.
  "Papers presented at the fourth annual conference of CeRP, 'Is mandatory retirement an outdated feature of pension systems?' held on 16 September 2003 in Turin"–Acknowledgements.
  Includes bibliographical references and index.
  1. Old age pensions–Cross-cultural studies–Congresses. 2. Retirement income–Cross-cultural studies–Congresses. 3. Retirement, Mandatory–Cross-cultural studies–Congresses. I. Fornero, Elsa. II. Sestito, Paolo. III. Center for Research on Pensions and Welfare Policies (Turin, Italy)
  HD7105.3.P4577 2005
  331.25'2–dc22

2005040690

ISBN 1 84376 947 6

Printed and bound in Great Britain by MPG Books Ltd, Bodmin, Cornwall

Contents

Figures

Tables

Contributors

Michele Belloni	Center for Research on Pensions and Welfare Policies (CeRP)
Barbara Berkel	Mannheim Institute for the Economics of Aging (MEA), Mannheim University
Margherita Borella	Center for Research on Pensions and Welfare Policies (CeRP)
Axel Börsch-Supan	Mannheim Institute for the Economics of Aging (MEA), Mannheim University and National Bureau of Economic Research (NBER), Cambridge, MA, USA
Sarah Bridges	University of Nottingham
Peter Diamond	Massachusetts Institute of Technology
Richard Disney	University of Nottingham and Institute for Fiscal Studies, London
Elsa Fornero	Department of Economics, University of Turin and Center for Research on Pensions and Welfare Policies (CeRP)
Michael Hurd	RAND
Angelo Marano	Department of Economic Affairs, Prime Minister's Office, Government of Italy and University of Tuscia

Mauro Mastrogiacomo   Netherlands Bureau for Economic Policy Analysis (CPB)

Cathal O'Donoghue   National University of Ireland, Galway, ICER, CHILD and IZA

Paolo Sestito   Ministry of Labour and Social Policies, Government of Italy and Bank of Italy

Acknowledgments

This book is a collection of papers presented at the fourth annual conference of CeRP,[1] 'Is Mandatory Retirement an Outdated Feature of Pension Systems?', held on 16 September 2003 in Turin.

The editors would like to thank the participants at this conference for stimulating discussion and helpful suggestions. CeRP gratefully acknowledges financial support for this event – and, in general, for the activities of the center – by the Foundation Compagnia di San Paolo.

A debt of gratitude goes to all contributors for carefully revising their chapters to fit into the book structure and for patiently answering the questions raised during the editing process.

We would also like to thank Onorato Castellino for reading and reviewing some of the chapters, Matteo Migheli and Pietro Ortoleva for editorial assistance, Vincenzo Maio for formatting the final typescript of the book and Silvia Maero for supervising all the stages of the realization of the volume. As always, CeRP researchers provided important support and encouragement.

Elsa Fornero and Paolo Sestito

---

1. Center for Research on Pensions and Welfare Policies (http://cerp.unito.it).

1. Introduction

Elsa Fornero and Paolo Sestito

1.1 PENSION REFORMS: THE PENDULUM SWINGS FROM FINANCIAL SUSTAINABILITY TO SOCIAL ADEQUACY

In the course of the last two decades, the prospects of swift population aging have led to a lively debate about the rationale of mandatory pension systems and the appropriateness of their rules. The many (and sometimes hardly coherent) roles in which public schemes have, in many countries, actually been cast – from insurance provider to tax-transfer program, from industrial restructuring tool to instrument for labor market policy – have been reconsidered in order to enhance the system's main task as a device for transferring resources from the active to the old age-inactive part of the life cycle.

Radical design changes – like the shift from a Defined-Benefit Pay-as-You-Go (DB PAYG) to a Defined Contribution Fully Funded (DC FF) system – are rare, both because the latter's long run advantages are less clear-cut than originally hoped and because of the sizable transition costs; partial shifts are however quite frequent.[1] Recourse to mixed (*multi-pillar*) systems based on partial funding and the establishment of a stricter relationship between contributions and benefits at the individual level, up to the introduction of actuarial fairness elements in the pension formulas, have indeed become rather widespread.

In this process, while the cornerstone function of the PAYG system has been reaffirmed, stringent budget constraints have forcedly directed attention towards financial sustainability goals, often pursued through piecemeal interventions consisting of a combination of i) *cuts in benefits level*; ii) *increases in contribution rates* and iii) *restrictions in eligibility conditions* (McMorrow and Roeger, 2002). In the still predominantly DB schemes, these three reform options are (roughly) substitutes as far as the financial outlook is concerned. They however entail very different outcomes as instruments of a *retirement income policy*, that is in terms of their implied retirement incentive structure, distributional effects and impact on pensioners' standard of living.[2]

After a decade of interventions mainly driven by financial sustainability considerations, the focus of the reform process is now shifting towards the *social adequacy* of pension systems, that is their capability to provide the elderly with a decent standard of living. Although not a straightforward concept, since the living standards of the elderly do not depend exclusively upon their mandatory pension income and countries traditionally differ in the orientation of their welfare systems, *adequacy* has become a European goal,[3] competing somewhat with financial sustainability. It is therefore hardly surprising that the search for a way out from what appears – particularly in the short–medium run – as a painful trade off between financial and social goals is causing a reconsideration of the three above-mentioned policy options.

In this wider perspective, reliance on the *first* policy option – cuts in benefits level – beyond a reduction of overly generous pension benefits directed at some privileged groups, would inevitably endanger the adequacy objective. It is obviously possible to ensure a financial equilibrium through sufficiently large cuts, but this is hardly a socially and politically feasible solution, as reducing unitary benefits in order to spread given resources over a longer life would negatively affect consumption in retirement. A way out might of course be represented by encouraging accumulation of additional savings during people's working life, so as to compensate for the reduced benefits provided by the public mandatory schemes. This strategy, however, seems to ignore that the very reason behind the mandatory nature of the public system rests upon the individuals' 'inadequate preparation' for retirement (Diamond 2004), that is their lack of capability to make efficient choices leading to insufficient savings and the difficulties to annuitize the accumulated resources, whatever their level.

A more effective approach implies the compensation of the reductions of unitary benefits in existing DB PAYG systems with parallel recourse to compulsory participation in DC funded schemes. Such an approach may provide a short cut for the mixed system initially referred to, and also 'soften' transition problems; however, besides the need to take into account the relative weights and the interactions between the two 'pillars', there would still remain the issue of financing, particularly in countries relying heavily on PAYG, if the resources are not somehow increased, that is if the process does not lead to higher savings.

The *second* policy option – increase in contribution rates – has also been extensively used in the past. Devoting more resources (as measured, in aggregate terms, by the share of GDP absorbed by pensions and, possibly, old age-related health expenditures) to retirees in response to an increase in life expectancy might well represent a more correct solution than the mere cutting of benefits; payroll tax rates increases, however, imply placing the burden of the adjustment disproportionately on the younger (and the still to be born) cohorts. Moreover, it has to be acknowledged that in many countries, where the contribution rates are already relatively high (as it is often the case in Europe), such a policy is hardly feasible because of its likely negative effects on labor costs and firms' competitiveness.[4] So, while it could still make sense in some countries or for some categories of workers, it is far from being generally commendable.

This leaves the *third* option – raising the effective retirement age – as a potentially more effective instrument to promote adequacy without jeopardizing the financial sustainability of the system. Indeed, the goal – in the form of 5 years' average retirement postponement by 2010 – has been adopted by the EU in the 2002 Barcelona Summit. For current generations of workers, the measure can amount to a partial repayment of the implicit debt towards future cohorts by working longer, paying higher overall contributions and enjoying a reduced retirement period, and thus is easily interpreted as a heavily penalizing restriction, motivating a strong opposition. Of course, it need not be, depending on how the pension formulas adapt to changes in longevity patterns. In any case, for the young and future cohorts, the measure could not be interpreted as a restriction of previous promises, but as the 'natural' consequence of a longer lifespan.

1.2 WORKING LIFE EXTENSION AS THE CORNERSTONE OF RETIREMENT INCOME POLICIES

For an average individual an increase in longevity implies a reconsideration of labor supply and saving plans, that is a reallocation of the extra lifespan between work and non-work time (including retirement), and of the extra income between present and future consumption. This re-planning obviously does not imply the maintenance of the former (before the rise in longevity was known) ratio between working and retirement years.

In general, the allocation of the additional lifespan depends not only on the level of resources already accumulated for retirement and on the time path of earning opportunities, but also on uncertain life occurrences over the extra lifetime. Apart from the fact that the 'average' lifespan gain can be far from uniformly distributed, so that differences in expectations would affect the outcome, these occurrences prominently include health contingencies: the prospect of healthy aging would tilt the scale towards more work, while poor health could induce to accept a *ceteris paribus* lower lifetime income and spread it upon both pre- and post-retirement consumption. Similarly, people differ in their accumulated savings and access to capital markets, and each of these factors will influence their decisions. Finally, a crucial factor is the age at which the lengthening of the lifespan is perceived: if this perception occurs at a youthful age the individual's decisions would probably include spending extra time (and money) on education; if it occurs relatively late in life the re-adjustment of plans can be less feasible because of previous commitments.

Nonetheless, quite clearly the direction of the 'natural' response to an increase in life expectancy will include some extra work, except for the cases of poor health outlook or particularly hazardous occupations, which can both be tackled with ad hoc policies.

The crucial question thus becomes whether the actual pension system does help people to make sensible decisions in response to an increase in life expectancy. As a matter of fact, it often happens that just the opposite is true: pension policy in Europe and elsewhere has de facto encouraged workers – through indulgent eligibility requirements and heavily biased pension formulas – to retire at comparatively young ages. This myopic approach probably owes much to the 'lump of labor fallacy', that is the belief that, in a period of relative scarcity of employment opportunities, early retirement helps the young in finding a job, while this is not the case, at least not in the medium–long run.

This issue is of course strictly connected to the pension formula: DB formulas with no actuarial adjustment mechanisms usually incorporate a high implicit tax on the continuation of work after some minimum requirements have been met. The introduction of *actuarial principles* in benefit calculation, as well as the indexation of future benefits to life expectancy (or at least providing for an automatic revision, linked to longevity patterns) seem a feasible solution, leading to more neutrality in the work/retirement choice. Italy and Sweden went along this route envisaging a (more or less gradual) transition to a Notional Defined Contribution (NDC) system

An actuarial-based NDC method has many other advantages, such as the possibility of reaching almost automatic financial equilibrium, thus reducing the need for socially and politically painful intermittent corrections; and of substituting uniformity of treatment to the maze of schemes typical of most PAYG systems in Europe, with privileges granted to the more politically influential categories. The use of an age-related incentive structure (including both compensations for postponement and penalties for early retirement) would also allow more flexibility and more freedom of choice, and call for more responsibility at the personal/family level. Further, flexibility-enhancing features would ease the transition towards a higher average effective retirement age in a world in which so many firms and workers are already committed to given retirement paths, by partly offsetting its costs.

1.3 BEYOND MANDATORY RETIREMENT AND ELIGIBILITY THRESHOLDS?

When looking at the retirement issue from the point of view of personal choices, however, one cannot but recognize that, in most countries, retiring from work – one of the most important decisions in the individual sphere – is still largely given over to the state or, at any rate, heavily regulated. Even in systems that fully incorporate the actuarial equivalence principle, not only are minimum thresholds usually established, but an 'upper' age at which retirement is *mandatory* is also sometimes contemplated.

It is reasonable to question the compatibility of these rules with the good functioning of a modern economy and with the kind of awareness and responsibility usually credited to or required from individuals in many other fields. If a pension system has to be interpreted mainly (if not exclusively) as a saving program, allowing workers to decide when, how and how much to draw from their accumulated pension wealth should not appear such an extraordinary feature. Indeed, a thorough examination of the issue has to start from the reasons why a set of retirement-related rules may be needed at all within a mandatory pension system.

There are, broadly speaking, two main economic reasons for such a regulation: individual myopia (with permanent negative effects both on individuals' income and on society) and market imperfections, in particular imperfections of insurance and financial markets. Therefore, just as children are required to get a minimum school education, workers are required not only to contribute towards their future pension by paying payroll taxes, a form of forced saving, but also to satisfy a series of minimal conditions, in order to be eligible for pension benefits. Since participation in the system is compulsory, changing the status of participation (from contributor to recipient) is just an aspect of the same mandate.

The presence of redistributive components in the system – partly naturally linked to the goals of the public pension system and partly inescapable as no actuarial adjustment factor may fully compensate for the differentials in longevity[5] – compounds these problems. Obviously, these components may imply that, for some workers and quite irrespective of their capacity to make rational forward-looking choices, the marginal incentives to postpone retirement are too weak and may need to be complemented by eligibility constraints.

Legislation could of course simply establish a *minimum age* – usually referred to as the earliest eligibility age (EEA), possibly linked to changes in longevity – in order to prevent people making short-sighted decisions and to avoid the situation where a fraction of the workforce falls below acceptable pension levels. It could complement this with an eligibility test defined in terms of an accrued minimum benefit, a threshold below which the pension cannot be obtained,[6] thus ensuring that workers do not retire with 'too low' a benefit, such a limitation obviously applying only within an age band. In the same vein, it could also separate retirement from work and access to pension benefits, so further increasing the room for flexible choices. As for the EEA itself, the provision of an automatic adjustment with respect to further increases in life expectancy is just another aspect of the reason to introduce it in the legislation, in the first place; it would help both the financial equilibrium of the system and the individual's planning, allowing for a better allocation of the demographic risk, and preventing myopic choices.[7]

In practice, legislation normally does much more, as shown by the fact that, while some separation is often allowed for, stringent earnings tests (that is reductions of individuals' earnings when they are receiving a pension) are used. Some moderate use of earnings tests may be a practical way to obtain additional resources by discriminating against 'workaholics' and healthy (and usually richer) very old persons characterized by a low labor supply elasticity. Going beyond that could easily imply a zero-one game (either one retires and gets one's pension or works and gets one's earnings) amounting to a total 'confiscation' of benefits, and inducing people to stop working completely or moonlighting.

As for the eligibility conditions – normally differentiated across working categories, sometimes with poor justification – these are often expressed in terms of age plus accumulated contributions (or, specularly, pensions entitlements), or age plus seniority, that is the length of the working (contributive) career. We have already pointed out the rationale of the former; however, eligibility defined in terms of seniority is more difficult to rationalize, as it doesn't seem to bear a direct connection to any goal of the pension system. A seniority requisite is normally used as a proxy for other relevant factors, as greater seniority is normally associated – *ceteris paribus* – with an early start and relatively low education and permanent income levels.[8] In principle, it is introduced in order to take care of more hazardous working conditions and possibly greater health risk; in practice, it often degenerates into arbitrary rules used to gain political consensus. Moreover, the pension system is hardly the appropriate instrument to compensate health problems or to circumvent the difficulties that workers with greater seniority may encounter in reconverting their productive ability in the event of unemployment. These kinds of problems are better dealt with by specific policy measures.

In any case, while the presence of a minimum age threshold is easily accounted for, less clear-cut seems the rationale for establishing an upper age threshold, that is an age at which retirement becomes *mandatory*. Such a rigid provision appears to be hardly reasonable, as it seems to act against the stated goal of postponing retirement and to weaken the aim of strengthening both the savings features of the pension scheme and the correlation, at the individual level, between contributions and benefits.

Strictly dominant solutions in the pension field, however, hardly exist. The question then is: in the overall design of a retirement policy, does it make more sense to establish an upper limit after which (even if work is not prohibited) no further adjustment of the conversion factor used to compute benefit occurs, than to have just a minimum age, plus the actuarial adjustment mechanism at work? Generally speaking, there are two kinds of argument in favor of a positive answer to this question. The first rests in the limitations of the actuarial method of calculating benefits; the second has to do with yet other aspects of people's diversity, that is their ability to make wise and prudent choices.

As for the first argument, as already stated, the actuarial method has undisputed merits, but also drawbacks, particularly in its implied bad redistribution effects (the rich live longer and thus get more). This points to the appropriateness of limiting the potential advantages granted to richer people – insofar as they enjoy a higher longevity and, possibly, a lower disutility of work – by adopting 'actuarial fairness'. As for the second, it would imply a kind of paternalistic intervention in order to influence people at the opposite end of the income spectrum, who might be induced to retire 'too late' because of lack of awareness about their expected longevity or because of capital markets imperfections.[9] In both cases, establishing an upper limit to the actuarial adjustment of the conversion mechanism and calling this the age of mandatory retirement can be an effective short cut to reach socially relevant goals without too much interference with the underlying good incentive structure. This upper limit should also be revised according to the same mechanism linking it to longevity, already mentioned for the EEA.

From the above considerations, it seems possible to derive four preliminary conclusions: a) a set of age-related eligibility conditions for retirement represents an integral part of the mandatory pension scheme; b) beyond an *earliest eligibility age*, an actuarial adjustment mechanism linking pensions benefits to life expectancy allows the combination of flexibility, neutrality in the work/retirement choice and good incentives to postpone retirement; c) the actuarial adjustments may be cut back (or completely frozen) beyond an upper age limit, consistent with the aim of limiting their implied 'bad' redistribution and as a paternalistic intervention to prevent possible poor choices of less fortunate workers; d) the above procedure may be further enriched by the introduction of a mild earnings test, well coordinated with the actuarial adjustment mechanisms operating beyond the EEA.

The specific design of the different features so far described depends in any case very much on the actual characteristics of each pension system. Moreover, it has to be noticed that, while this design cannot be solely driven by considerations of labor supply of the elderly, the conditions actually prevailing in the labor market for the individuals close to retirement are quite important in establishing which combination of eligibility constraints and marginal incentives to postpone retirement has to be selected.

This book is devoted to this complex set of issues. It is based upon the proceedings of the fourth annual CeRP conference: 'Is Mandatory Retirement an Outdated Feature of Pension Systems?', held in Turin, in September 2003. This volume does not provide easy answers to the questions concerning the extent and nature of collective decision-making processes needed to allocate the extended life expectation between work and retirement periods, and the means to achieve a prolonged work period through the combination of more stringent age eligibility thresholds and incentives to postpone retirement. While easy answers to these questions obviously do not exist, the book provides a wide array of views both about the normative issues and the substantive empirical relevance of retirement postponement in the future evolution of mandatory pension systems.

1.4   AGE VARYING RULES

In Chapter 2 Peter Diamond derives some principles of 'good pension design' by concentrating on the rules that could help people to make sensible retirement choices, and thus on the relationships between benefit eligibility and age, on the one hand, and benefit level and age, on the other. He starts from a microeconomic perspective, but sensibly avoids both the hypotheses of a fully rational, representative individual, and of perfect insurance markets. On the contrary, he insists on individual diversity with respect not only to the earning opportunities and disutility of work, but also to the ability to plan for the future; and he stresses the imperfections in the market for annuities. Perhaps because of this more realistic attitude, his analysis is not too sympathetic with the so-called *neutrality view*, that is with those arguments conducive to a policy mainly based upon endorsing the principle of actuarial equivalence, establishing a minimum eligible age (possibly supplemented with the requirement that a minimum pension level has been accrued), and then letting incentives work.[10]

He uses two main arguments to rationalize his preference for an articulated regulation of retirement chances: workers' heterogeneity and redistributive scope. In order not to reduce welfare, legislation should accommodate people's diversity as much as possible. In order to redistribute resources within cohorts, the pension system should effectively complement the usual tax-transfer programs; given that it affects *life resources,* it may at least partially correct for the perverse redistribution implicit in different longevity patterns (with richer people living longer).

His analysis carefully separates the various aspects of the decisions to be made by an individual, like whether to retire (stop working) and whether to access benefits (drawing down pension wealth). In analyzing how to replicate individual 'sensible' choices into policy rules, that is into principles of benefit eligibility and benefit level within a mandatory system, he is equally careful in considering the likely consequences of the different rules, identifying both good outcomes – like having more insurance – and bad ones – like unnecessary distortions and perverse redistribution.

An example of this is the increase in the earliest eligibility age in response to the lengthening of life expectancy. This would work, first of all, as an appropriate measure to cope with myopic individual choices, as those made by people who simply decide, as a rule of thumb, to retire as soon as possible. Furthermore, provided workers are not over-annuitized already, it would also (assuming a constant present discounted value of benefits) grant more insurance, given that a later start implies a higher annuity. On the other hand, at least for some workers, it could also worsen liquidity conditions, tilting consumption towards older ages, and thus acting just as an imperfection of capital markets. It would also originate more redistribution, including the perverse one referred to before, which consists of transferring resources from people who have a lower life expectancy (typically, the poor) to people who live longer (typically, the rich).

The analysis is applied to various possible rules (age only; age plus an earnings requirement; age-varying eligibility rules) and various ways to change benefits regarding the age at which they start. From a political point of view, it also helps to clarify the reasons why what appears quite the obvious response to increases in life expectancy, that is working longer, is normally very much opposed, and thus difficult to accomplish. On the opposite front, it is also useful in checking the perhaps too easy enthusiasm about the effectiveness of actuarial fairness in providing not only sustainable pension systems, but also an adequate pension level. Diamond is fully aware that the complexities of the real world and individuals' heterogeneity suggest more prudence in deriving policy implications, and warns against all-too-easy solutions. Providing people with the right incentives and making the explicit redistribution embedded in the system transparent are good objectives, but they are not necessarily the only elements of a good income retirement policy. The implicit redistribution, operating through the correlation of mortality patterns with wealth, is not less important, although, since the correlation is not well understood, trying to offset it by means of the pension system could reduce overall social well-being, as Mike Hurd observes in his comments.

From an empirical perspective, we could finally remark that Diamond's arguments about an articulated set of rules concerning retirement options (and pension formulas) do not obviously imply any optimality of the currently stratified rules characterizing existing pension systems, or even that they are not in need of repair. All too often, in fact, such a web of rules simply reflects – whatever the originally stated high motives – the overlapping of privileges for different categories, groups or cohorts. It is to remedy this and perhaps also to start afresh from a less inefficient system that more neutral and transparent pension formulas and more coherent requirements are called for.

1.5   AN AGGREGATE PERSPECTIVE ON EXTENDING WORKING LIVES

However much the incentive structure may affect the supply side of the labor market, one should never forget the demand side. This reminder is perhaps the main point in Disney and Bridges' cross-country analysis of retirement patterns, in Chapter 3.

Paralleling Diamond's emphasis on individual heterogeneity, Disney and Bridges stress country diversity, even within a supposedly rather uniform area, like the EU. This diversity, in their view, is such as to undermine the usefulness of the money's worth measures of retirement incentives (such as the pension wealth, the accrual, the tax rate) customarily computed. Despite their limited informative content, these 'monetary' measures are typically used to explain retirement patterns. Disney and Bridges challenge this view both methodologically and empirically. Under the first perspective, they point out that these measures should take account of the main, if not all, tax-transfer programs, and not just of those which make up the pension system. For example, even if one limits the consideration to the differences between gross and net effective tax rates, calculations for a few countries reported in the chapter show quite a large – and dissimilar among countries – variability. More importantly, the calculated implicit taxes do not summarize all factors and conditions inducing people to choose early retirement; apart from the fact that they only have relevance in the 'age window' when retirement is allowed, earnings tests and deferral conditions are equally important.

After considering the intrinsic limitations of money's worth measures, from an empirical point of view the authors raise doubts about their relevance in explaining the observed changes in retirement patterns; in particular, they examine the changes induced, in the last decade, by the (partial) shift towards more neutral and flexible pension formulas. Since the late 1990s, in contrast to the preceding trend, empirical observations exhibit increases in the activity rates of older workers, almost everywhere in Europe. Country differences, moreover, are shown to be strongly correlated with relative GDP growth rates, with the correlation being stronger for younger workers in the group (within the age category 50+) and (from the UK experience) higher-skilled ones. The macro-evidence which is provided thus points to an important role played by the demand side (that is by the attitude of firms), in explaining retirement patterns, a factor which is somewhat overlooked by proponents of the view that monetary incentives 'matter'.

The point is important, although the evidence cannot be interpreted as conclusive. Apart from the exceptions noticed by the authors themselves (first of all Italy, on which more will be said later), one could question the rather simple specification adopted. Demand side factors are captured by considering the GDP growth rate, which is an endogenous variable in itself, and one which is likely to differ, for structural reasons, across countries. Other methodologies, such as an output gap approach or a joint examination of both employment and unemployment among the older workers, could provide further corroboration to the argument. Moreover, a 'demand-shifts' interpretation should imply a rise in employment across all age groups, while changes in retirement rules operating through a supply channel are likely to fall disproportionately upon the age groups most directly affected, which are presumably the 50–54 and the 55–59 ones.

Although this kind of analysis requires further investigation, the evidence presented is strongly 'suggestive' and reminds us of the fact that correcting the 'distortions' embedded in the pension system may be not enough to boost elderly people's employment, as demand side factors are also an essential ingredient. As Mike Hurd, in his comments, remarks: 'pension reform may not work if the demand side is not sufficiently flexible to accommodate late retirement in response to policy change', which might require changes, and flexibility, in the pay structure. The Disney and Bridges story, thus, is not to be read as an assertion that financial incentives and retirement rules do not matter; rather as a healthy warning on customarily computed measures, particularly in their application to cross-country panel regressions along with a (small) vector of control variables including both economic and institutional factors. As the authors stress, this approach – commonly used by international organizations – has two drawbacks: first, the indicator variables of the retirement regimes summarize heterogeneous within-country distributions of marginal rates, and this is likely to induce measurement errors; second, the linear specification implausibly assumes that the impact of variations in the regime indicators is independent of control variables (typically, institutional indicators). More promising, in theory, but excessively demanding, in practice, is the use of detailed country-specific micro-econometric models of retirement behavior, fully specifying the 'option value' of continued work (Stock and Wise, 1990).

The preference of the authors is for a '*quasi-experiments*' strategy, where the *difference* in the outcome variable before and after a policy change for a group affected by that change (the 'treated group') is measured relative to the outcome change for a 'control group', unaffected by policy actions. This strategy has merits but is not free from shortcomings, as the treatment effect may be specific to those groups or countries that have undergone the policy change, which may prevent any general lesson from being learned. Moreover, it is of course difficult to separate the effects of the policy change from those which result from 'anticipation' of the change itself by the workers. For this, as the authors rightly contend, Italy is again a case in point.

1.6   COUNTRY STUDIES

The problem of encouraging (or imposing) longer working lives is common throughout Europe, irrespective of differences in demographic scenarios, institutional framework and political preferences. In this book, we do not pretend, of course, to cover this diversity, but only aim at providing a few significant examples of countries' policies meant to reduce the distortions hidden in the pension system, and make less disadvantageous (if at all), for older workers, to continue their activity, plus an example (the Netherlands) pointing to a possible negative impact of mandatory retirement on workers' income expectations at retirement, even in the context of a rather generous system.[11]

In Chapter 5, Barbara Berkel and Axel Börsch-Supan analyze the German case. They start by describing the (quite common) story of a progressive 'loosening' of the social security's features in the 1990s (in parallel with the democratic party being in government for the first time since 1933), with the introduction of more 'flexible' eligibility requirements – allowing early retirement practically without any actuarial correction of benefits – and the extension of exit possibilities through other forms of benefits – mainly disability and survivor benefits. As expected, workers were quick in taking advantage of the new rules, which strongly contributed to a significant reduction in the average retirement age and to a steady increase in expenditure. As in other countries, worries of unsustainability eventually led to reforms in the 1990s, by which eligibility requirements were restricted; the correlation of benefits to contributions was strengthened; privileges were curbed.

Berkel and Börsch-Supan then use an option value model to estimate the probability of retirement for older workers, assuming social security wealth plus a set of age-specific dummy variables, financial and real wealth and self-assessed health measure as explanatory variables. The option value – that is the value of continuing to work as opposed to retiring – has a highly significant, negative effect on the probability to retire. The age dummies are again highly significant for both genders, indicating that being 60, 63 or 65 (that is the age limits for entering specific retirement paths) clearly raises the probability of being retired. Self-reported health is also highly significant: healthier workers retire substantially later than those who report poor health. Marriage status is not significant for men, while it is for women; the presence of a child in the household has a significant negative effect on the probability to retire. As for education, the effect of a college degree is also very strong, and negative, even controlling for income. The wealth effects are weak and barely significant. High labor income weakens labor force attachment; the status of self-employement has a negative effect, while being a civil servant has a positive effect.

Using the estimated parameters, the authors then simulate the steady state properties of different reform options, which involve first a modification of parameters and then the more radical change consisting of the adoption of a notional defined contribution (NDC) scheme. These are compared to the status quo benchmark (represented by the original social security design, modified by the 1992 and 1999 corrections). In general, the simulation shows a remarkable rise in the average retirement age for men and a weaker one for women.

Different reform scenarios are considered, like: i) increases in the EEA and in statutory retirement ages; ii) increases in benefit reductions for early retirement; iii) establishment of an NDC regime. The model shows responses of average retirement age which respect the ranking: increasing the age requirements (both the EEA and the statutory retirement age) by two years raises the average by 9 months; deductions to pension benefits operate in the same direction, but more strongly: when their level is increased to 6 percent, the average retirement age for men reaches the statutory level (65 years). Possibly due to the existence of easier disability options, women's responses are weaker in both cases. The third variant, that is the introduction of actuarial fairness, appears to be the most effective to induce workers to postpone retirement; as before the effect is stronger for men.

The exercise is a confirmation of the potential impact of retirement incentives on the supply side. Of course, if one takes the Disney and Bridges critique into account, these simulated outcomes would also require a favorable evolution of demand in order to materialize.

Cathal O'Donoghue illustrates, in Chapter 6, the Irish system and reform. In the European context, Ireland represents rather an exception under many perspectives, including, in particular, demography and growth. Though also characterized by an aging population, the country is still relatively young, and projections of both dependency ratios and expenditures are far less worrying than in most other European countries. This is due not only to the high migration flows of the first half of the twentieth century, but also to the rather severe rules of the pension system. Eligibility requirements for old-age pensions were set at 70 until the early 1970s, when they were lowered at 65/66 (today's level), a change which can hardly be dubbed a 'slackening' of rules, particularly when compared to the innovations which characterized other countries, more or less in the same period. Moreover, somewhat according to the Anglo-Saxon model, the Irish system integrates the PAYG system with two fully funded components: occupational funds (publicly or privately managed, and widespread) and private individual accounts (relatively infrequent).

As for the PAYG system, it exhibits typical features of a 'liberal' welfare state: contributions are earnings-related while benefits are flat rate and relatively low, so that supplementing them with the other components or with means-tested social assistance benefits (for those not eligible for other systems) is quite essential. A further feature is that the (already rather low) average replacement ratio decreased in recent years because of the country's good economic performance, with productivity and (net) earnings increasing rapidly and pensions (not indexed to wages) lagging behind. Finally, early retirement is contemplated but data do not give the impression that recourse to it was an abuse or a privilege. In this context, it thus seems that the main factor driving the pension reform was not so much the sustainability of the system, but rather its 'adequacy' in meeting the objective of preventing poverty among the elderly.

Using a dynamic micro-simulation model that mimics life-cycle processes of different cohorts, having regard to personal and family characteristics, demographic variables, labor market circumstances, pension and tax rules, O'Donoghue provides an illustration of the likely effects of various 'parametric' reforms on retirement age and on poverty reduction. The results of the simulation are not always clear-cut, in terms of the two goals. The chapter, however, provides an interesting example of the relatively new micro-simulation technique; it also shows its limits, in that as much as the stochastic paths of individual life cycles are complicated to replicate 'real' processes, they only capture part of the supply side of the story about employment of older workers. Again, one should consider both 'demand effects' and the possibility of macroeconomic shocks, which can unpredictably affect individual trajectories.

The two Chapters 7 and 8 are meant to offer, together, a broad perspective on retirement rules and patterns in Italy. In Chapter 7, Marano and Sestito provide a survey of the various reforms enacted since 1992, up to the very recent one approved in July 2004. They do so by considering both the pension system and the labor market, with the explicit aim of looking at the reform process through the lenses of the 'working longer' issue, in itself recognized as something far from being uniquely related to the pension domain. The authors, consequently, also give a brief presentation of the current, and prospective, labor market performance of the Italian elderly, conditioned by a sizable (even if possibly declining) human capital gap, by institutions traditionally geared to protect adult male workers and, at the same time, relatively unaccustomed to dealing with the re-entrance difficulties of older workers, given the widespread use of special programs designed to accompany them towards their pension in case of difficulties at the firm or sector level.

Pension reforms ratified in the 1990s were directed at correcting the main structural defects of the system: a regular deficit of contributions; an excess of 'bad' redistribution and relatively young retirement ages. They have significantly curbed expenditure, although in the short run this is mainly because pension indexation has been downgraded from wages to prices. As for the medium and long run, the decrease in benefits implied by the gradual phasing in of the reform, that is by the progressive injection of the new NDC method, does not appear sufficient to counter the effects of the sizable demographic changes. Moreover, the lengthy transition and the maintenance of the so-called 'seniority pensions' create different retirement regimes over time and hardly acceptable inequities across cohorts. Finally, insofar as the old defined benefit formula will continue to apply (which will be the case for almost three decades for the new pensions and much longer for the stock of benefits in payment), both the relatively high benefit accrued to workers with good seniority (that is 35 years) and the implicit tax on work continuation will prevent a significant increase in the average retirement age.

In the longer run, a reduced replacement ratio and the much higher neutrality of the actuarial-based benefit should encourage a lengthening of the working life. However, taking account of both the labor market functioning and the pension rules, it would be quite optimistic to assume an increase in the average retirement age approximating that in life expectancy.

It is to correct this overly lengthy and, with respect to the age of retirement, too timid reform path that a new act was approved in July 2004. Essentially, this is aimed at refocusing the target, from the previous 'cuts in benefits' approach to a more aggressive strategy directed at increasing the average retirement age.

The authors argue that this shift represents an important and welcome novelty. Two notable caveats are nonetheless introduced. The first concerns the *abruptness* and *timing* of the change in the seniority requirements, which will produce further inequalities across cohorts and a sizable, even if expected, supply shock to be accommodated by the labor market. A smoother approach and allowance of greater room for individuals' choices would have enhanced both the efficiency and the equity features of the measure. The second concerns the lack of coherence with the NDC system and consequently the loss of some of its positive features, like the flexibility in retirement age. Under this perspective, the establishment of an automatic link between the earliest eligibility age and life expectancy would have been a more efficient measure than a compulsory increase in retirement ages.

Complementing the normative analysis of Marano and Sestito, Chapter 8, by Belloni, Borella and Fornero, contains an empirical investigation into Italian retirement patterns. In order to understand workers' choices and the likely impact of the major 1995 reform, the authors first estimate a model in a relatively stable period and then use the obtained parameters to simulate future patterns. As for the past, a descriptive analysis of the years covered by the data set (1985–98) suggests that a demarcation line should be drawn in 1992, the year of the first pension reform, in order to separate the rather stable, pre-reform period and the unstable one, essentially covering the 1990s, characterized by intense pension legislation.

In the 'stable' period, money's worth measures appear an important determinant of retirement. Two caveats apply, however: first, 'round ages' like 60 and 65 matter, possibly revealing the social relevance of typical ages; second, the empirical performance of the model shows discrepancies with respect to a priori reasoning based on an intertemporal optimization approach; in particular, social security wealth is confirmed to be highly significant, while marginal effects – that is implicit taxes – are not. In the unstable years of reform, instead, uncertainty about possible future restrictions seems to dominate behavior, causing, as an anticipation effect, a much larger recourse to early retirement, whenever an 'exit-window' (which was periodically established by law in a context of rather sharp restrictions) is opened.

As for the future, characterized by the progressive phasing in of the new formula, based on *actuarial equivalence*, simulation is rather robust in showing that, assuming no change in workers' preferences, the mere modification in the pension rules will not by itself bring about the increase in the average retirement age which is called for by population aging (a result which might be due to the rather low earliest eligibility age, fixed at 57). In a broad sense, the analysis thus provides ground for further reform, although the authors share the reservations, already advanced in Chapter 7, concerning the unjustified roughness of the 2004 interventions.

The analysis has relevant policy implications. The adoption of the principle of flexible retirement – as a counterpart to the principle of actuarial fairness in benefit determination – would inevitably reduce the constraints created by the institutional framework and possibly drive workers' behavior towards closer adherence to the economic model of retirement (like the option value model), but enhance the role of family variable and considerations. However, the substitution of the easy-to-apply 'rules of thumb' of the past (for example retiring at 60 with a replacement ratio of, say, 70 or 80 percent) with a new decision framework will take time and require extensive information. It also will require a more widespread 'culture of decision making', which in its turn will call for a resolute educational effort.

The three countries up to now considered provide examples in the tradition of seeing the pension systems as having a large influence in determining the employment rate of older workers; in two of them (Germany and Italy), correcting the past distortions is considered a crucial step in order to strengthen the financial sustainability of pension systems, particularly in the face of rapidly aging populations; in the third (Ireland) the driving force for reform seems to rest instead more on the aim of preventing the (relative) poverty of the elderly. All three cases point to the distortions embedded in pension rules and the potential gain of their eradication. Of course, the validity of the Disney and Bridges critique casts doubt on the efficacy of pension reform per se to sustain the employment rate of elderly people.

The Netherlands – addressed under a different perspective by Mauro Mastrogiacomo, in Chapter 9 – provides a case study more conducive to Diamond's arguments about workers' diversity and their limited rationality and knowledge with respect to their retirement rights. The perspective Mastrogiacomo is interested in is how individuals' expectations of income around retirement age fare with respect to realizations. The Dutch system is characterized by an overall high level of income protection, the coexistence of relatively modest social security benefits and quite generous private provisions, and the presence of somewhat lax exit routes at earlier ages than the statutory retirement age. The issue of expectations is relevant not only per se, but also because it bears important consequences for the question of the eligibility conditions for retirement. From the former standpoint, anticipations are shown to be systematically worse than realizations, which might be due to the intrinsic pessimism characterizing the entrance 'into a new non revertible phase of their life' or to imperfect information about the true generosity of the retirement income provisions. Under the second, the Netherlands offers grounds to the argument that there are different ways to grant workers generous options to withdraw at relatively young ages from the labor market, and that these options are usually resorted to by a substantial number of workers, so that what appears prima facie a set of rather tight eligibility conditions reveals instead a number of loopholes, when considering the whole context of exit possibilities.

As in the case of other European countries, in the Netherlands the statutory mandatory retirement age is 65. Early retirement, however, is allowed from the age of 60 and almost 80 percent of workers between ages 60 and 64 take advantage of this rather generous option (which can be ascribed to firm-specific early retirement plans). The majority of workers, however, leave their job *before* the age of 60, in that they exploit the very generous legislation concerning disability and unemployment benefits for older workers.

As for expectations, an anticipated drop in income at retirement is not an uncommon finding in empirical surveys. Dutch data confirm this finding, but comparisons to realizations prove that anticipations are systematically biased downward. More precisely, workers do expect a decline in income, but only to discover, at retirement, that realizations fare better than expected; a worsening in expectations is detectable at both ages 60 and 65, with a sharp negative peak for the second threshold. This reveals a pessimistic attitude with respect to the time of retirement, and also implies that a significant improvement in anticipations after age 65 is quite common. When the same phenomenon is studied across the years, data show an increasing trend in both expectations and realizations, with the former constantly below the latter.

The analysis is substantiated by an econometric model which confirms the anticipated drops in the mandatory retirement age and a significant positive 'time effect', perhaps attributable to the fact that the Dutch pension system – contrary to most other European countries – did not undergo a major structural reform.

The expected fall in income at retirement is then decomposed according to the two main factors supposedly at its origin: coming closer to the mandatory retirement age and personal characteristics, where it is estimated that about 55 percent is due to the first, while the rest is accounted for by 'taste shifters'. As for the mismatch between expectations and realizations, it is plausible that – apart from the pessimistic bias that seems to characterize older workers – its origin lies in incomplete information about a fragmented but on the whole rather generous system.

The lesson that can be derived is that even financially stable systems could improve their underlying incentive structure, make the eligibility requirements more transparent and increase the correlation between contributions and benefits, as well as the coherence between different schemes. This could positively influence households' welfare by making it easier for them to plan their retirement on the basis of a better forecast of their retirement income.

In conclusion, the European objective of significantly increasing the effective retirement age is an ambitious one, not easy to reach. To this end, interventions on the different factors that result in retirement patterns heavily biased towards relatively young ages are required. These factors affect the labor supply, where economic incentives and psychological motivations overlap, as well as the demand side, where high overall labor costs coexist with possible distortions in the wage structures between the young and the old. Pension systems throughout Europe are in fact moving towards granting more flexibility, personal responsibility and greater (actuarial) fairness to the retirement decision. This is an important step. It should not be forgotten, however, that a considerable fraction of older workers possibly go through a troubled period in the years preceding retirement, somewhat challenging the stereotype of the 55-year-olds happily living their few remaining years of work simply in anticipation of becoming a retiree and drawing down their pension wealth. Such a moment is frequently determined not by a personal choice but rather by company crisis, often dealt with through ad hoc social programs. The combination of the supply side, possibly less conditioned by biased pension formulas, with the demand side, offers new challenges and interesting perspectives for further research.

NOTES

1. In the comparison between the returns of PAYG and FF systems, steady state situations are frequently considered. However, these analyses have severe limitations, and do not lend themselves easily to policy recommendations. In practice, given that the uncertain returns from both systems are not perfectly correlated, the choice of an optimal risk–return combination should lead rational, risk-averse individuals to participate in both systems, that is to diversify their social security portfolio. This seems to be the main rationale for a partial shift to a funded system.
2. In any case they are interconnected by the endogeneity of the work–retirement choice. The impact of pension entitlements rules has been examined using actuarial fairness and a perfect annuity market as benchmarks in the cross-country studies presented in Gruber and Wise (1999).
3. Along with pursuing the financial sustainability and the (perhaps even more ambiguous than social adequacy) 'modernization' of the pension systems. These are indirect goals, governed by the so-called 'open method of coordination', given that the 'subsidiarity principle' leaves legislation to member states. As early as Autumn 2002, EU countries were asked to present a Strategy Report, focused upon these broad goals. The financial sustainability of pension systems has been included in a list of long-term sustainability factors to be considered in the future 'refocusing' of the Stability and Growth Pact.
4. Furthermore, in a DB system characterized by a weak correlation, at the individual level, between benefits and contributions, the increase in payroll tax rates would create all the distortions of tax rises, including tax evasion, so as to jeopardize the very aim of the policy.
5. On the topic see Hurd, Chapter 4 of this volume.

6.   As will be the case, for example, in Italy, with the new NDC rules.
7.   See Munnell et al. (2004).
8.   In firm/industry-based schemes seniority may complement age eligibility thresholds in order to avoid free riders taking advantage of the system, but such a role does not arise in nationwide systems.
9.   Notice also that the possible rationale for the mandatory retirement threshold just sketched differs very much from the rationale of mandatory retirement in private firm based pension schemes. To the extent that those private schemes are to be interpreted as a deferred wage payment system, capable as such of providing correct incentives to workers and firms, the mandatory retirement threshold has a role in discouraging the firm from being tempted to renege on its promise (see for instance Lazear, 1979).
10. For example, he asks (p. 37) 'whether social goals across groups are optimized by actuarial fairness' by using break-even pricing, corresponding to the use of a uniform annuitization factor for individuals.
11. According to sociological classifications, (see Esping-Andersen, 1990 and SCP-CeRP, 2004), it could be argued that the countries included in the survey are representatives of different 'welfare regimes': Germany (corporatist regime), Ireland (liberal regime), the Netherlands (hybrid regime) and Italy (Mediterranean regime). This book does not, however, exploit this classification, and only considers the pension system (and not, for example, reforms of the labor market aimed at facilitating older workers' activity).

REFERENCES

Diamond, P. (2004), 'Social Security', Presidential Address delivered at the 115th meeting of the American Economic Association, 4 January 2004, San Diego, CA.
Esping-Andersen, G. (1990), *The Three Worlds of Welfare Capitalism*, Princeton: Princeton University Press.
Gruber, J. and D.A. Wise (eds) (1999), *Social Security and Retirement around the World*, Chicago: University of Chicago Press.
Lazear, E.P. (1979), 'Why is there Mandatory Retirement?', *Journal of Political Economy*, **87**, pp.1261–64.
McMorrow, K. and W. Roeger (2002), 'EU Pension Reform – An Overview of the Debate and an Empirical Assessment of the Main Policy Reform Options', Economic Papers No. 162, European Commission, DG Economic and Financial Affairs, Brussels.
Munnell, A.H., K.B. Meme, N.A. Jivan and K.E. Cahill (2004), 'Should we Raise Social Security Earliest Eligibility Age?', Center for Retirement Research at Boston College, Issue in brief, no. 18, June.
SCP-CeRP (2004), *Unequal Welfare States. Distributional Consequences of Population Ageing in Six European Countries*, joint report by the Social and Cultural Planning Office, The Hague and CeRP, Turin.
Stock, J.H. and D.A. Wise (eds) (1990), *Issues in the Economics of Aging*, Chicago: University of Chicago Press.

PART 1

Increasing retirement age: principles and practice

2. Social security rules that vary with age*

Peter Diamond

2.1 INTRODUCTION

Some workers enjoy their work and want to continue working beyond what many consider a suitable retirement age. Others no longer enjoy their work (if they ever did) and are eager to stop working as soon as they can afford a decent retirement.[1] A good retirement income system will not overly discourage the first group from continuing to work at ages at which the second group will indeed retire.[2]

Some workers would save adequately and work long enough for a comfortable retirement even if there were no government- or employer-provided retirement income. Other workers would do little or no saving for retirement and would choose to retire with insufficient assets to finance a reasonable retirement for themselves and their spouses. A mandatory public system of retirement income provision needs to recognize the presence of both types of workers when designing detailed rules.

Public systems can address diversity in the working population by having rules relating *benefit eligibility* to some combination of the age of a worker and the level of the worker's continuing earnings and by relating *benefit levels* to the age at which the benefits start as well as the history of past earnings.[3]

This chapter begins by considering how a sensible worker might carry out retirement planning. This shows the considerations behind some workers' retirement decisions. It also shows that many workers would not want to start retirement benefits until they stop working (or cut back significantly) while other workers would sensibly start retirement benefits while continuing to work. Then we consider some principles of the design of a mandatory public system of retirement income. These relate to setting benefit eligibility rules and benefit levels (relative to the age at which they start) to balance concerns coming from workers showing different bases for decisions and experiencing different work opportunities.[4]

The focus is primarily on rules that explicitly relate to age around the age at which benefit eligibility starts. Thus there are several (implicit) age-varying rules that are not considered. Any method of benefit determination that is based on the history of earnings in different years is implicitly adjusting for different ages by how it weights the earnings in different years. For example, a notional defined contribution system (NDC) aggregates taxes on earnings in different years using some measure of wage growth. This treats different ages differently from a defined contribution (DC) system which aggregates taxes on earnings in different years using the rate of return on assets in the account. Not addressed are issues raised by differences in weights given to different years,[5] the time shape of benefits after retirement, which is also an issue that varies implicitly with age, nor issues raised by the families of workers (particularly widows).[6]

The focus is on the impact on individual workers, not on others. For a policy design applying to many years it is a major mistake to discourage work by older workers in the hope of generating more work for younger workers. The economy adapts (through wage adjustments and labor demands) to the supply of workers. It is simply not the case that countries that most discourage work by older workers have systematically lower unemployment rates among younger workers.

There is a large difference in approach between US Social Security, which has a non-linear (progressive) benefit formula and the typical European (and Canadian) system which has a linear benefit system. While all of these countries have minimum income systems for the elderly, that in the US is far less generous than those in Europe (and Canada). Thus US Social Security has been used as an important tool in fighting elderly poverty, while the higher level of support of the poor elderly through the minimum income system makes this unnecessary in many other countries. But there is more to the difference between linear and non-linear systems than just fighting poverty. Progressivity in the benefit formula can be seen as part of a country's general redistributive system since it redistributes on a lifetime basis, while typically tax-transfer systems (for example, progressive income taxes) are based on annual evaluations and thus can be usefully supplemented by redistribution on a lifetime basis.

While a linear system is not overtly redistributive, it needs to be kept in mind that this does not imply that the system is not redistributive. In any system providing annuitized benefits there is a redistributive component coming from the systematic differences in life expectancy in the population. In particular, women tend to live longer than men, making a gender-neutral system redistributive toward women collectively. It is also the case that within each gender high earners tend to live longer than low earners, with large (and increasing) differences in some countries. This makes a linear system regressive within each gender. A proper analysis of this aspect of redistribution needs a proper counterfactual of what annuitization, if any, would happen without the mandatory program. The simplest setting is to imagine that everyone would have annuitized anyway and the mandatory program substitutes uniform pricing for the risk-adjusted pricing that would occur in a private market. In this case the pattern of redistribution is easy to see, being based on price differences. Once we recognize that there is very little voluntary annuitization in the world, then the discussion needs to incorporate the insurance value of annuitization (which varies with income level) as well as the differences in life expectancy.[7]

This chapter simply assumes a linear benefit formula. This still leaves open the determination of additional benefits from additional years of work and the issue of how benefits should vary with the age at which they start. This also leaves the important issue of the use of system design to provide insurance of earnings risk. That is, even if we consider a population with the same *ex ante* wage opportunities, different stochastic realizations of both opportunities and difficulty of work raise an insurance issue that closely resembles analyses from a redistributive perspective. Providing insurance to those who have shorter careers because of poor stochastic realizations (assuming that they have greater unmet needs) is an important dimension of the public provision of retirement income, one that remains present even if the basic benefit formula is constrained to be linear. Thus the typical European approach is considered as a constraint to being a linear benefit formula rather than a choice to ignore insurance opportunities.

2.2 INDIVIDUAL CHOICE WITHOUT A MANDATORY SYSTEM

In a world where all retirement decisions were unconstrained by public or private programs, each worker would decide how much to save (for retirement and other future expenditures), when to stop working, when to start drawing down accumulated balances, and whether to make use of annuities, in some form. A worker choosing to annuitize has choices about when to purchase the annuities, when to have the benefits start, and what time shape and indexing structure to give to benefits.[8]

In modern advanced economies, workers are required to pay taxes while working (to help finance retirement benefits), they are required to receive benefits in a given form (commonly as an annuity), and are restricted as to when they can receive benefits. The restrictions on benefit receipt may depend on age or a combination of age and earnings levels. Workers may or may not have some choice of assets during accumulation.

Individuals with complete freedom of choice (subject to market availabilities) who follow the standard life-cycle model under uncertainty would start drawing down accumulations for retirement under three circumstances – at the same time at which they stop working; when work has become lucrative enough or life expectancy short enough that the retirement accumulation is best spent over a longer period than just after stopping work; and when there are some particularly important expenditure opportunities, perhaps for a consumer good, such as world travel, or perhaps for a need, such as medical expenses. For simplicity, assume that the end of work is a once-and-for-all decision (although many workers in the US do return to work after self-described retirement) and that the work decision is a zero-one choice – full-time work with no variation in hours or full retirement (although many workers in the US use 'bridge jobs' in a transition between a career job and full retirement). Moreover, assume that the opportunity set and the arrival of information are such that the choice problem is well-behaved so that one can consider first-order conditions for decisions without needing to compare two distinctly different planned retirement dates as alternatives.

Individuals planning their own retirement and sensibly looking ahead would contemplate the end of work by comparing the utility from consuming the earnings from additional work with the disutility from additional work. Such individuals continuing to work need to decide whether to save or dissave out of earnings, that is, whether to add to their retirement accumulation or subtract from it (in addition to interest earnings). This savings decision would contrast the marginal utility of consumption while continuing to work with the marginal utility from the consumption affordable after retirement. This is similar to the decision for a worker in a retirement income system between starting retirement benefits now or waiting to start them later. In either setting, a worker would recognize the implications of a delay in the start of benefits in terms of a higher flow of per-period benefits that would start later. How much higher depends on the arrangements for retirement income flows and the behavior of the market. For example, an individual contemplating purchase of a real annuity would recognize that a delay of a year in the purchase of an immediate annuity would mean another year of stochastic accumulation on the existing balance, and a change in the pricing of annuities reflecting both being a year older and the changes in the bases of annuity pricing in general – developments in cohort mortality estimates and in interest rates.

Of course, not all retirement benefits need to be consumed – some could be saved. Alternatively, not starting benefits may be accompanied by further savings from earnings. Implicit in this formulation is the assumption that individuals do not engage in complex asset market transactions to separate out decisions that are made contingent on a retirement decision from decisions that could be made separately. That is, I assume that workers accumulate balances in some portfolio (with unchanging balance) and annuitize at retirement. While economic theory makes it clear that it is advantageous to annuitize earlier (or on a rolling basis) (Brugiavini, 1993; Sheshinski, 2001) this does not usually seem to be done. Similarly, most workers do not engage in sophisticated hedging actions. Thus I do the analysis around a simple behavioral model, which seems more useful than considering what super-sophisticated workers might find to do, although the latter analysis can also help inform the design of mandatory systems.

In the familiar life-cycle model under certainty, a forward-looking worker retires when the disutility of continued work equals the marginal utility of the additional lifetime consumption that could be financed as a consequence of additional work. Adding uncertainty about life expectancy does not change this analysis if the individual fully annuitizes as may make sense in a setting with no other uncertainty (Yaari, 1965; Davidoff et al., 2003). Randomness in interest rates and in annuity pricing would complicate the story, adding reality and additional interactions, but adding little to the basic character of the retirement decision. In a certainty setting, the start of drawing on assets for consumption and the end of work occur at the same moment provided the wage is non-decreasing. (With a constant interest rate, drawing on asset income and decumulating occur at the same time; with varying interest, this need not be the case.)

However, it is straightforward to construct models where assets are drawn on before retirement. What can accomplish this is the arrival of opportunities or information. Either a surprisingly good wage opportunity or learning that life expectancy will be short can result in this pattern. Of course, the arrival of a temporary spending need (for example, medical expenses) or opportunity (for example, a good time for world travel) can do the same (in the absence of insurance covering this event).

From the perspective of a mandatory retirement income policy, there are two issues here. One, not discussed but apparent in practice, is that without strict mandates discouraging it, different sensible people want to retire at different ages since they can differ in many ways. Second, there may be a difference in timing between when workers want to stop working and when they want to start drawing on their 'retirement' benefits.

2.3 MANDATORY SYSTEMS: AGE-VARYING PAYROLL TAXES AND ANNUITIZATION

A mandatory system starts (chronologically) with a requirement to pay taxes. In practice, taxes are levied on earnings and taxes are proportional to earnings for any worker, possibly between a floor and a ceiling. The tax rate can vary with age (and does in Switzerland). The advantage of an age-varying tax is to have the tax relatively lower when more workers are having liquidity problems than happens later in life. That is, typically younger workers have lower earnings than they will have later, and may have higher needs to prepare for home ownership and to build up precautionary balances, and possibly young children to finance. When older they are more likely to have an easier time setting aside a larger fraction of earnings for retirement purposes. The disadvantage of an age-varying payroll tax is added administrative burden. There is a potential here for a useful age-varying policy, but I do not know empirical work that spells out in detail the extent to which liquidity problems vary by age and so the ideal shape of such a policy.

At the other end of the life cycle, one could lower the payroll tax rate (or drop it totally) for workers who have not yet stopped working by the age at which they can start collecting retirement benefits. In Chile, compulsory savings in individual accounts stops on reaching the point of being able to start drawing benefits at age 65. In a system without insurance related to earnings or redistribution across workers, it is not clear what is gained by continuing taxes on workers who have access to their retirement accumulations. That is, if a country lets workers start benefits while continuing to work, there is little apparent gain (apart from simplicity) from continued taxation of earnings in a system without redistribution across workers based on earnings histories. In a system that does explicitly redistribute (as does the US and do rules that contain implicit taxes that depend on the length of a career), then continued earnings do represent an addition to lifetime resources and so a greater ability to pay taxes on average. Note I refer to explicit redistribution – there is no way to design a compulsory system that does not involve some redistribution, as noted above.

For the continued analysis, assume a single payroll tax rate that does not vary with age and continues either until benefit eligibility or as long as work has not stopped, depending on which assumption helps make the analysis clearer.

2.3.1 Annuitization

Different countries have different rules governing whether benefits must be received as an annuity or how large a fraction of accumulations must be annuitized or with strong incentives encouraging a particular degree of annuitization. I will not explore this choice of public design of benefit structure, which generally does not vary with age, although the UK has rules requiring annuitization by a particular age.[9]

Different countries have different rules for the change over time in a benefit level that is already in the payment phase with the passage of time. Some vary benefits with prices, some with wages, some with a combination of prices and wages, and some include a tilt relative to the chosen index. There are good arguments for each of these choices and I will not explore the alternatives. Note that the greater the increase in benefits with age (time), the lower the initial benefits for a given availability of finances. A steeper pattern with a lower initial benefit can be particularly valuable in influencing decisions to stop working by short-sighted workers.

Different countries also vary in the protection offered to a surviving spouse, either in the form of a benefit for a spouse who never worked or a change in benefit level for a spouse who also receives a benefit from past work. Protection of surviving family members, particularly widows, is an important part of the design of a good retirement income system. Again, this issue is not explored here.

And some countries allow some choice in some of the details of annuitization.

To continue the analysis, assume that once benefits start, they are paid as a real annuity. A critical issue is how much benefits increase if they start later, assuming workers are free to delay the start of benefits. Before discussing this issue, we need to consider what age or combination of age and earnings results in eligibility to start benefits.

2.4 MANDATORY SYSTEMS: CONDITIONS FOR THE START OF BENEFITS

There are multiple possibilities for a system to determine whether a worker is eligible to start benefits. The simplest rule is an age at which benefits start – no choice, no requirement of stopping work. A variant on this approach would allow a worker to defer the start of benefits in order to receive larger benefits once they do start. Alternative to this approach, the start of benefits might require both a minimum age and a test of retirement (perhaps measured as some allowed level of earnings), with benefits increased for workers who do not stop work and so do not start benefits.[10] This approach could also be modified to allow a deferral of the start of benefits for a worker who could start benefits, again associated with larger benefits. And, the above possibilities can be combined into an age-varying rule, as in the US, where low earnings are required for the start of benefits between two ages, benefits are allowed to start despite continued work beyond the upper age, and deferral of the start of benefits despite eligibility is allowed up to a third age.[11] These possibilities are shown in Table 2.1, raising three questions: how to choose among approaches, for each approach, how to choose the age or ages that make up the rule, and how much to vary benefits with the age at which they start.

Table 2.1 Starting benefits

	Benefit eligibility rule	
Benefit start rule	Age only	Age and earnings
Must start at eligibility	1	3
Can defer	2	4

Note: The size of the increase in benefits for a deferral forms an effective continuum from 'must start' to and beyond 'actuarially fair.'

In addition to rules relying on age and earnings, there are rules that also include a measure of years of service. Offhand, I find it hard to think of a good reason for a national system to include a rule based on years of service, however sensible that might be in some industries. I return to that issue below.

2.4.1 Age-only Eligibility Rules

The simplest case to consider is where benefit eligibility is an age-only rule. Assume there is an earliest entitlement age, EEA, at which benefits start, whether continuing to work or not. Assume there is no opportunity for a worker to delay the start of benefits in order to receive larger ones. Then the remaining individual decisions are when to stop working and how much saving, if any, to do in addition to payments to the mandatory program. In thinking about how to set EEA, there are two dimensions to the effects of alternative levels of EEA – what happens to the cash flow to different workers and how worker behavior varies with the level of EEA.

Assume that the level of resources flowing to retirement incomes is independent of EEA (in present discounted value, PDV). Then, the higher the EEA, the higher the benefits per month once they start. This has three implications. With the PDV of benefits the same, a higher level starting later implies fewer earlier payments and more later payments. With the same timing on tax collection, that would be an increase in national savings. Second, every worker would be receiving a higher level of annuitized benefits. If workers are not overannuitized, that represents providing more insurance against the risk associated with length of life. Third, there is a redistribution of lifetime benefits in that those with longer life expectancy gain at the expense of those with shorter life expectancy. Or, assuming that everyone gains from more annuitization at an individual break-even, those with longer lives have a further gain, while those with shorter lives have an offsetting loss. Since higher earners (of each gender) tend to have longer expected lives, the higher the EEA, the more regressive the system is within gender. On the other hand, since women tend to live longer than men, and women tend to have lower earnings than men, a higher EEA is more progressive on this basis. A full examination is more complex given the presence of marriage and the tendency of couples to share their resources somewhat.

There are two aspects to this increase in EEA – a disappearance of benefit cash flow at some ages and an increase in the level of annuitized benefits at higher ages. Some workers have greater needs earlier, for example those with poor or no earnings opportunities and little other income or wealth. Other workers have greater needs later, for example those with jobs paying well (relative to past earnings) and a pension benefit replacement rate well below one. Thus, a critical question is which EEA does better in providing a larger cash flow when it is needed more. Plausibly the relative weight in the two concerns shifts monotonically with the level of EEA, making analysis of this aspect of the choice of EEA straightforward.

The next step is to consider how the change in flows affects individual worker behavior. To focus on the non-redistributive aspect of this, we analyze the case for a worker who has the same present discounted value of benefits independent of EEA.[12] To proceed we need to consider different models of how workers might react to different choices of EEA.

Forward-looking workers who behave along the lines of the life-cycle model are mostly unaffected by an increase in EEA if the increased EEA is earlier than the date at which they stop working. The exceptions would be the workers who will work so long relative to life expectancy that they would like to use some of their retirement benefits for consumption while still working. In contrast, a life-cycle worker who would retire at or before the original EEA may find it optimal to work longer than otherwise (unless savings levels were already adequate to finance consumption from the end of work to the start of benefits). Overall, for such sensible workers, the presence of limited access to retirement benefits is a form of capital market imperfection. By itself, the earlier the EEA, the better from this perspective.

However, insofar as individual savings do not get annuitized, or get annuitized with a heavier administrative load than is provided by the public system (at the margin), then, there is a gain from delay through the mechanism of providing more insurance. That is, with a market imperfection of poorly priced or non-existent private annuities, the larger annuities from a later EEA can have value for offsetting this market imperfection. Thus this consideration tends to support an EEA in the interior of the set of times when sensible forward-looking workers would choose to stop working without an EEA restriction.

This analysis would be different if we were considering offering a particular level of monthly benefits and varying the tax rate to finance different levels of EEA. In that case the focus would be on the level of retirement savings that was optimal for different workers rather than the level of annuitization. Again, we would balance those who wanted more savings against those who wanted less, again assuming that the private market did not offer as attractive an alternative (for example through poor functioning of the annuities market from either the supply or demand side).

The analysis takes on a different flavor when we consider some alternative models of behavior, models that show plausibility for some workers given empirical studies of consumption and retirement. Some workers may retire as soon as benefits become available even if that implies inadequate resources for the full remaining expected life. Some indirect evidence for workers like this appears in the large spike of workers retiring as soon as benefits become available, even in systems that provide a generous increase in benefits for a delayed start, as in the US. Direct evidence would focus on consumption trajectories given a belief that some patterns of declining consumption are not plausibly *ex ante* optimal. Studies of consumption and resources at different ages are suggestive. Increasing EEA then protects some workers (and their spouses) from retiring sooner than would be sensible given their resources and the remaining life expectancy of the worker and spouse. On the other hand, raising EEA too high would force some workers who do not save to continue working longer than may be optimal given the PDV of their future benefits.

A second form of inefficiency arises for workers who do continue working if they consume too much from the combination of ongoing wages and the start of retirement benefits relative to their later needs. Again one would look at the pattern of consumption over the lifetime to identify the presence of this concern.

Formal modeling of an optimal EEA would evaluate the gains to different types of workers associated with different levels of EEA. While variation in life expectancy is measurable and the correlation of life expectancy with incomes is measurable, there are aspects of this issue that are very hard to measure. In particular, it is hard to know how many workers gain from working longer (because they have too few resources for a fully comfortable retirement), as opposed to how many lose (because they would sensibly retire earlier if they had earlier access to retirement resources).

Note that insofar as the choice of EEA affects the extent of work, and insofar as the extra benefits as a result of extra work differ from the extra payroll taxes paid, the system will gain or lose additional net revenues from an increase in EEA that induces more work. It is important to recognize that delaying the EEA may be of little (or even negative) consequence to Social Security finances depending on how much benefits increase with an increase in the age at which they start. That is, with actuarial adjustment of benefits for the age at which they start, EEA is primarily an issue of pension adequacy, not of pension finance. In practice both adequacy and finance are considered together along with the EEA. Similarly, inducing more work by actually subsidizing a longer career hurts finances (unless packaged with other elements that more than offset this).

Assume that an EEA is chosen based on some evaluation of the issues discussed above. Then, it is natural to ask how that EEA should change over time. Note that a change in EEA is likely to have little impact on system net fiscal balance if the adjustment of benefits for a delayed start is roughly actuarial. This is very different from a change in the age at which benefits are paid subject to the basic formula (an age for what are sometimes called full benefits). The latter is equivalent to some pattern of benefit cuts in that benefits are lower at any given retirement age.

2.4.2 Allowing Deferral of the Start of Benefits

One could readily amend the system described above by allowing larger benefits for a later start for workers who choose to delay the start.[13] Workers might choose to delay the start of benefits for several reasons.[14] One is that they are still working (and so not liquidity constrained) and value either the additional insurance that comes with higher monthly benefits or are concerned about their self-control with a larger cash flow and choose to have higher benefits starting later to avoid the temptation of spending too much earlier in their lives.

The other incentive comes from believing one has a long enough life expectancy that one sees profit in expected present discounted value (that is, ignoring risk aversion) from a delay. This adverse selection effect implies that there is a difficult actuarial estimation in designing a system that is revenue neutral (actuarially fair). If an equilibrium can be found with this property, then the additional choice given to workers is purely a gain (apart from some workers who perversely save too much – which is not normally seen as a widespread concern).[15] Of course the result that with break-even pricing there will be a Pareto (or near-Pareto) gain in expected utilities, if delay is priced actuarially for those delaying, does not imply that this is the optimal pricing. By being slightly less favorable in benefit increases it would discourage some who would defer (an efficiency cost) but would permit a redistribution from those who defer to those who do not, based on the gain from those still deferring. Since those deferring are plausibly likely to be better off than those not deferring, such a deviation from actuarially fair pricing may be worthwhile in social welfare terms (Sheshinski, 2001).

2.4.3 Age and Earnings Eligibility Rules

Starting from an age-only rule, we can consider adding a requirement (at least for a period of time) that one must stop work (or a very low level of earnings to allow part-time work and work by those with very low earnings) in order to start receiving benefits. The effect of adding such a retirement test (or earnings test) runs differently through different models of worker behavior.

For most people following the life-cycle model, requiring an end to work in order to start benefits would be of little consequence since mostly they do not start using the benefits to finance consumption until they do stop work. If everyone were like this, then adding a requirement of stopping work would open up the possibility of improved insurance (Diamond and Mirrlees, 1978; 1986; forthcoming). That is, some people stop working because of poor realizations of random outcomes such as work opportunities or the utility cost of continuing work. By providing a less than actuarial increase in benefits for a delayed start associated with continued work, the system can provide higher benefits for those who stop work earlier out of the resources freed up by lower benefits (in PDV) for those working longer. In this way more insurance is provided against the poor realizations that shorten working life. That is, one can use earnings as an observable variable correlated with unobservables such as earnings opportunities or work disutilities. Of course, there is some labor market disincentive associated with this, but as is always the case with second-best insurance, some distortion of the labor market in order to have more insurance is worthwhile in simple settings. This is likely to carry over quite generally.

This analysis does need adjustment to recognize that some life-cycle savers might want to start drawing on retirement funding to finance higher consumption while continuing to work, as noted above. Limiting this availability would then have an efficiency cost in two senses – it would make consumption less efficient for those who do continue working and it would add to the responsiveness of premature retirement in order to start receiving benefits.

Also interesting is the response of workers who are less forward looking. For those who do not alter their work experience, providing benefits while they continue to work runs the danger of greater early consumption than is optimal, resulting in declining living standards after they do stop working.[16] Thus a requirement of retirement helps these workers on a lifetime basis. Offsetting this is the discouragement of further work since stopping work is needed to start getting these benefits. This may be particularly costly if these workers are prone to retire 'too soon' for their own good anyway – so that encouraging further decreases in working life has a sizable effect right from the start.

In other words, we expect a spike in the retirement hazard at the EEA. Part of this spike comes from life-cycle workers who wanted to retire earlier but waited for liquidity reasons, and from life-cycle workers with short life expectancies so that the increase in benefits for a delayed start involves an implicit tax for them even if it is actuarially fair on average. (Offsetting this spike is the set of people who would have retired by EEA but delay retirement because of the implicit subsidy in actuarially fair benefit increases when one has above average life expectancy.) Part of the spike comes from workers who stop work short-sightedly as early as they are able to access benefits. Adding to this spike by requiring a stop of work in order to collect benefits has a social cost that is not second order.

Consideration of these short-sighted workers raises the issue of whether there is some design of benefit provision that would result in more work without as large a resource cost as simply paying much more for additional work. That is, is there a way of providing benefits different from the rule that they are real annuities starting with the end of work that would result in more efficient decisions? One possibility is to have benefits that start smaller and grow faster than real annuities (with the same PDV). In addition to influencing career-length decisions, this has income distribution implications based on length of expected life. Further examples lie in the realm of behavioral economics. There have been proposals, although I have not seen a derivation of such proposals from basic psychological premises that have been empirically supported. Henry Aaron suggested offering a sizable lump sum benefit after a period of time (three years, say) for those continuing to work beyond EEA (Fetherstonhaugh and Ross, 1999). The argument is that a lump sum in the future would be perceived as a larger incentive than an increase in monthly benefits with the same PDV. If the lump sum payment is age related then one has to recognize that it is provided before some people would retire anyway. A smoother incentive does not play off the difference in perceptions between lump sums and monthly flows, but in the tendency to pay too much attention to short run considerations. This proposal (Diamond, 1981) is to pay a steadily growing fraction of benefits independent of stopping work, while holding back the remaining fraction, with an increase in future benefits financed by the withheld sum. The idea is that the perception of steadily growing total income while continuing to work makes continued work more attractive. These ideas, and others that might come from further analysis based on behavioral analysis should be explored. Whether we can have the sort of success that has happened in encouraging contributions to individual pension accounts (Benartzi and Thaler, 2004) is unclear, and any experiment may be harder to organize.

My bottom line here is that it is plausible that some creative use of withholding benefits in response to continued work may be able to make a well-designed social insurance program better. It is plausible that the choice of EEA would be different with and without an earnings test. A system that withholds benefits until work stops but imposes very large implicit taxes through inadequate or non-existent increases in benefits for a delayed start is a very poor design, and one that has historically been far too common.

2.4.4   Age-varying Eligibility Rules

It is natural that the mix of worker types being influenced by rules governing the payment of benefits would change with age. Thus it seems plausible that the rules for benefit eligibility should vary systematically with age. Without in any way endorsing the particular ages used in the US (which have come historically from legislative parallels, not a detailed policy study), it seems to me plausible that having an earnings test over some range of ages and then paying benefits without regard to continued work makes sense.

2.4.5   Varying Benefits with the Age at Which They Start

With a defined contribution system, assuming no change in interest rates or cohort mortality expectations or degree of price competition, the change in level of monthly benefits from a delayed start in benefits would be roughly 'actuarially fair' in the sense that the expected present discounted value of benefits would be roughly the same whether there was a delay in starting benefits or not for the pool of annuitants who are combined in a single risk classification. Continued contributions while working would raise the benefit level as would a delayed start in benefits. A public defined benefit system could adjust benefits on the same basis (and an NDC system is designed in parallel with a DC system).

It should be noted that a system that is actuarially fair for a group of workers will give a better return than would be fair for some and a lower return than would be fair for others. This is true whether or not there is risk classification with separate pricing for separate groups. Moreover, workers would be aware on average of their differences in life expectancy (Hurd and McGarry, 1995). Generally public systems use the same annuitization factors for individuals, independent of both easily measured factors that are correlated with life expectancy, such as sex and earnings level, and the possibility of trying to measure health or health practices (for example special prices for smokers).

There are two questions about the social desirability of break-even pricing for each risk classification. One is whether even with uniform life expectancy within a risk class, social goals across groups are optimized by actuarial fairness. The other is whether the heterogeneity in the population within each classification is a basis for pricing that varies from actuarial fairness. There are research papers that have addressed both issues (Sheshinski, 2001).

But in order to make sense of the question, we need to put it in the context of retirement decisions. Workers have three options assuming that retirement is required for the start of benefits (at least over some range of ages). One option is to retire and start benefits. A second option is to continue work and delay benefits. The third option is to retire and still defer the start of benefits. In the US, while most workers do one of the first two, a small but significant fraction of workers do the last option. I will not run through how workers conforming to different behavioral models contribute to different choices for both the EEA and the size of the increase in benefits for a delayed start.

2.4.6 Benefit Eligibility Based on Length of Service

It is common in industry- or firm-based defined benefit plans to make use of years-of-service as a key variable in determining benefits. Some national systems do this as well. I can see how this may make sense in a single type of job, but have trouble seeing that it makes sense in a national system applying to a wide range of different types of work. Of course the level of benefits should vary with the length of career (as happens with DC and NDC systems and some other DB systems) but should the age for full benefits or the EEA vary with length of career? This raises a question of whether to think of the ability/difficulty of work in terms of age or in terms of years of service – with those starting later (for additional education or time spent with children) significantly more able to continue working than others of the same age who had an earlier start.[17] The ability to hold jobs that make it sensible to work to later ages is plausibly correlated with length of education. Thus this is a vehicle for explicit or implicit redistribution. I do not know of research sorting this issue out, but I am skeptical of the value of relying on years of service.

2.5 CONCLUDING REMARKS

It is common for national pension systems to have poorly designed rules, causing more labor market distortions than are appropriate given the insurance and redistribution goals of the system. While designing optimal systems is beyond current research capability given complexity, data availability, and population diversity, improving many existing systems is not beyond our capability.

2.A APPENDIX: MODELS OF RETIREMENT DECISIONS

2.A.1 Individual Choice

Consider an $n+3$ period model. Assume that everyone works in the first n periods which are identical and referred to collectively as period 1, no one works in periods 3 and 4, and work in period 2 is the choice variable of concern. These assumptions could be derived from more fundamental assumptions about preferences and opportunities. Assume also that everyone survives to period 3 and there may be a positive probability of death prior to period 4.

2.A.1.1 Certainty model

For convenience I assume a zero utility discount rate and zero interest rate. Denote the utility of consumption when working at age z by $u[c] - a_z$. Denote the utility of consumption when retired by $v[x]$. Using separate notation for consumption whether working or not is convenient. Denote the wage at age z by w_z, with the same wage (and same labor disutility) in the first n periods, and assume no lump sum income. Then utility maximization can be written as the choice between an n period career and an $n+1$ period career. In both cases consumption will be the same in periods of work and in periods of retirement. With an n-period career, using a superscript 0 to denote choice variables, utility maximization is

$$Maximize_{c,x} \quad nu[c^0] - na_1 + 3v[x^0]$$

$$\text{subject to: } nc^0 + 3x^0 = nw_1$$

(2.1)

With $n+1$ periods of work, using a superscript 1 to denote choice variables, we have

$$Maximize_{c,x} \ (n+1)u[c^1] - na_1 - a_2 + 2v[x^1]$$

$$(2.2)$$

$$\text{subject to: } (n+1)c^1 + 2x^1 = nw_1 + w_2$$

Given the utility-of-consumption functions, u and v, the choice of length of career depends on the disutility of labor and wage in period 2. Consumption in period 2 might be higher or lower than w_2, with a sufficient condition for it to be lower (to not decumulate) being $w_1 \leq w_2$.

To see the outcome most simply, let us assume that the two utility-of-consumption functions, u and v are the same. Then, in this certainty setting, consumption is the same in every period. With an n-period career, lifetime utility is $(n+3)u[nw_1 /(n+3)] - na_1$.

With an $n+1$-period career, lifetime utility is $(n+3)u[(nw_1 + w_2)/(n+3)]$ $-na_1 - na_2$.

Comparing these two expressions makes clear the role of both the wage and the disutility of labor in choosing the length of a career; w_2 is added to lifetime resources and a_2 is subtracted from lifetime utility.

Note that depending on the size of these two parameters, consumption in period 2 might be higher or lower than earnings in period 2 for someone with an $n+1$-period career. That is, a worker might want access to asset accumulation for retirement while continuing to work. With a zero interest rate, having consumption exceed the wage is equivalent to having asset values decline. With positive interest, this equivalence does not apply. The focus is on the sign of the wage less consumption.

2.A.1.2 Uncertainty model

Adding uncertainty about a_2 and w_2 would add realism and more readily allow for decumulation while working. That is, with certainty, earlier consumption adapts to planned career length as influenced by a_2 and w_2. With uncertainty, prior consumption is necessarily independent of the realization of these variables in period 2. Thus there is less scope for adaptation to a better career opportunity (higher wages or lower disutility), resulting in a larger impact of work on consumption in period 2 while continuing to work.

Similarly, adding the arrival of information about life expectancy at the start of period 2 (assuming no insurance) opens up a similar opportunity as can be seen by assuming that the information changes the probability of survival to period 4 from 1 to 0. The realization of the shorter life and so altered budget constraint may result in a prompt retirement or may result in work and asset decumulation, even if there would have been continued accumulation if the news was of survival to period 4. A similar possibility would arise with stochastic interest rates – a surprise increase in rates could also lead to decumulation while continuing work.

NOTES

*   I am grateful to Elsa Fornero for helpful comments.
1.   Both stopping work and starting retirement benefits are often referred to as 'retiring'. Yet these are distinct concepts and I will avoid referring to either as the start of retirement.
2.   This chapter considers rules for national systems that apply to many different industries. To an economist it seems obvious that such a system should not have a single mandatory retirement age. Whether such a rule is appropriate and useful in some particular industries requires different analysis.
3.   This chapter considers rules for retirement benefits without also considering rules for disability benefits. The interaction between disability and retirement rules is an important subject. See, for example, Diamond and Sheshinski (1995). I also do not consider programs that provide minimum income guarantees to the poor elderly. These also interact with retirement income rules, particularly if retirement income is not annuitized. Not that these issues are unimportant – it is just that this is a limited chapter.
4.   This chapter does not consider the optimal overall level of benefits, just the relative levels for different ages. On the former, see Diamond (1995). It is also limited in considering retirement income systems without acknowledging the presence of other institutions, such as annual income taxes, that affect the implications and interpretation of behavioral responses to the retirement income system.
5.   Existing systems tend to count or not count earnings in individual years. A more complex weighting scheme could likely do better in insuring the risk associated with the earnings trajectory.
6.   For some discussion of issues in the treatment of widows, see Diamond (1995; 2004).
7.   For a systematic study of this issue, see Brown (2003).
8.   The latter includes choices such as whether to index, whether to have a flat benefit or a sloped benefit relative to the index, whether to use single-life or some form of joint-life annuities, and whether to include a contingent bequest in the annuity contract (often referred to as a guarantee).
9.   In the US, withdrawals from tax-favored retirement accounts must start by age 70½..
10.   For those earnings just a little more than the exempt amount, benefits would be reduced to offset some fraction of those earnings, and later benefits would be increased to counterbalance the decrease.
11.   In the US benefits are subject to an earnings test between age 62 and what is called the Normal Retirement Age (but would more accurately be called the Age for Full Benefits), which is in the process of changing from 65 to 67. There is no earnings test after the Normal Retirement Age, and the ability to defer benefits in order to receive larger ones stops at age 70, when benefits simply begin.
12.   If a worker works longer as a consequence of a change in EEA, there is also a change in benefits and taxes as a consequence. We assume these just balance, not including an implicit tax.
13.   I assume that the adjustment factor is the same for everyone.
14.   For evidence that some workers delay benefits that could be claimed in the US, see Coile et al. (2002).
15.   On having more choice generating a Pareto gain with all workers rational, see Diamond (1992).
16.   There have been estimates of the implications of consuming benefits while continuing to work at different ages in the US as part of the discussion leading up to the legislation that removed the earnings test between the Normal Retirement Age and age 70, but did not remove it between age 62 and the Normal Retirement Age (Gruber and Orszag, 2000).

17. Such a distinction is defeated if credits are given for time in higher education.

REFERENCES

Benartzi, S. and R. Thaler (2004), 'Save More Tomorrow: Using Behavioral Economics to Increase Employee Saving', *Journal of Political Economy*, **112**(1), pp. S164–87.

Brown, J. (2003), 'Redistribution and Insurance: Mandatory Annuitization with Mortality Heterogeneity', *Journal of Risk and Insurance*, **70**(1), pp. 19–43.

Brugiavini, A. (1993), 'Uncertainty Resolution and the Timing of Annuity Purchases', *Journal of Public Economics*, **50**, pp. 31–62.

Coile, C. and J. Gruber (2001), 'Social Security Incentives for Retirement', in D. Wise (ed.), *Themes in the Economics of Aging*, Chicago: University of Chicago Press, pp. 311–41.

Coile, C., P. Diamond, A. Jousten and J. Gruber (2002), 'Delays in Claiming Social Security Benefits', *Journal of Public Economics*, **84**, pp. 357–85.

Davidoff, T., J. Brown and P. Diamond (2003), 'Annuities and Individual Welfare', NBER Working Papers 9714.

Diamond, P. (1981), 'Social Security: A Case for Changing the Earnings Test But Not the Normal Retirement Age', unpublished.

Diamond, P. (1992), 'Organizing the Health Insurance Market', *Econometrica*, **60**, pp. 1233–54.

Diamond, P. (1995), 'Government Provision and Regulation of Economic Support in Old Age', in M Bruno and B. Pleskovic (eds), *Annual Bank Conference on Development Economics*, Washington, DC: The World Bank, pp. 83–103.

Diamond, P. (2004), 'Social Security', *American Economic Review*, **94**, pp. 1–24.

Diamond, P. and J. Mirrlees (1978), 'A Model of Social Insurance with Variable Retirement', *Journal of Public Economics*, **10**, pp. 295–36.

Diamond, P. and J. Mirrlees (1986), 'Payroll-tax Financed Social Insurance with Variable Retirement', *Scandinavian Journal of Economics*, **88**(1), pp. 25–50.

Diamond, P. and J. Mirrlees (forthcoming), 'Social Insurance with Variable Retirement and Private Saving', *Journal of Public Economics*.

Diamond, P. and E. Sheshinski (1995), 'Economic Aspects of Optimal Disability Benefits', *Journal of Public Economics*, **57**(1), pp. 1–23.

Fetherstonhaugh, D. and L. Ross (1999), 'Framing Defects and Income Flow Preferences in Decisions about Social Security', in H. J. Aaron (ed.), *Behavioral Dimensions of Retirement Economics*, Brookings and Russell Sage Foundation, pp. 187–208.

Gruber, J. and P. Orszag (2000), 'Does the Social Security Earnings Test Affect Labor Supply and Benefits Receipt?', NBER Working Paper 7923.

Hurd, M. and K. McGarry (1995), 'Evaluation of the Subjective Probabilities of Survival in the HRS', *Journal of Human Resources*, **30**, pp. S268–92.

Sheshinski, E. (2001), 'Optimum and Risk-Class Pricing of Annuities', unpublished.

Yaari, M. (1965), 'Uncertain Lifetime, Life Insurance, and the Theory of the Consumer', *Review of Economic Studies*, **32**(2), pp. 137–50.

3. Retirement incentives and retirement*

Sarah Bridges and Richard Disney

3.1 INTRODUCTION

Demographic ageing in OECD countries poses a problem for the viability of unfunded public pension programmes. A number of strategies to cap programme spending are regularly discussed but several have proved difficult to implement in practice. For example, reductions in programme generosity that enforce benefit reductions on existing recipients have often proved to be politically infeasible. And there are both political and economic limits to the scope for spreading the costs of paying for pensions by increased labour force participation rates or accelerated immigration. Given these constraints, an attractive response to demographic ageing is to combat the long run downward trend in economic activity rates amongst workers of 50 and over, thereby raising the ratio of contributors to pensioners (the 'support ratio'). For example, the Stockholm European Council has set a target to increase the average European Union employment rate for older men and women (aged 55–64) to 50 per cent by 2010.[1]

Falling employment rates of older people of working age can be curbed, it is argued, by supply-side measures designed to increase the incentives for people to retire later. This approach is central to a number of studies under the auspices of OECD, the genesis of which can be traced back to the influential 'Jobs Study' of the mid-1990s (OECD, 1995), and underlies the international project on retirement developed at the National Bureau of Economic Research (Gruber and Wise, 1999). Since disincentives to continue work beyond a certain age are often directly embedded in the public tax and benefit regime, governments have an innate capacity to initiate reforms in this field. Studies suggest that the pay-off, in terms of higher economic activity rates, from reforming retirement incentives could be quite considerable. For example, the results of the OECD cross-country simulations of policy reforms conducted by Blöndal and Scarpetta (1997, 1998) suggest that moving to a regime in which there were no specific incentives to retire early (which will be defined as 'actuarial neutrality' shortly) would raise participation rates of 55–64-year-olds to over 60 per cent in all but three of the surveyed OECD countries (Blöndal and Scarpetta, 1998, par. 109).

In general, there is almost universal acceptance among economists that getting fiscal and tax incentives 'right' is a central aim of economic policy. In the present context, legal barriers to work for those people who wish to work later in life, such as mandatory retirement, are incompatible with individual choice and ignore the consequences of population ageing. However, countries differ in their institutional features, and it is important to design policy measures and to measure policy effectiveness in ways that capture this heterogeneity of programme design and programme response.

In addition to considering the 'supply side', it is also important not to lose sight of the impact of the demand side of the labour market on the economic activity of older workers. A buoyant macroeconomy facilitates the achievement of supply-side targets, such as higher employment rates. Indeed, shocks to aggregate demand may have disproportionate effects on the employment of more 'marginal' workers (that is those that face attractive outside options) such as older people through encouraged/discouraged worker effects. The size of these responses is likely to depend on institutional factors, such as the activities of trade unions and the forms of pay bargaining (Bertola et al., 2003). Some supply-side policies (such as changing the explicit costs of hiring older workers) may have effects on both the demand and the supply side of the labour market. Other policies, such as abolishing a mandatory retirement age, primarily operate through the supply side of the market, and the impact on employment should ideally be analysed in a macroeconomic framework, where relative wage rates vary to match changes in supply to the relative demands for different types of labour. Understanding these various interactions in each institutional context is a challenging research agenda.

This chapter considers three issues. First, it focuses on recent trends in the *demand* for older workers. Demand factors should not be forgotten in the quest to get incentives 'right'. Section 3.2 of the chapter shows that there has been a recovery in participation rates among older workers in many OECD countries since the mid-1990s. In fact there is little evidence that the countries that have seen the fastest rising participation rates have done disproportionately more to reform their public pension programmes, or their retirement incentives, than countries that have not done so (Italy, and perhaps Germany in earlier periods, seem to be clear and important exceptions to this generalisation). We argue that, in general, the most plausible reason for the increased economic activity rates among older workers in recent years is increased demand for older workers. In particular, cross-country variation in real GDP growth is strongly associated with changes in economic activity rates. The nature of the employment response strongly suggests that this is largely an 'encouraged worker effect' in most countries rather than a supply-side driven response.

The remainder of the chapter reverts to the question of how we measure the economic (dis)incentives to work arising from public pension programmes, and the behavioural response of participants to such (dis)incentives. Section 3.3 of the chapter first follows the standard approach in deriving a benchmark of 'actuarial neutrality' against which to judge programme incentives to retire early or later. The 'implicit tax rate' then defines the cost of deferring retirement, relative to the benchmark of actuarial neutrality. Calculating 'implicit tax rates' on work later in life has been central to much of the empirical analysis that has been undertaken in recent years.

Section 3.3 makes the simple (and unoriginal) point that this 'implicit tax rate' is only relevant to retirement decisions under certain conditions: there must be a 'window' in which the individual has choice as to when to retire, and retirement must be a condition for receipt of public pension benefits. There are some countries where one or both of these features are absent. In those countries, simple and transparent policies for improving economic activity amongst older workers, such as lengthening the retirement 'window' (for example, linking state pension age to expected longevity improvements) and abandoning retirement tests, may prove most successful in the long run. Again, institutional differences matter in designing and implementing supply-side policies: a 'one size fits all' policy agenda is not appropriate. [2]

Given this variety in the design of retirement incentives across countries, Section 3.4 of the chapter considers strategies for the empirical modelling of the impact of changes in retirement incentives. Policy reforms, whether simulated or observed, can be thought of as 'quasi-experiments' or treatments, by which participants are subject to alternative external regimes and the responses monitored. In this respect, the chapter argues, simulations of behavioural responses derived from cross-country regressions should be treated with caution. In contrast, there are other methods of measuring policy responses that utilise explicit control groups against which to measure the effects of policies. Such 'controlled experiments' provide a more precise measure of outcomes. Inevitably, however, such treatments are limited in scope, both temporally and geographically. Methodologically, alternative modelling procedures are trading generality for precision – a common problem in economic modelling. Overall, however, the analysis argues for care in modelling disparate retirement regimes. These arguments are developed utilising case studies of policy changes in a number of countries, including Italy, the UK and the US.

3.2 RECENT EVIDENCE ON PARTICIPATION RATES OF OLDER WORKERS

It is well known that economic activity rates of older workers in almost all developed countries have fallen substantially over the last century, but especially in the period from the early 1970s to the mid-1990s.[3] In general terms, the fall in activity rates has been attributed to income effects arising from increased household wealth, and to increased generosity of (and, in some cases, earlier eligibility for) public pension benefits. Mandatory retirement may also have played a role in particular institutional settings.

The demand side of the market for older workers has been less extensively modelled, although there is qualitative and quantitative evidence that workers of different ages are imperfect substitutes, both in type and extent of skill (Disney, 1996). Moreover, there are grounds for believing, particularly under certain institutional conditions, that demand as well as supply elasticities for older workers are higher than, for example, among prime age males (Bertola et al., 2003).

In the light of these forces from both sides of the market, it is interesting to note that the period since the mid-1990s has seen a reversal of the trend towards lower economic activity rates among older workers. Table 3.1 plots changes in the employment–population ratios for two older age groups each of men and women, for the period 1996–2001, as well as real GDP growth in each country over the period 1995–2001. It will be seen that employment–population growth rates have generally been positive – substantially so for women in a number of countries – and significantly so overall if one abstracts from the performance of the transition economies of Central Europe where, with the exception of Hungary, employment–population rates of older workers have declined significantly.

Is there any pattern to these changes across countries? Certainly the countries of the European Union seem to have done rather better than those outside the EU in terms of increased economic activity rates. For example, for men the average rise in the employment–population ratio for 50–54-year-olds in the EU was 2.8 per cent compared to 0.7 per cent for the countries as a whole, and 2.6 per cent for 55–59-year-olds compared to 1.2 per cent for the overall average. This growth precedes the Stockholm target.[4] Inspection suggests that these disparities between EU and non-EU countries are not eliminated by removing the underperforming Central European countries: compare Denmark and Sweden on the one hand with Norway and Iceland on the other, or EU members with the group 'Other developed OECD'.[5] Nor is it because of differential real economic growth between EU and non-EU countries – overall real GDP growth from 1995–2001 was 22.1 per cent for the countries as a whole and 22.8 per cent for the EU countries.

Table 3.1 Changes in employment–population ratios of older workers and GDP growth rates, OECD countries, 1996–2001 (percentage points)

Country	Men 50–54	Men 55–59	Women 50–54	Women 55–59	GDP growth 1995-2001(%)
Scandinavia					
Denmark	2.3	3.4	7.6	17.6	16
Iceland	0.1	2.3	1.3	3.7	29
Norway	0.2	0.8	3	5.5	21
Sweden	3.1	−0.7	2.8	0.2	19
NW Europe					
Austria	0.9	−0.2	6.4	0.1	15
Belgium	2.4	3.4	11.4	6.7	15
France	1	1.7	3.1	3.9	16
Germany	0.5	1.1	5.2	1.1	10
Ireland	6.6	6.6	13.1	7.9	67
Luxembourg	3.3	2.6	9.7	7.8	40
Netherlands	4.8	12.2	12.1	9.1	21
UK	2.8	4.7	3.7	5	18
S. Europe					
Greece	−1.5	−2.9	2.4	−1.3	23
Italy	4.4	−5.1	3.8	1.9	12
Portugal	2.9	2.6	8.9	2.5	23
Spain	5.9	7.3	7.6	5	25
Other developed OECD					
Australia	1.9	1.3	6.3	1.3	25
Canada	1.6	2.2	7.7	5.6	23
Japan	−2.8	−2.6	0.5	−0.4	7
New Zealand	1.6	1.3	1.6	3.8	17
US	−0.3	−0.5	2.7	2.1	22
Europe transition economies					
Czech Republic	−1.5	−2.1	−1.9	−0.2	10
Hungary	3.3	8.2	9.9	8.7	27
Poland	−8	−3.6	−4.2	−3.3	30
Slovak Rep	−5.5	−1.4	1.9	−1.2	25
Turkey	−10	−8.4	−7.4	−10.5	12

Source: OECD website.

At an individual country level, however, individual GDP performance plays a major part in explaining the differences in the growth of employment–population ratios since 1996. There are individual countries that fit a GDP-driven 'story' particularly well – Ireland, which has had a rapid increase in GDP, has seen the employment–population ratio of older workers rise very sharply, whereas Japan has seen both low economic growth and a falling employment–population ratio amongst older workers.[6] More formally, we can examine the cross-country correlations between GDP growth and changes in employment–population rates across countries. These are provided in Table 3.2.

Table 3.2 Cross-country correlations of changes in employment–population ratios and real GDP growth

	Men aged 50–54	Men aged 55–59	Women aged 50–54	Women aged 55–59
All countries	0.310	0.388	0.434	0.279
Excluding transition economies	0.512	0.396	0.514	0.268

The correlations are positive and significant. They are even stronger when we look only at the European economies excluding the transition states. Given measurement error in aggregates, we could not expect to see coefficients close to unity, so these results are strongly indicative of GDP growth being a key driver of employment–population rates among these age groups. Of course, correlation is not causation and these results are not prima facie evidence of demand-side factors dominating – if incentives were improved, one might expect to see greater real output as a result of the higher rates of employment. Without more structure, we cannot tell whether the dominant factor is output driving employment or the converse, but the results are certainly consistent with standard 'stories' such as encouraged worker effects.

Note that these results are weaker for workers aged 55–59, closer to normal retirement age, compared to those aged 50–54. This confirms the more detailed analysis for the United Kingdom in Disney and Hawkes (2003), which suggests that the response of employment of older workers to GDP growth declines with age for those aged over 50 – elasticities of employment growth to GDP growth fall from around 0.2 at age 50 to around 0.02 at age 65. The UK research also provides evidence that responsiveness varies by skill category – elasticities are generally around 0.05 higher for skilled than unskilled workers (defined as whether workers have qualifications beyond first school leaving age). Again, these discrepancies in responses across age and skill groups suggest that we are not primarily observing responses to incentive structures, but differential responses to changes in demand conditions.

Is there any evidence from Table 3.1 that countries where employment–population responses are higher have introduced wide-ranging programme reforms, especially reforms that have increased the incentive to work later in life? Italy, Sweden and the UK introduced substantial reforms of their pension programmes over this period, while New Zealand raised the retirement age significantly and countries such as Belgium made some efforts to change retirement incentives to encourage later retirement. Of all these countries, perhaps Italy is the only one where a reform impact is observable from Table 3.1, since there are quite different trends in employment–population ratios for 50–54-year-olds and 55–59-year-olds (and which cannot therefore simply be explained by demand conditions). The changes to early retirement ('seniority pension') provisions in the reforms of the mid-1990s are almost certainly reflected in these data, and we return to the Italian case later. There is little other evidence of institutional conditions underpinning these results – for example, those across the broad groupings of countries. Again, the main exception is the group of transition economies that have, with the exception of Hungary, seen substantial falls in employment–population ratios. The two countries with substantial pension reforms among this group are Hungary and Poland – both, but especially Hungary, introducing a private component into the pension programme.

To sum up the argument of this section: in contrast to trends for the preceding decades, the period of the late 1990s onwards saw rises in economic activity rates amongst older individuals of working age. Differences in these rises across countries are strongly associated with relative rates of real GDP growth. Moreover, greater sensitivity to GDP growth is associated with younger workers (within the age category 50+) and (from the UK experience) skills. These facts suggest that the employment growth of older workers in the period is primarily demand-led rather than driven by changes in retirement policy. The exception in this period appears to be Italy, where the differential rates of employment growth of those above and below age 55 is probably associated with the regime reforms of the early and mid-1990s.

3.3   MEASURING RETIREMENT INCENTIVES

We now consider the issue of retirement incentives in more detail. In recent years, a number of studies have implied that workers are sophisticated enough to evaluate the value of foregone retirement opportunities by comparing accrued pension rights to current earnings and increments to prospective pension wealth from deferring retirement. Depending on the structure of these implicit incentives or 'option values', this dynamic framework of analysis calculates substitution effects as well as income effects that may deter older individuals from continued work.

To discuss whether pension programmes discourage individuals from continuing in work, we need a benchmark against which to evaluate 'distortions' that encourage individuals to bring forward (or indeed defer) retirement. We term this (in common with a number of other studies) 'actuarial neutrality'.[7] Departures from actuarial neutrality imply that there are implicit tax rates on continued work.[8] The concept is discussed more fully in the next sub-section.

The second sub-section illustrates departures from 'actuarial neutrality' with two clear case studies (from Germany and Italy). It then makes two substantive points: (i) in a number of countries, people can both work and receive a state pension, so the 'implicit tax rate' does not bind, and (ii) measures of 'actuarial neutrality' should incorporate the whole tax and benefit regime. Countries that appear to be approximately 'actuarially neutral' when only the pension programme incentives are considered may not be neutral when other taxes (such as income taxes) are included as well as other benefits, and vice versa. Moving the pension programme towards 'actuarial neutrality' is desirable (for many reasons) but is but one of a package of policies that should be pursued.

3.3.1 Actuarial Neutrality

A static measure of the incentive to retire is the standard 'replacement rate' – measured as the ratio of pension benefits to earnings (the measured replacement rate will of course depend on whether the calculation is done before or after tax, the measure of 'earnings' and so on). A superior measure is forward-looking – examining the opportunity cost of continuing to work relative to current and expected benefits (which may themselves be affected by postponing the retirement decision) after the age at which the individual is first entitled to a public pension. This is commonly measured as the (marginal) implicit tax rate on (continued) employment. This calculated tax rate can be greater, less than or equal to zero. A benchmark for the retirement decision is where this implicit tax rate is zero and the individual's budget constraint gives an equal value to continuing to work and retiring now (in which case the retirement decision will wholly be determined by preferences). We term this actuarial benchmark where retirement age is flexible as *actuarial neutrality*.

To illustrate this point, define the expected effective tax rate, m, from one more year's work at age a at some time t as the *marginal implicit tax rate* = $m(t,a) = -\Delta p(t,a)/w(1 - x_w)(t,a)$ where the change in pension wealth at age a is Δp, the wage is w, and both are defined net of other personal taxes, x. Clearly the sign of m depends on the sign of Δp.

If we further define s_i as the probability of surviving from one period to the next, then $\Delta p = \sum_{i=a+1}^{\infty} s_i [p_{a+1} - p_a](1-x_p)(1+r)^{-(i-a)} - [c_a + p_a(1-x_p)]$ where c is the contribution rate. The first term represents the increased prospective pension benefit stream × the probability of surviving from a to $a+1$ (parameter s), and the second the costs of continuing to work as the contribution plus foregone pension at that age. When these are equal Δp is zero and so is m.

Note that the marginal implicit tax rate does not directly determine the retirement decision. It defines the budget constraint for every future date at which there is a choice between work and retirement (p_a gives the 'wealth effect', as a current annuity value). Within the 'window' during which the retirement date can be chosen, the pension accrual Δp will depend on the benefit formula (for example, whether an extra year of contributions 'count' towards benefits) as well as the possibility of deferring benefits, and at what rate.

The retirement decision depends on the rate at which the individual discounts benefits, which is a product of the interest rate, r, and the year-on-year probability of dying, ρ, which will be time varying. Write the rate of pension accrual as $\Delta p/p$. If $\Delta p/p \geq (r + \rho)$, then the implicit tax rate does not bind, as the individual would not have chosen to retire in that period. Nor does it bind if retirement is *not* a condition of public pension receipt or where individuals have the opportunity to defer retirement and accrue benefits at a rate $\Delta p/p \geq (r + \rho)$ (Burkhauser and Turner, 1978; Johnson, 2000). The implicit tax rate 'model' is therefore most pertinent in countries where (a) there is a retirement age 'window', (b) where receipt of the pension requires some degree of retirement from paid activity and (c) where deferral is non-existent or less than the 'actuarially neutral' rate. Stylised implicit tax rates for a range of OECD countries can be found in Gruber and Wise (1999), Table 1 and Blöndal and Scarpetta (1997), Table 5.

3.3.2 Empirical Illustrations

The relation of actual pension accrual rates to retirement age relative to a 'neutral' rate that takes account of age-specific mortality rates has been calculated for a number of countries. The chapter in this volume by Berkel and Börsch-Supan provides a clear illustration for Germany.

Italy, in Table 3.3, provides a particularly interesting illustration, in so far as these accrual rates change over time as a result of programme reforms. The 1995 reform introduced several regimes, which provide different retirement accrual rates for successive cohorts. Earlier cohorts remain within the 'redistributive' programme, in which there are generous early retirement provisions and therefore a positive implicit tax rate on continued work beyond the first age of attaining any retirement benefits. There are then 'transition' cohorts, whose benefit calculations are based on a mixture of the 'redistributive' programme and the post-1995 'contribution-based' calculation of benefits. Later cohorts will wholly come under the 'contributory' programme, in which pension accruals by age are broadly calculated by actuarial factors that adjust pension benefits to remaining average life expectancy. Given the parameter values chosen by the authors, the calculated implicit tax rate for the representative worker is approximately zero. Weaknesses of the 1995 reform include the long transition period, and the failure to index the first age of eligibility to subsequent growing life expectancy (Fornero and Castellino, 2001).

Table 3.3 Pension accrual rates and implicit tax rates for private sector workers in Italy by cohort and years of contribution

		Δpension accrual (m. lire 2000)			Implicit tax rate (%)		
		Years of contribution			Years of contribution		
Regime	Cohort	35	37	40	35	37	40
Redistributive	b. 1943	−19.44	−23.63	−31.05	43	52	72
	b. 1948	−24.78	−27.76	−32.88	52	59	72
	b. 1953	−25.65	−28.88	−32.94	53	61	72
Pro rata	b. 1958	−14.28	−14.25	−13.92	29	29	29
(transition)	b. 1963	−10.00	−9.86	−9.50	20	20	20
	b. 1968	−5.80	−5.56	−5.16	11	11	10
	b. 1973	−1.92	−1.63	−1.24	4	3	2
Contributory	b. 1978	−1.93	−1.64	−1.24	4	3	2
	b. 1983	−2.08	−1.79	−1.35	4	3	2
	b. 1988	−2.24	−1.90	−1.44	4	3	2

Notes:
Δpension accrual refers to the net gain in the pension stream from deferring retirement for one year. The implicit tax rate is also as defined there.

The calculations assume real income growth of 1.5 per cent and a real interest rate of 2 per cent. The worker started work at age 22 and therefore has 35 years of contributions at age 57.

Source: Fornero and Castellino (2001), Table 2.2.

A growing literature on retirement takes the modelling of the 'implicit tax rate' on work late in life as its centrepiece. However, as mentioned in the previous section, implicit tax rates will be a pertinent factor in retirement decisions only so long as there is some form of 'retirement test' and where incentives to defer are less than actuarially fair to the individual. Moreover, they only apply within the age 'window' in which retirement is permitted.

Other incentive considerations arise in countries that impose significant restrictions on retirement at any time other than a 'normal' age (that is where the retirement 'window' is very narrow) and, conversely, for countries that are much more flexible in permitting pension receipt without full retirement.

Table 3.4 provides evidence from OECD countries on these three parameters: retirement test, deferral rate and flexibility of retirement. The 'implicit tax rate' framework is most pertinent to the countries that have some form of earnings or retirement test (the first two categories) and in which there is some 'window' of retirement ages between which retirement is possible. Amongst these countries, only Japan has a reasonably generous deferral rate that is likely to satisfy the condition $\Delta p/p \geq (r + \rho)$, so the key conditions are only the existence of the retirement test and the retirement window. It is hard to think of a sensible rationale for enforcing retirement tests in the face of demographic ageing, other than as a second-best policy to offset other distortions, such as permitting early retirement at an excessively young age.

For other countries (the third category), the 'implicit tax' framework is less pertinent since individuals can both claim their public pension and work. A forward-looking individual who is not liquidity constrained should then choose the date of retiring from work independently from the date at which the public pension is available (of course, changes to 'retirement tests' thereby provide an excellent policy 'experiment' through which to investigate labour supply responses – see section 3.4). For example, in the United Kingdom there has been no retirement test since 1989 and no early retirement 'window' below 'normal' state pension age. The only parameter that is pertinent to the retirement decision in the public pension programme in the UK is the age of first receipt of the state pension – and a simple policy option should be to consider linking this explicitly to changes in average longevity.[9]

Finally, it should be noted that calculations of measures of 'actuarial neutrality' should take account of other taxes and benefits, and not just those implicit in the public pension programme. Figure 3.1 illustrates 'effective tax rates' calculated by Whitehouse (2002) for four countries, by age for representative income levels, when income taxes are included in the tax measure in addition to pension contributions. In some cases, the inclusion of personal taxes simply raises the tax rate proportionally at all ages. However, the effects may be non-proportional with age where, for example, Social Security contributions are only levied on the economically active, or only on those below a certain age, or where income tax structures (such as the value of tax allowances) vary by age and/or economic status.[10] This general point is illustrated in the case of Finland. In Japan, the inclusion of additional taxes actually shifts the regime closer to actuarial neutrality until age 65, but exacerbates the jump in the implicit tax rate thereafter. Germany from age 62

Table 3.4 Earnings tests and retirement flexibility in OECD countries

Earnings test	Disregard (% of average earnings)	Withdrawal rate (%)	Early/standard/ latest age of retirement	Pension adjustment
Yes + Deferral not possible				
Greece	116	Full	60/65/65	0.5% per month
Denmark	50	60	60/67/67	Pro rata maximum
Austria	30	Full	60/65/65	Yes
Belgium	33	100	60/65/65	UI credits
Norway	18	50	67/67/67	
Australia	8	50	65	
Ireland	18	Full	55/65/65	Means-tested
Portugal	None	Full	60/65/65	UI credits
Spain	None	Full	60/65/65	0.67% per month
Yes + Deferral possible				
Canada	160	15	60/65/70	0.5% per month
Italy	23	100	57/65/70	Varies by cohort
Japan	17–90/90	20/full	60/60/70	1–2% per month
United States	38	33–50	62/65/70	0.5% per month
No restrictions on work				
France, Germany, Finland, the Netherlands, New Zealand, Sweden, Switzerland, the UK				

Notes:
'Disregard' is the earnings level exempt from the application of the earnings test. The 'withdrawal rate' says, for every euro of outside earnings, the percentage of a euro in benefit withdrawn. 'Full' means that all benefit is withdrawn if the person has earnings (above the exemption level).

Pension receipt in Ireland, Portugal and Spain is conditional on withdrawal from work; France conditional on withdrawal from normal work. Canada – the test only applies on the earnings-rated segment and for Japan, pension adjustment only applies to part of the pension. Pension withdrawn at a 100 per cent rate between 29 and 33 per cent of average earnings in Belgium. Italy gives a higher disregard for self-employment incomes (which are an important income source) and has different applications of the test for seniority pensions and the old age pension. Australia has a means-tested Social Security system. The 'earnings test' in the US only applies between ages 62 and 64 from 2000.

Source: Blöndal and Scarpetta (1998), updated from Social Security Administration (1999), and by the US reform.

Finland

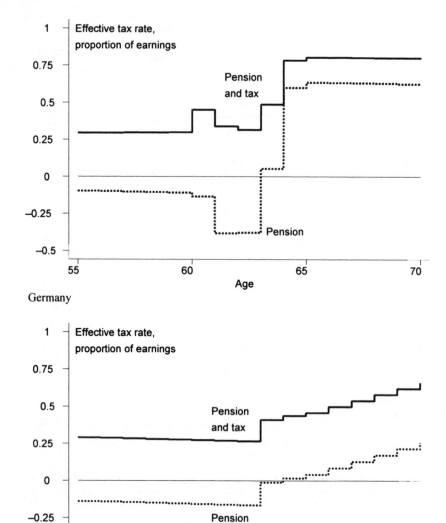

Figure 3.1 Average effective tax rates of continuing work by age including pension contributions and income taxes, selected countries

Japan

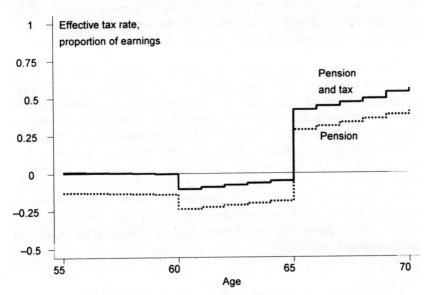

Sweden

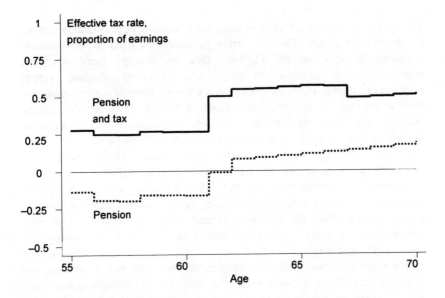

Figure 3.1 (continued)

in Figure 3.1 illustrates again the evidence in Berkel and Börsch-Supan's chapter. Sweden, after the 1998 reform, is indeed approximately neutral by age when additional income taxes are ignored but the inclusion of such taxes raises the measured effective tax rate, in particular exacerbating its rise at age 62.

To conclude the argument of this section, therefore: disincentives to continued work are often summarised by the 'implicit tax on work' constructed in a number of studies by OECD and the Gruber and Wise (1999) project. This serves as a useful benchmark for policy measures, and studies utilising cross-country differences and changes in these tax rates over time indeed show that these tax rates affect retirement behaviour. However, such calculations should take account of *all* household taxes and benefits: 'neutrality' in the pension programme can co-exist with significant non-neutralities in other taxes paid and benefits received by households. Where countries have no retirement tests, and narrow retirement 'windows', other simple reform options make more sense, such as linking first state pension age to expected longevity.

3.4 EMPIRICAL MODELLING OF RETIREMENT REGIMES AND RETIREMENT BEHAVIOUR

This section describes several strategies for estimating behavioural responses to retirement regimes. The first strategy, commonly used by international organisations such as OECD, uses data on average pension regime characteristics in each country and/or time period to calculate average responses to regime changes, exploiting variations across countries and over time in regimes to identify behavioural responses. The second strategy, broadly, uses micro-econometric methods to construct 'quasi-structural' models of labour supply across households with different characteristics. In the absence of regime changes within the sampling period, behavioural responses to reforms are estimated by imposing different regimes on participants and simulating outcomes. A third strategy uses the limited number of observed regime changes as 'experiments', either utilising a simple 'before–after' framework to measure the treatment effect, or more sophisticated strategies where 'controls' can be used to identify the 'treatment' more precisely.

We argue that each of these strategies has its merits and limitations, and that it is desirable to utilise a variety of measures of behavioural responses and to compare the magnitudes derived from different methodological approaches. The section provides examples of some studies that utilise the third strategy to identify 'treatment effects'. In particular, it provides some new evidence on the impact of the 1992 pension reform on the retirement behaviour of private sector workers in Italy.

3.4.1 Modelling Strategies

There are various methods by which estimates of behavioural responses to changes in retirement regimes are obtained. Several studies utilise cross-country panels containing various indicators of the retirement regime (such as a stylised 'average' replacement or implicit tax rate at time t), along with a vector of control variables including both economic and institutional factors. Time and/or cross-country variation in regime variables are then used to identify average policy responses. Blöndal and Scarpetta (1997, 1998) are the most well-known and comprehensive studies that adopt this approach to the modelling of retirement behaviour in OECD countries, although the general approach is applied in many studies to a number of related issues concerning tax and benefit regimes (Disney, 2004). These studies of retirement incentives suggest that departures from 'revenue neutrality' have large and significant impacts on retirement behaviour.

In general terms, studies of this type estimate the model:

$$\bar{y}_{it} = f_i + \beta I_{it} + \bar{z}_{it}'\gamma + \varepsilon_{it} \tag{3.1}$$

where $\bar{y}_{it}$ is, say, the economic activity rate of older workers in country i at time t, f_i is a country fixed effect, I is one or more indicator variables of the retirement regime (this can include categorical variables, or numerical variables such as average replacement or implicit tax rates) and $\bar{z}_{it}$ is a vector of categorical and continuous controls proxying underlying economic and institutional conditions. Cross-country estimates of the effect of the retirement regime on retirement are obtained from the association between economic activity rates and the within-country variation in regime indicators.

There are two difficulties with this approach. First, the indicator variables (such as 'the' average replacement rate) summarise heterogeneous within-country distributions of marginal rates. This is likely to induce measurement error, the effect of which will be compounded by identifying response of the within-country variation in the indicators over time. Whilst it is true that measurement error in general biases downwards coefficient estimates, we can make no a priori predictions as to the effect of the within-country aggregation procedure on the size and direction of the error.

Second, the linear specification assumes that the impact of variations in the regime indicators on outcomes (here, economic activity) is independent of the control variables, which typically include other institutional indicators such as whether there is coordinated or decentralised bargaining, strength of unionisation, and so on. All cross-country studies of this type suggest that these institutional factors are highly important determinants of labour market outcomes, but the implication of the chosen specification is that the impact of changes in the retirement regime is independent of the institutional setting. Put simply, an x per cent change in the average replacement rate or the implicit tax rate has exactly the same impact in Germany and the UK on retirement, despite their very different institutions. This would seem to be a strong and implausible assumption. It can be avoided by introducing further non-linearities – for example by interacting retirement regime indicators with other institutional indicators, but the limited dimensionality of the data and the difficulties in interpreting the ensuing parameter estimates militate against such a strategy.

A second modelling strategy, utilised in later 'rounds' of the Gruber–Wise international comparisons of Social Security regimes, is to estimate country-specific micro-econometric models of retirement behaviour in which the 'option value' of continued work is central to the modelling (Gruber and Wise, 2002). The attraction of this strategy, if successful, is that it identifies the parameters of the underlying model of labour supply. Model parameters are then used to simulate policy reforms (for example, changing retirement incentives, or deferring the first age of receiving the state pension). In a number of these studies, retirement incentives indeed have strong impacts on retirement behaviour, although responses seem to be country-specific. [11] A minor problem in such models is that the 'option values' are assumed to contain all the necessary information to model retirement. But where households have more complex portfolios (such as privately accrued retirement wealth), wealth effects have to be grafted onto the core model to obtain plausible parameter experiments. Nevertheless, such studies use household heterogeneity to identify retirement behaviour, before using the results to simulate policy reforms, and therefore permit more heterogeneity in the measurement of behavioural responses.

The final strategy is to use 'quasi-experiments' such as past policy reforms to estimate behavioural responses to regime changes (for an introduction, see, for example, Meyer, 1995). At its simplest, a 'before–after' design identifies the effect of the reform by assuming that no other changes occurred over the period that contaminated the measured effect. This is unlikely to hold where both the outcome variable and the controls are time-varying (for example, economic activity rates are clearly changing over time). A more attractive strategy is the so-called 'differences of differences' methodology where the 'before–after' outcome change of the group 'treated' by the policy measure is measured relative to the outcome change for a 'control group' (whether a sub-set of households, or a country). Write:

$$y_{it}^j = \alpha_0 + \alpha_1 d_t + \alpha_2 d^j + \beta d_t^j + z_{it}^j{'}\gamma + \varepsilon_{it}^j \tag{3.2}$$

As with (3.1), the parameter of particular interest is β: the impact of a policy on the treated group $j=1$ relative to the outcome for a group unaffected by the policy $j=0$. The d_t term refers to the common 'before–after' change and d^j is equivalent to the fixed effect – the between-group difference in the outcome variable, conditioned on the control vector z. This approach makes explicit the 'policy experiment' that is being examined.[12] Its weakness is that the treatment effect is specific to those groups or countries that have undergone the policy change. The results can be generalised only to the extent that the policy changes affect a representative sub-set of groups (countries) and yield similar responses across the 'experiments'.

3.4.2 Empirical Evidence on Specific Reform of Retirement Regimes

We know of no studies that explicitly adopt this last strategy to measure the impact of reforms that change average implicit tax rates on retirement (the studies in Gruber and Wise (2002) use micro-econometric estimation and then simulate policy reforms). Nevertheless, there are studies that use comparable methodologies to explore changes in explicit taxes on retirement – so-called 'earnings tests' and 'retirement tests' – and to model changes in state pension ages. This section illustrates some results from these studies and also investigates the 1992 Italian public pension reform. In doing so, it also describes a potential pitfall in examining the outcome of a reform process (and one which is well known in the evaluation literature).

The first selection of studies presented in Table 3.5 examines the policy impact of changes in explicit tax rates on older workers. Two are based on actual policy changes, one on extending a limited policy change, and the other is pure simulation. In all three countries considered (Canada, the UK and the US), the 'earnings test' is, or was, levied on people who wished to consider working whilst also receiving their public pension. If they do so, all or part of their pension is withdrawn. The test generates a non-linear budget constraint with an exemption level of earnings and a high marginal tax rate over the relevant budget segment.

Both the studies by Disney and Smith, and Baker and Benjamin, use a 'differences of differences' methodology. In the UK study, the 1989 reform abolished the 'earnings test' on work for people for five years beyond state pension age, so reducing the relevant marginal tax rate by 100 per cent. The control groups are the age groups bracketing the group that were affected by the reform. The Baker and Benjamin study exploits the fact that the change to the retirement test occurred at different times between Quebec and the rest of Canada. This allows them to exploit both the pretest–post-test periods and the period when the test partially covered the population. Both results find small but significant impacts of the changes on hours supplied.

Table 3.5 Impact of retirement tests on labour supply of the elderly

Author(s)/group	Event and data	Methodology	Results
Friedberg (2000): *US*, older men	Simulates impact of earnings test in US using Current Population Surveys	Piecewise linear econometric modelling; identification from time variation in earnings test rules	i) Earnings test abolition would raise hours for people at or above kink by +5.3% ii) earnings at kink from abolition +50%, above kink −4%; net effect positive
Baker and Benjamin (1999): *Canada*, older men	Survey of Consumer Finances 1972–80	'Differences of differences'; identifies from joint 'quasi experiment' of abolition of earnings test in CPP 1975 and QPP 1973–77 and from other age groups unaffected by test	i) Abolition increases annual weeks worked by +5–6 weeks ii) main source of Δweeks is that people move from part-year to full-year work
Zabalza et al. (1980): *UK*, older men and women	Retirement Survey, 1977 (cross–section)	Explicit CES utility function, estimates discrete choice model; reform results by simulation	Abolition of earnings test would increase annual hours by: Men: +10.2 Women: +7.0
Disney and Smith (2002): *UK*, older men and women	Family Expenditure Surveys 1984–94	'Differences of differences' on actual abolition 1989; identification of older and younger age groups not directly affected by earnings test	i) Abolition of earnings test increased annual hours of *working* men in age band by four hours a week ii) the impact for women is weaker at around 2 hours a week for working women

The Freidberg (2000) paper on the US captures the non-linearity of the budget constraint, since the hours response varies according to the marginal tax rate facing the individual along the budget segment. The study exploits the changes over time in thresholds and effective tax rates to model abolition of the test. Finally, the Zabalza et al. study is a more conventional study (but innovative at the time) that applies a discrete choice quasi-structural model of labour supply to the choice between part-time, full-time work and retirement, and simulates the abolition of the 'earnings test'.

Examining the impact of earnings and retirement tests is an attractive strategy because they generate high measured marginal tax rates that are typically changed dramatically by the policy. (There is no uncertainty as to whether the measured tax rate is the 'true' rate and the correct budget constraint can be derived.) Even so, such tests tend only to affect the small sub-set of people who want to work beyond 'normal' state pension age.

Examining policy reforms that change the state pension age directly are more attractive as an 'experiment', in the sense that more people are likely to be affected. The second group of studies, described in Table 3.6, is representative of a large literature that examines the impact of changes in retirement ages – either the introduction of 'early retirement' (or its abolition) or changes in the 'normal' age at which the individual can first receive benefits. [13] The first two studies use the traditional 'before–after' approach to examine the effects of changing the first age of eligibility for state pensions. In Germany, there seems to be a large effect, with the average age of retirement falling by three years in response to the introduction of an early retirement 'window' of two years.[14] Note, too, that the average age of retirement is lower than the first age of state pension eligibility both before and after the reform. The New Zealand case study is interesting because it shows that these impacts of state pension age on participation rates are symmetrical – raising the state pension age by two years increases participation not just in the 'affected' age band, but also at ages either side of the age band.[15]

These results are reported as 'differences' in average ages of retirement and participation rate changes. However, Johnson (2000) uses a 'differences of differences' methodology using 'similar' countries that did not reform retirement (state pension) age as the 'controls'. Two of the six 'experiments' that he discusses are those already described. For example, he compares New Zealand, which had policy changes in both 1938 and 1991 onwards with Australia, which did not. Some of the 'controls' (such as the United Kingdom for France) seem implausible on the grounds of both pension programme design and economic circumstances. Nevertheless, the results in Table 3.6 are of some interest: in particular, the study strongly confirms the effects of the New Zealand and German reforms for 60–64-year-olds. There also seems to be a large and significant effect of the Danish reform. Other country-by-country comparisons are less convincing, and results are also less clear-cut for the 55–59 age group.

Table 3.6 Impact of changes in retirement (state pension) age on labour supply of the elderly: selected studies

Country/author(s)	Event	Results
Germany Börsch-Supan and Schnabel (1999)	Normal age of retirement 65 In 1972 – introduction of 'flexible retirement' from 63 onwards, for those with long careers Also retirement at 60 permitted for women, unemployed, disabled	Average retirement age: 1971 61.5 years 1981 58.5 years
New Zealand St. John, in Disney and Johnson (2001), Chapter 8, Table 8.11	State pension age to be raised gradually over ten years from 1991 from 60 to 65 By 1996, the state pension age had risen to 62	Increase in employment rates 1991–96 (% points): Age Men Women 59 +7 +11 60 +19 +15 61 +20 +14 62 +15 +12 63 +8 +8
Johnson (2000) Men Six 'diffs of diffs' experiments: ten-year changes in participation rates across reforms	*Denmark v. Norway* ('control') A) Denmark **1979** cuts eligibility age from 67 to 60 for early pension	Denmark 60–64 Norway 60–64 −21.4% −3.8% ΔΔ −17.6% (−1.4) Denmark 55–59 Norway 55–59 −3.3% −0.7% ΔΔ −4.0% (−1.0)
	New Zealand v. Australia ('control') B) NZ **1938** cuts eligibility age from 65 to 60	NZ 60–64 Australia 60–64 −13.4% −6.7% ΔΔ −6.7% (−0.7) NZ 55–59 Australia 55–59 −5.1% −2.3% ΔΔ −3.8% (−1.4)
	C) NZ **1991–97** raises state pension age from 60 to 63	NZ 60–64 Australia 60–64 +14.7% −6.2% ΔΔ +20.9% (2.3) NZ 55–59 Australia 55–59 +3.0% +1.2% ΔΔ +4.2% (0.6)
	France v. United Kingdom ('control') D) France **1983** Benefits raised at 60–64 & earnings test introduced	France 60–64 UK 60–64 −17.8% −17.8% ΔΔ +0.0% (0.0) France 55–59 UK 55–59 −7.3% −11.4% ΔΔ 4.4% (1.1)
	Austria v. West Germany ('control')	Austria 60–64 WG 60–64 −21.1% +2.4% ΔΔ −23.50% (−2.8) Austria 55–59 WG 55–59

E) Austria **1961–6** cuts eligibility age from 65 to 60	−3.2% +0.5% ΔΔ −3.7% (−1.2)
W. Germany v. Switzerland ('control')	WG 60–64 Swiss 60–64 −30.5% −4.6% ΔΔ −25.9% (−2.1)
F) W. Germany **1973** cuts eligibility age from 65 to 63	WG 55–59 Swiss 55–59 −5.7% −1.3% ΔΔ−4.4% (−1.1)

To understand this 'differences of differences' framework, take the example of Denmark and Norway. Denmark (the 'treatment') introduced more generous early retirement provisions than Norway had (the 'control'). Over a ten-year period either side of the reform, participation rates among Danes aged 60–64 fell by 21.4 per cent compared to 3.8 per cent in Norway. The 'treatment effect' is therefore calculated as a 17.6 per cent reduction (the bracketed standard error suggests this is a highly significant change). Compare this with the France ('treatment') and UK ('control') illustration which suggests no significant effect of the reform (or else that the UK is a bad 'control' to utilise).

A caveat to the 'treatment' approach, well known in the evaluation literature, is that pre-experiment behaviour of participants (and, possibly, non-participants) is affected by the onset of the experiment so that care has to be taken in utilising appropriate *ex-ante* and *ex-post* data. These changes can occur from selection, where the treated group are non-randomly selected (see Ashenfelter, 1978) or from policy anticipation (not necessarily just announcement). For example, if it is known that the government is considering a reform to the pension programme that will adversely affect the wealth of a particular cohort, it is possible that they might adopt behaviour (for example, retiring immediately under the 'old' regime) to minimise its impact. The general problem of policy endogeneity, which is the most pertinent form of the selection issue in this context, of course also qualifies the analysis.[16]

The 1992 reform of the Italian Social Security programme provides a nice illustration of the issue of policy anticipation. The 1992 reform raised 'normal' retirement age for women from 55 to 60 and that of men from 60 to 65 (see Brugiavini and Fornero, 2001, Table 6.2) – the provisions coming into operation over a subsequent ten-year period. However, the reform that was enacted froze for one year after the reform the provisions for retiring early once a certain number of years of service had been completed (the 'seniority pension' provisions). Given that participants treated the 1992 reform as a signal that early retirement would become more difficult in the future (a correct prediction given still further tightening in 1995), the immediate effect of the reform was to induce an increase in *immediate* retirement for those who wanted to avoid the subsequent rise in the retirement age, while its subsequent effect was to cut retirement rates in the next year due to the freezing of early retirement provisions.

Using data on age and actual dates of retirements of participants within the programme covering private sector workers from 1986 to 1998, we constructed a proportional hazard model of exit from the workforce. Since we did not have individual characteristics, the only control variables are age and gender. We also do not know elapsed tenure at the start of the data period (1985) – in other words the data are left censored. We assume that individuals that retired before the 'normal' retirement age must have had enough years of service to qualify for the seniority pension; for the rest, we randomised elapsed tenures at the start of the period.[17] The resulting time coefficients for the proportional hazard are plotted in Figure 3.2.

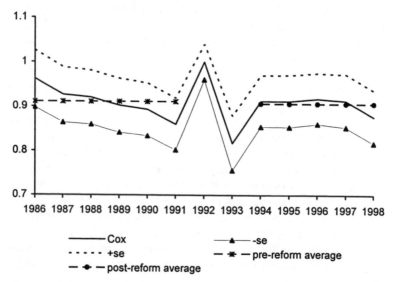

Figure 3.2 Retirement hazard, Italy 1986–98, public sector workers (Cox proportional hazard + or – 1 std. error)

Figure 3.2 shows how the announcement of the 1992 reform induces a 'jump' in the hazard, succeeded by a negative spike in the hazard when early retirement provisions were frozen in 1993. The point of this lies in the interpretation of the effect of the 'treatment' (reform). Clearly a simple 1992– 93 'before–after' interpretation would greatly exaggerate the impact of the reform – in fact the pre- and post-reforms averages are barely different – the post-1993 average hazard is slightly (but not significantly) lower than the pre-1992 hazard. The evidence on distribution of retirement ages in Italy discussed in this volume by Borella, Belloni and Fornero further illustrates this finding.

The Italian reform process therefore offers a good illustration of the 'treatment' methodology, and it would be interesting to compare estimates of the impact of the reform with estimates derived from more structural estimation. Overall, this section has examined alternative modelling approaches to examine retirement incentives. These are cross-country analyses, from which average 'responses' are recovered, micro-econometric studies using within-period reforms of simulation to recover response parameters, and 'quasi-experimental' studies which utilise actual policy reforms to identify local 'treatment effects'. The weaknesses and strengths of some of these approaches are described – in particular, the chapter has pointed to the pitfalls in using within-country variation to characterise 'average' responses, and of using simple 'before–after' measures of effects. The studies cited show clear impacts of changes in pension age and affect tax rates on retirement behaviour, although the magnitudes of the responses are not always large.

3.5 CONCLUSION

The chapter examines a number of interlinked issues concerning retirement incentives and retirement, in the context of declining economic activity rates among older workers. The thrust of much recent literature has been to focus on the issue of reforming retirement incentives as a means of reversing this trend, illustrating the potential benefits by studies based on cross-country panels of average measures of these (dis)incentives.

The chapter makes three points. First, in many OECD countries since the mid-1990s, employment–population rates of older workers have been rising, not falling. The rises strongly correlate with real GDP growth differences across countries. The reason for thinking that these correlations are demand-driven, not supply-driven, is that responses have been greater among the 50–54 group, rather than those closest to state pension ages, and among skilled workers. Were reforms of incentives to be the dominant explanation, one might have expected those closest to eligibility for benefits to be most affected, and there to be little differentiation in other dimensions. Only in Italy is there a pattern of economic activity rate changes consistent with the outcome of a reform process.

Second, the chapter considered the theory of retirement incentives. It described a benchmark of 'actuarial neutrality' and a measure of deviations from this benchmark. It suggested that the model of incentives was most pertinent in countries where there was a long 'retirement window', and in which there were effective (explicit) taxes that deterred individuals from working and receiving a pension, or from deferring retirement. Some countries satisfied these criteria (such as Germany and Italy). Others did not (such as the United Kingdom). Cross-country measures of policy responses should take account of this country heterogeneity.

Finally the chapter considered alternative modelling techniques for examining the effect of retirement incentives. It argued that the conditions required to interpret the results of cross-country regressions as 'response elasticities' were stringent. Suitable country-specific studies using micro-econometric techniques, especially over periods containing significant reforms, were much more attractive, but out-of-sample simulations of major reforms were always more difficult. The chapter advocated greater emphasis on using 'quasi-experiments' to identify policy responses and provided a number of illustrations from countries such as Canada, Italy, New Zealand, the UK and the US. The chapter points to two dangers in using such studies: first, generality, in that each reform has to be interpreted as a 'local treatment' and generality can only be obtained by a sufficient large number of similar 'experiments'. Second, the chapter describes the dangers inherent in simple 'before–after' measures when announcements affect pre-'treatment' and outcomes, and (a common criticism of all studies of retirement incentives) where reforms themselves may not be strictly exogenous. There is therefore scope for a good deal more empirical work in this important field.

NOTES

* This is a revised version of a longer paper presented at the fourth annual conference of CeRP (Center for Research on Pensions and Welfare Policies) in Turin on 16 September 2003: 'Is Mandatory Retirement an Outdated Feature of Pension Systems?' A complementary paper (Disney, 2004) contains some of the other material in the paper presented at the CeRP conference. Disney is grateful to CeRP, and especially Margherita Borella, Onorato Castellino, Bruno Contini and Elsa Fornero, for enabling him to visit CeRP in May 2003 to discuss various aspects of the Italian pension reform and for providing some of the data used in the present chapter. Axel Börsch-Supan is thanked for comments on an earlier draft. Olga Babouchkina provided able research assistance.

1. In 2001, the employment rate for this age group in the EU was 38.6 per cent, compared to 58 per cent in the United States (Economic Policy Committee, 2003, p. 41).
2. We emphasise that such policy options as lifting retirement tests and raising state pension ages are also advocated by those, such as OECD and Gruber and Wise (1999), that want to lower 'implicit tax rates' on older workers.
3. There are interesting exceptions, such as Iceland and, for much of the period, Japan.
4. Indeed the growth might have permitted the Stockholm target to be established.
5. In general, however, EU economic activity rates for older workers have been lower than those of non-EU countries, giving more 'scope' for increases.
6. Finland would be another good case study of a faster-growing economy, but unfortunately the age-employment data is not classified in the same age bands.

7. This is distinct from 'actuarial fairness', which takes retirement age as fixed and examines differences in the 'return' on contributions to different programme participants: see Disney (2004).
8. We use the concept of the implicit tax rate in exactly the same sense as that of the OECD studies. Confusingly, some studies of public pension programmes use the concept in a totally different sense, closer to that of a generational accounting framework – for example Fenge and Werding (2003).
9. However, there are early retirement incentives that are pertinent in the UK within company pension schemes – see Blundell et al. (2002). Early retirement is also possible through the disability insurance programme although, as with the Netherlands, the degree of 'toughness' of the enforcement of medical criteria has proven to be the main policy issue in recent years. See Disney et al. (2003) on this question in the United Kingdom.
10. For 15 OECD countries described by Keenay and Whitehouse (2003), ten exempt pensioners from Social Security contributions, five levy contributions on health insurance benefits only and one also on survivors' pensions.
11. It is not therefore possible to replicate this finding using the cross-country pooled approach.
12. At its simplest, a specification such as (3.1) above is removing all 'untreated' groups (countries) by identifying responses only of the variation in 'treatments' and then assigning the average measured effect to the treated and untreated group alike. It might be possible however to recast the cross-country studies as a multi-treatment model but the specification would look somewhat different from (3.1).
13. But again, much of this literature relies on simulating policy changes, rather than actual policy changes. Only studies of the latter are considered in the table.
14. The average age of retirement is lower than 63 because of other 'routes' into retirement such as receipt of disability benefits.
15. For example, there is an increase in the fraction of people working at 63 after the age of receiving benefits is raised from 60 to 62.
16. In the specific context of pension reform, see Galasso and Profeta (2002).
17. The object of the randomisation technique is to separate tenure effects (the age profile of the hazard) from time effects. We are only interested in the latter. We assumed that tenures were uniformly distributed across three bands.

REFERENCES

Ashenfelter, O. (1978), 'Estimating the Effect of Training Programs on Earnings', *Review of Economics and Statistics*, **60**, pp. 47–57.

Baker, M. and D. Benjamin (1999), 'How Do Retirement Tests Affect the Labour Supply of Older Men?', *Journal of Public Economics*, **71**, pp. 27–51.

Bertola, G., F. D. Blau and L. M. Kahn (2003), 'Labour Market Institutions and Demographic Employment Patterns', Cornell University, mimeo.

Blöndal, S. and S. Scarpetta (1997), 'Early Retirement in OECD Countries: The Role of Social Security Systems', *OECD Economic Studies*, **29**, pp. 7–54.

Blöndal, S. and S. Scarpetta (1998), 'The Retirement Decisions in OECD Countries', OECD Economics Department Working Papers No. 202, Paris.

Blundell, R., G. Meghir and S. Smith (2002), 'Pension Incentives and the Pattern of Early Retirement', *Economic Journal*, **112**, pp. C153–70.

Börsch-Supan, A. and R. Schnabel (1999) 'Social Security and Retirement in Germany', in J. Gruber and D. Wise (eds), *Social Security and Retirement around the World*, Chicago: Chicago University Press for National Bureau of Economic Research.

Brugiavini, A. and E. Fornero (2001), 'Pension Provision in Italy', in Richard Disney and Paul Johnson (eds), *Pension Systems and Retirement Incomes Across OECD Countries*, Cheltenham, UK and Northampton, MA, USA: Edward Elgar.

Burkhauser, R. and J. Turner (1978), 'A Time Series Analysis of Social Security and its Effect on the Market Work of Men at Younger Ages', *Journal of Political Economy*, **86**, pp. 701–16.

Disney, R. (1996), *Can We Afford to Grow Older? A Perspective on the Economics of Aging*, Cambridge: MIT Press.

Disney, R. (2004), 'Are Public Pension Contributions a Tax on Employment?' *Economic Policy*, **39**, pp. 267–311.

Disney, R., C. Emmerson and M. Wakefield (2003), 'Ill Health and Retirement: A Panel Data-based Analysis', Institute for Fiscal Studies Working Paper W03/02, London.

Disney, R. and D. Hawkes (2003), 'Why Has Employment Recently Risen Among Older Workers in Britain?' in R. Dickens, P. Gregg and J. Wadsworth (eds), *The Labour Market under New Labour*, Palgrave: Macmillan, pp. 53–69.

Disney, R. and P. Johnson (2001), (eds) *Pensions Systems and Retirement Incomes across OECD Countries*, Cheltenham, UK and Northampton, MA, USA: Edward Elgar.

Disney, R. and S. Smith (2002), 'The Labour Supply Effect of the Abolition of the Earnings Rule for Older Workers in the United Kingdom', *Economic Journal*, **112**, pp. C136–52.

Economic Policy Committee (2003), *Annual Report on Structural Reforms*, ECFIN/EPC/083/03-EN, European Commission, Brussels.

Fenge, R. and M. Werding (2003), 'Ageing and Fiscal Imbalances Across Generations: Concepts of Measurement', CESifo Working Paper No. 842, Munich.

Fornero, E. and O. Castellino (2001), *La Riforma del Sistema Previdenziale Italiano*, Bologna: Il Mulino, Studi e Ricerche.

Freidberg, L. (2000), 'The Labor Supply Effects of the Social Security Earnings Test', *Review of Economics and Statistics*, **82**, pp. 48–63.

Galasso, V. and P. Profeta (2002), 'The Political Economy of Social Security: A Survey', *European Journal of Political Economy*, **18**, pp. 1–29.

Gruber, J. and D. Wise (eds) (1999), *Social Security and Retirement around the World*, Chicago: Chicago UP for NBER.

Gruber, J. and D. Wise (2002), 'Social Security Programs and Retirement Around the World: Micro Estimation', National Bureau of Economic Research Working Paper w9407.

Johnson, R. (2000), 'The Effect of Old-age Insurance on Male Retirement: Evidence from Historical Cross-country Data', Research Division, Federal Reserve Bank of Kansas City, Working Paper 00–09, Kansas City.

Keenay, G. and E. Whitehouse (2003), 'The Role of the Personal Tax System in Old-age Support: A Survey of 15 Countries', *Fiscal Studies*, **24**, pp. 1–21.

Meyer, B. (1995), 'Natural and Quasi-experiments in Economics', *Journal of Business and Economic Statistics*, **13**, pp. 151–62.

OECD (1995), *The OECD Jobs Study: Taxation, Employment and Unemployment*, Paris: OECD.

Whitehouse, E. (2002), *Retirement Incentives in 15 OECD Countries*, Axia Economics, London, mimeo.

Zabalza, A., C. Pissarides and M. Barton (1980), 'Social Security and the Choice between Full-time work, Part-time work and Retirement', *Journal of Public Economics*, **14**, pp. 245–76.

4. A discussion

Michael Hurd

4.1 INTRODUCTION

Richard Disney and Sarah Bridges make the important point that most of the discussion about retirement outcomes focuses on the response of individual workers to the incentives they face, or more broadly to their choice set; yet, the demand side also helps determine retirement outcomes. They illustrate the point by noting that growth rates in GDP are relatively strongly correlated with the employment of older workers. Of course, expanding economies are associated with declines in unemployment and increases in employment, so it would be surprising if this association did not carry over to older workers. In my view the more interesting issue is: holding constant the level of economic activity what is the long run demand for older workers and where on that demand curve is a particular economy located? Or put differently, what is the substitution elasticity between older and younger workers and what are the relative costs of employing them? Here I will mention some issues without distinguishing between these two aspects. But first it should be pointed out that pension reform may not work if the demand side is not sufficiently flexible to accommodate late retirement in response to policy change.

Employers will not want to retain older workers if the pay structure is rigid, in particular if pay increases with seniority at a faster pace than productivity increases. More generally we need to know the cost of employing older workers including pay, additional benefits, and age-related taxes relative to their productivity. The non-financial aspects of work are important. Workers will want to retire earlier if work is physically demanding or has overly challenging technical requirements. Flexibility in hours of work will encourage later retirement. The availability of rewarding part-time work is particularly important as revealed by surveys of workers. Optimal pension policy should aim to alter the demand side including workplace conditions as well as financial incentives because retention in the workplace will require both the cooperation of employers and a willingness to work by employees.

The implicit tax rate from continued work has been used for at least 20 years in studies of retirement behavior, and, as a first-order approximation it is a very useful tool. For example, in cases such as Germany prior to 1992 or Italy in the redistributive regime (Table 3.3 of Bridges and Disney) no fine-tuned measurements are necessary to see the obvious financial disadvantage from continued work. Where one wants to estimate retirement models within country some subtleties become pertinent which make application of the model difficult. For example, Disney and Bridges discuss a comparison between the change in pension wealth and the sum of the interest rate and the mortality rate as an important determinant of retirement. However, from the point of view of the individual the financial calculation will not depend on a single interest rate but on alternative uses of money which, because of differing portfolios, will vary from person to person. The calculation will not depend on population mortality rates but on subjective survival which, according to measures in the Health and Retirement Study, varies substantially from person to person. Further, for a comparison of the utility from retirement today with the utility of retirement a year from today addition factors such as wealth and the strength of a bequest motive become relevant. If someone is liquidity constrained, the subjective time rate of discount rather than the interest rate is a partial determinant. If there are non-convexities which can be found in employer-sponsored defined benefit pension plans, the marginal approach will not be completely appropriate.

Possibly because of these difficulties and others, the implicit tax method has been of limited usefulness in estimation based on US data. There is a large retirement hazard rate at age 62 which cannot be explained by the marginal tax on work: based on life tables and conventional interest rates the Social Security system is approximately neutral and even positive in some cases. Thus the marginal tax rate predicts smoothly increasing retirement hazards over the ages 61, 62 and 63, but that is not observed in the data. What is the explanation for the large hazard at 62? Liquidity constraints undoubtedly play a role for part of the population, but not for all. More likely workers do not understand the value of greater annuitization that results from delayed claiming of Social Security benefits. Financial education is probably called for.

Despite these reservations, I believe the implicit tax method is useful because of its simplicity and because it probably is approximately what is used by most workers. The challenges revolve around finding the information that workers use such as interest and mortality rates, and how they process the information.

The use of natural experiments to better understand the response of retirement behavior to changes in the public pension program is valuable. But I doubt they will ever replace the use of economic theory.[1] The main problem with natural experiments is that they are not the actual experiment we would like to see done, which is the actual policy under consideration. For example, we might like to predict the effect of increasing the normal retirement age from 65 to 66, but that policy experiment has not been done; rather for some sub-set of the population or under some other circumstances the normal retirement age was changed. We would like to take the result of that policy change to find the effect of increasing the normal retirement age from 65 to 66 in the entire population today. We might have confidence in using the qualitative effect from the prior policy change as evidence about the qualitative effect of the anticipated policy change, but often the main product of this exercise is a demonstration that incentives work. We would properly be more cautious about using the quantitative effect as a prediction.

I was very interested in the summary of evidence about the earnings test on labor market activity (Bridges and Disney's Table 3.5). Despite my reservations about natural experiments and the difficulties of model-based estimation which they discuss, there seems to be qualitative agreement about the effect of the earnings test. It is difficult to understand from the table whether the estimated effects are in quantitative agreement: it would be a valuable addition to the chapter were the authors to undertake such a comparison.

Diamond mainly considers how a public pension system will affect two decisions: when to stop working (retire) and when to begin drawing pension benefits (pension claiming). From the work of Gruber and Wise and many others it is clear that the characteristics of the system have strong effects on these decisions and that these choices by workers have important effects on welfare. In principle we would not want a system to force the decisions of all workers to be the same either through mandate or through very strong financial incentives, and we would not want to force the retirement and claiming ages of a particular worker to be the same. For example, someone who enjoys working should, at some age, be allowed to claim benefits even though they continue to work, and someone who retires early should be able to increase their ultimate level of benefits by delaying claiming.

Before discussing some points of disagreement, I will mention several (of many) points of agreement. In my view Diamond rightly criticizes public pension policy which uses retirement incentives to 'create' jobs as has been found in Europe at times. As he points out, such economics are not noted for lower unemployment rates. A related point concerns retirement systems that offer little or no increase in benefits once the normal retirement age is reached. Such systems punish financially anyone who wants to work longer, with the result that labor force participation at older ages is very low.

4.2   WELFARE, RETIREMENT AND ANNUITIZATION

Diamond is mainly concerned with two outcomes: the welfare of workers who retire early (whom he characterizes as being poor); and the welfare of those with few resources at advanced old age due to insufficient annuitization at younger ages. To address the first problem he suggests a system in which benefits are increased at a rate that is less than actuarially fair. Thus those who retire later will receive less in lifetime benefits (expected present value) than under a neutral system, and this shortfall can be used to increase the benefits of those who retire earlier. To address the second problem one might want a system in which benefits increase rapidly with a delay in claiming, thus through incentives encouraging delays in claiming and hence more annuitization. Obviously these remedies are in conflict. Furthermore, the labor supply effects in the first situation could be rather large depending on the magnitude of the under-adjustment. Indeed the extreme case of little or no additional pension benefit from delayed retirement is criticized by Diamond.

In my view reducing the benefits from additional work is the wrong mechanism: if the benefit redistribution is large enough to have a significant impact on the well-being of the early retirees, it is likely to have significant and costly labor supply effects. Any policy that encourages earlier retirement should be viewed with suspicion when we should be finding policies that encourage later retirement. Furthermore, I believe that Diamond's characterization of earlier retirees is incorrect, at least in the US. While poor health is associated with retirement before the age of 62, generous employment-based pensions and high wealth are also associated with early retirement. Thus the statement by Diamond that earnings are an indicator of (reduced) earnings opportunities or work disability is true, but earnings are also an indicator of a number of other determinants of early retirement such as high assets and pension entitlements. A rough approximation is that about half of those who retire before 62 are in the first group and about half in the second. Thus, increasing public pension benefits for early retirees as a group would miss the target a significant fraction of the time and simply give an undesirable windfall gain to many who are already well off.

A second mechanism of a pension system is the earnings test. As an illustration of its operation consider a worker in the US who retires at 62, and then at 63 returns to work. At the point during the work-year when earnings have reached the exempt amount (the amount of earnings that are not subject to the earnings test), his Social Security benefits are reduced by one dollar for every two dollars of earnings above the exempt amount.[2] With increased earnings Social Security benefits are reduced until they have been reduced to zero. Viewed solely within the year, the earnings test appears to be a 50 percent tax on earnings, and empirical studies as well as anecdotal evidence suggest that workers view the earnings test to be a tax. In fact, Social Security benefits that are lost via the earnings test are restored on an approximately fair basis when the worker reaches the normal retirement age (65 until very recently). Thus the earnings test is forced saving, although at a slightly lower rate of return than the implicit rate of return from delayed claiming.[3] Regardless of its actual operation in the law, the empirical evidence that I am aware of suggests that it is viewed as a substantial tax and has labor supply effects that may be large.

Diamond favors the earnings test because of his judgment that it increases annuitization. For this to be the case and for it to be the determining factor in deciding in favor of an earnings test requires that a significant number of workers would claim Social Security benefits while continuing to work and that there be no large offsetting labor supply effects. We can identify four classes of workers:

1. Workers who retire before 62 and have no desire to return to the labor force. They will not be affected: their decision is whether to delay claiming, which is not affected by the earnings test.
2. Workers who now work from 62 to 65. They would continue to work but in the absence of an earnings test might claim Social Security benefits while they continue to work. This is the group Diamond worries about.
3. Workers who now retire at the ages 62 through 65. Because of the large retirement hazard at 62 this is a relatively numerous group.
4. Those already retired who might contemplate returning to the labor force. An example would be someone who retired unexpectedly because of a health event but has recovered and is capable of returning to work. The return of some members of this group should be encouraged by social policy.

Diamond advocates a policy that prevents those in group two from claiming benefits even though they may desire to do so. The justification is that they would be making a mistake. The cost of the policy (beyond any utility loss they might incur) is the labor supply effect on groups three and four which results from the perceived (and partly real) taxation effects. Beyond the loss in earnings and taxes, there is the additional reduction in annuitization which would offset any annuitization gains by group two. In the US there has been a considerable amount of research studying the effect of the earnings test on labor supply, and the typical finding is that it does have an effect, although it is difficult to quantify its importance.[4] For example, Bac Tran finds an increase of about six percentage points in the labor force participation of 65-year-olds following the elimination of the earnings test for those 65–69 in 2000.[5] As this increase propagates over time through the ages up to 70, I expect to see a fairly large labor supply effect. Of course, as my discussion of Bridges and Disney suggests, it would not be appropriate to apply immediately these results to find how the earnings test would affect the labor force participation of 62–64-year-olds. Nonetheless, the magnitude is impressive. Even lacking a precise quantification, I can see little utility in a policy that would be likely to reduce labor supply at older ages.

4.3   THE WEALTHY LIVE LONGER THAN THE POOR: REDISTRIBUTION VIA THE PUBLIC PENSION SYSTEM

Diamond mentions but does not discuss in detail some effects of differential mortality. Across many populations and over many time periods there is a positive correlation between health and socio-economic statuses (SES), whether SES is measured by education, income, wealth or occupational class. Health can be measured by mortality rates or life expectancy or by health conditions or self-rated health, and the correlation remains. This correlation means that the well-to-do live longer on average than the poor, and that, therefore, they will draw greater lifetime benefits from an identical annual pension benefit. It has been said that this tendency for greater lifetime benefits to the well-to-do reduces the progressive aspects of many public pension systems such as the Social Security system in the US and that it may even cause the overall system to be regressive.

I will argue that the terms 'regressive' and 'progressive' have different meanings in this context from their usual meanings in welfare analysis and that redistribution tied to differential mortality could in some circumstances reduce overall social well-being.

The most basic argument for redistribution from the well-to-do to the poor is based on two ideas: people are alike and the marginal utility of consumption declines in consumption. Then a dollar of consumption reallocated from a well-to-do person to a poor person will cause a small utility loss to the well-to-do person and a large utility gain to the poor person. Total utility will increase.[6] The result that total utility increases can be accepted by most people because it rests on assumptions that are so simple and appealing that they do not require empirical validation.

In a multi-time period problem the situation is not straightforward. Suppose that person B lives substantially longer than person A and, hence, has greater lifetime pension benefits (pension wealth) based on the same annual pension flow. Consider the same type of progressive reallocation as in the one-period case. To equalize pension wealth the flow of pension benefits to B may have to be reduced substantially, so much so that annual consumption by person B would be considerably lower than consumption by A. If the marginal utility of consumption declines sharply in consumption it may be that the utility loss of B is greater than the utility gain of A. Then total utility would be reduced by the progressive reallocation.

A simple numerical example is shown in Table 4.1. Person A lives one period and has no wealth. Person B lives two periods and has wealth. Initially they both have the small pension flow.

Table 4.1 Example of pension income and consumption

	Person A			Person B		
	Period			Period		
	1	2	total	1	2	total
Wealth of B = 100						
Initial						
pension income	100	–	100	100	100	200
consumption	100	–	100	150	150	300
Redistribution						
pension income	150	–	150	75	75	150
consumption	150	–	150	125	125	250
Wealth of B = 50						
Initial						
pension income	100	–	100	100	100	200
consumption	100	–	100	125	125	250
Redistribution						
pension income	150	–	150	75	75	150
consumption	150	–	150	100	100	200

As shown in the first three lines, Person A will consume his pension income of 100 and because he lives for just one period his pension wealth is 100. If B has wealth of 100 and the desired consumption path is flat, she will consume her pension income of 100 and half of her wealth each period. Her pension wealth will be 200 and total lifetime consumption will be 300.

Now consider a redistribution of pension income to equalize pension wealth. As shown in the next three lines, A will have pension income of 150; B will have pension income of 75 and consumption per period of 125. Because B now has smaller consumption in period one than A whether total utility has increased or decreased cannot be said without reference to a statement about the variation in marginal utility. For example, if marginal utility declines sharply with increases in consumption beyond 125, the gain for A may be less than the loss for B. As a specific example suppose utility is constant relative risk aversion

$$u(c) = \frac{c^{1-\gamma}}{1-\gamma}$$

and that γ is 1.2.[7] Then total utility would be increased by the redistribution.[8] This happens because the reduction in consumption by B is from a relatively high level where the marginal utility of consumption is low.

The last two panels of the table repeat the analysis of the first two panels but now wealth of B is 50. Under the redistribution total utility is reduced. This happens because the marginal utility of consumption at the initial consumption level of B is higher than in the first example, so that the loss to B is greater than the gain by A.

Of course this example is artificial, and even if the risk aversion parameter approximates a population average, the other aspects are not very realistic. But the main point is that unlike the simple single period example, we need to have a great deal of information to know whether a redistribution is welfare improving.

Should we have public policy to reduce the differences in pension wealth that result from SES-related differential mortality? It seems to me that the example says we should not. But even were we certain that overall utility would be increased from a redistribution, I think other aspects of the problem argue against such a policy. First, we do not understand the relative magnitudes of the causal flows that produce the SES–health correlation. In the sociology literature which first studied the topic it is generally accepted that the main causal flow is from SES to health. The mechanisms involve greater access to health care services as a result of higher income or wealth, or as a result of a better understanding of the health care delivery system as a result of higher education. In the economics literature, which came later, greater emphasis is given to a causal flow from health to income and wealth: poor health results in poor job performance, lower income and lower wealth. Health shocks cause reduced health, interruptions to income and lower wealth, increasing the correlation between health and income and wealth. A third model places emphasis on a latent model of fitness. Latent fitness produces success in education, in the workplace, and good health.

While most researchers, regardless of field, would say that there is some validity to all of these explanations, there is substantial disagreement about the quantitative importance of each. Establishing the relative magnitudes of the flows of causality is important for any policy that links SES to longevity and adjusts pension levels toward an equalization of expected lifetime benefits. For example, if wealth causes health, a windfall gain from the stock market will increase longevity, so the policy would call for a decrease in benefits to offset the greater life expectancy. But if both health and wealth are the result of latent fitness the wealth gain will not increase longevity and pensions should not be reduced.

A related aspect of our not knowing the causal mechanism is that we do not know whether the quantitative relationship between SES and health is stable over time. Thus a policy that anticipates a particular quantitative relationship could turn out to have very different effects from what was envisioned.

I believe that having a progressive public pension system to insure against lifetime earnings risk is valuable. However, the progressivity should be accomplished via taxation and the relationship between earnings and benefits, not by relying on an empirical correlation between socio-economic status and longevity, which is not well understood.

NOTES

1. I expect that Bridges and Disney would agree with this statement, but some economic studies seem to have given up on using theory entirely.
2. The exempt amount was $11 280 in 2002.
3. Due to the fact that the benefit level is not recalculated until age 65.
4. See Bridges and Disney, Chapter 3 in this volume.
5. Tran (2004).
6. Of course, this benefit must be balanced against goals of fairness and efficiency.
7. This is approximately the value of the risk aversion parameter estimated by Hurd (1989).
8. With no discounting.

REFERENCES

Hurd, M. (1989), 'Mortality Risk and Bequests', *Econometrica*, **57**, pp. 779–813.
Tran, B.V. (2004), 'The Effect of the Repeal of the Retirement Earnings Test on the Labor Supply of Older Workers,' typescript, Economics Department, University of Maryland, College Park, US.

PART 2

Country experiences

5. Patterns of retirement in Germany: how they emerged, and how to change them*

Barbara Berkel and Axel Börsch-Supan

5.1 INTRODUCTION

Germans retire early. While the statutory 'normal' retirement age for men and women is age 65, the actual average retirement age is much earlier. Only about 20 percent of all entrants used the 'normal' pathway of an old-age pension at age 65. The most popular retirement age is 60. The average retirement age in 1999 was 59.7 years for men and 60.7 years for women. These numbers refer to West Germany. In the East, retirement age was 57.9 years for men and 58.2 years for women.

Early retirement is popular. But times have changed. With an increasingly aging population and the precarious financial state of the public pension system, the costs of early retirement have received increased scrutiny. Recently, the reform discussion has shifted once again to the pivotal 'normal' retirement age, currently age 65, and the earliest possible qualifying age for specific forms of retirement pension, currently age 60. Bearing increasing life expectancy in nd, raising the age of retirement would appear to be an obvious reform option.

Raising the average retirement age is particularly attractive from a financial point of view, as an increase in the age of retirement would boost the number of contributors to the system whilst simultaneously reducing the number of beneficiaries. In a pension system, which is not actuarially fair – Gruber and Wise (1999) show that almost all public pay-as-you-go systems in Europe fail to be actuarially fair – this increases revenues and decreases outpayments. Börsch-Supan and Schnabel (1998) provide estimates of the actuarial imbalance for the German, and Brugiavini (1999) for the Italian, pension system.

What is more, there is no sign that an increase in the age of retirement is likely to be prevented by deteriorating health. On the contrary, age-specific rates of illness have dropped even faster than mortality rates (Cutler und Sheiner, 1998).

The aim of this chapter is to depict current patterns of retirement in Germany, how they are likely to change in response to recent legislation which is currently phased in, and how one might change them further. In order to do so, we employ an econometric model which relates the actual retirement decisions of older workers, as observed in the data provided by the 1984–97 German Socio-Economic Panel (GSOEP), to the relevant statutory pension rules. Drawing on the work by Berkel and Börsch-Supan (2004), we then use this model to predict future retirement decisions under alternative rules for early and normal retirement.

The chapter sets the stage with a description of current retirement patterns. Section 5.3 then describes the institutional framework which explains much of the observed retirement patterns in Germany. Section 5.4 introduces a set of reform options which might change these retirement patterns. Section 5.5 briefly presents data and methodology. Section 5.6 discusses the predicted retirement patterns under the alternative retirement regimes. Section 5.7 concludes.

5.2   RETIREMENT PATTERNS IN GERMANY

In this section, we depict the retirement patterns that have emerged since the 1970s in Germany. Data for the historical trends comes from the German association of public pension providers ('Verband der deutschen Rentenversicherungsträger', VDR). Cross-sectional data for recent years has mainly been drawn from the German Socio-Economic Panel (GSOEP).

Germany shares the rapid decrease of old-age labor force participation with most other industrialized countries; see Figure 5.1. This decrease accelerated after 1970. We will argue further below that the dramatic decline after 1970 is to a great extent due to the introduction of 'flexible' retirement arrangements in 1972 that did not adjust benefits according to actuarial tables. It is interesting to note that male labor force participation declined from 1970 to 1990 for all ages above 50, and increasingly so for older persons.

Female labor force participation increased for all ages below 60; see Figure 5.2. The increase for the age range from 50 to 59 is noteworthy because it contrasts with the decline in male labor force participation due to a high share of disability claims among male workers.

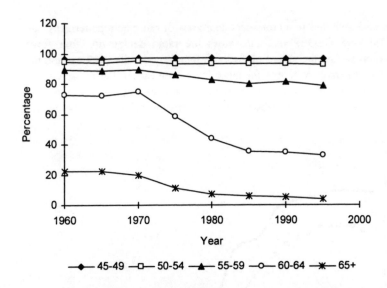

Source: Börsch-Supan and Schnabel (1998).

Figure 5.1 Male labor force participation rates, 1960–95

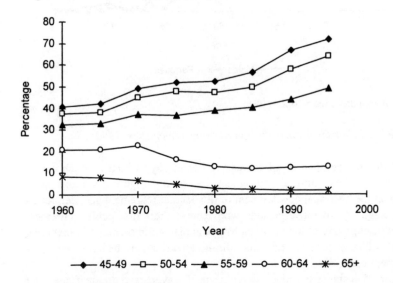

Source: Börsch-Supan and Schnabel (1998).

Figure 5.2 Female labor force participation rates, 1960–95

Figure 5.3 switches to a cross-sectional view of retirement patterns by age in the 1993–95 GSOEP data. It shows the rapid decline in labor force participation around the age of 60 for both female and male workers, and the large share of persons who exit the labor force even earlier. Particularly sharp declines in labor force participation are visible at ages 56 (male only), 60 and 65. By the age of 66, male labor force participation has dropped below 7.5 percent.

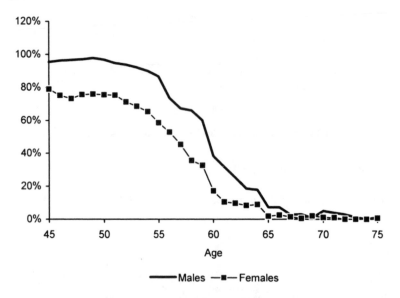

Source: Börsch-Supan and Schnabel (1998).

Figure 5.3 Labor force participation rates by age and sex, 1993–95

All this has resulted in an average retirement age which is much earlier than the statutory 'normal' retirement age of 65. Figure 5.4 looks more closely at the historical development of this factual retirement age, defined as the average age of those persons who receive their first public retirement benefit through one of the many pathways explained in section 5.3, including normal old-age pension benefits, disability insurance benefits and pre-retirement benefits.

Figure 5.4 shows a sudden decrease in the average retirement age after 1972, dropping steadily by about 3.5 years.

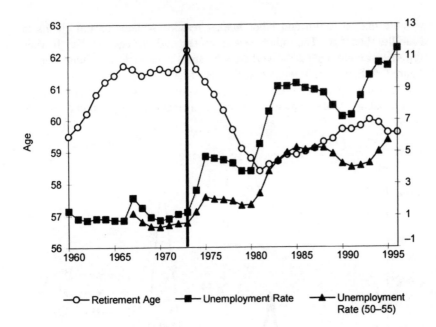

Notes: 'Retirement Age' is the average age of all new entries into the public pension system. 'Unemployment Rate' is the general national unemployment rate. 'Unemployment Rate (50–55)' refers to male unemployed age 50–55.

Source: VDR (1997).

Figure 5.4 Average retirement age of male workers, 1960–95

The core hypothesis in this chapter is that this sudden decline is no sudden change in preferences (a suddenly increased demand for leisure) or an effect of declining labor demand (paralleling an increase in unemployment). Rather, so we argue, it is created by the 1972 pension reform which introduced early retirement without actuarial adjustments, in effect giving workers almost the same annual pensions independent of how early they retire.

Figure 5.5 shows that the cross-sectional distribution of retirement ages among male workers has changed very systematically after 1972. Before 1972, the distribution of retirement ages had only one spike. In 1970, age 65 was the retirement age (thin line with hollow square). In 1975, only two years after the 1972 reform became effective, about half of the retirees preferred to retire earlier, and the retirement age distribution had two spikes (dotted line, hollow circles). In 1980, another five years later, a three-spike pattern had emerged (thick lines, full square). Since then, there was little change in this distribution (thick lines, full triangle for 1995). The distribution of retirement ages has its maximum at age 60, the earliest age at which retirement is possible due to health and labor market reasons without formal claims to disability benefits. The other spikes correspond to age 63 for flexible retirement and to age 65 for workers with short work histories. Quite clearly, Figure 5.5 shows that workers take the very first legal opportunity to retire. A similar striking pattern has evolved among women. However, the spike at age 63 is missing – since women could enter a normal old-age pension already at age 60.

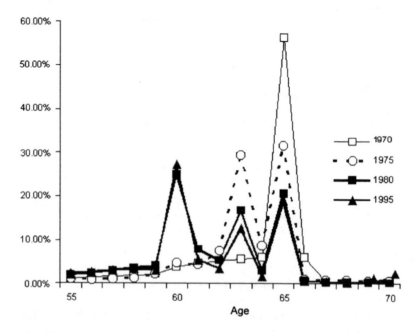

Source: VDR (1997).

Figure 5.5 Distribution of retirement ages, men, 1970, 1975, 1980 and 1995

One might argue that the shift in retirement age and the corresponding decline in old-age labor force participation after the 1972 reform was mainly a demand reaction to rising unemployment rather than a supply response to early retirement incentives.

We have two reasons to believe that this was not the case. First, the reform was part of the general expansion of the welfare state after the social democrats took power for the first time in the postwar period. The reform was designed at a time when unemployment was very low while the first steep increase in unemployment (1973 to 1975) happened after the 1972 reform had already been introduced. One might interpret this reform as a reaction to a long-term preference change towards more leisure or to the secular wealth increase after the West German 'economic miracle'.

Second, the time-series evidence does not support the view of a demand-induced change in retirement age. In Figure 5.4, we showed the suddenness of the decrease in the average retirement age after the 1972 reform. It dropped steadily by about 3.5 years while unemployment first rose and then fell from 1975 to 1980. Thus, there is no time-series correlation between mean retirement age and unemployment between the reform and 1980. After 1980, a positive time-series correlation between retirement age and unemployment is the opposite of what a demand-induced change in old-age labor supply would suggest.

5.3 INSTITUTIONAL EXPLANATIONS FOR THE GERMAN RETIREMENT PATTERNS

The evidence in section 5.2 points to the power of institutional rules to generate quite distinct retirement patterns. In order to understand this power, this section describes the retirement rules of the German public pension system as it has shaped the retirement patterns visible in section 5.2 and relevant for our retrospective econometric analysis in sections 5.5 and 5.6. They are based on the 1972 legislation. Where relevant, however, we mention the many institutional changes which have been ratified in the 1992 and 1999 reforms and are now slowly phased in. A detailed description of the recent history of institutional changes can be found in Börsch-Supan and Wilke (2003).

The public pension system or 'retirement insurance' ('Gesetzliche Rentenversicherung', GRV) covers about 85 percent of the German workforce. Most of these are private sector workers but the GRV also includes those public sector workers who are not civil servants. Civil servants, about 7 percent of the workforce, have their own pension system; the self-employed, about 9 percent of the workforce, are mainly self-insured although some of them also participate in the public retirement insurance system. For the average worker, occupational pensions do not play a major role in the German system of old-age provision, neither do individual retirement accounts yet, but their importance is increasing since the last reform in 1999/2001.

5.3.1 Private Sector Pensions

First, we describe *old-age pensions*. Until 1972, retirement was mandatory at age 65. In 1972, several early retirement options were introduced, 'early' defined as before age 65, the 'normal' retirement age. Since then the system of the GRV pays old-age pensions for employees from age 60 onwards if certain conditions are met. A main feature of the German old-age pensions is 'flexible retirement' from age 63 for workers with a long service history. Moreover, retirement at age 60 is possible for women, the unemployed and workers who cannot be appropriately employed for health or labor market reasons.

In addition, pre-retirement (that is, retirement before age 60) is possible using other parts of the public transfer system, mainly unemployment compensation. Labor force exit before age 60 is frequent: about 45 percent of all men call themselves 'retired' at age 59. Only about half of them retire because of disability; the other 50 percent make use of one of the many official and unofficial pre-retirement schemes, that is unemployment compensation in combination with severance pay.

Because of the numerous exceptions that enable retirement entry before age 65, the reforms of 1992 and 1999 introduced an increase of retirement age limits to age 65. The system has been simplified, because there will be no exceptions for the unemployed, part-time employees and women any more. After a transitional period, retirement entry rules of these persons will be adjusted to those of the long-time insured. If deductions (see below) are accepted, the long-time insured can choose early retirement from age 62 onwards. Similarly disabled people can obtain old-age pensions at age 63 and with deductions even at age 60.

Moreover the 1992 reform introduced explicit deductions for retirement before age 65. Before 1992, adjustment of benefits to retirement age was only implicit via years of service. There were no actuarial adjustments at all. The 1992 Social Security reform will change this stepwise by the year 2004. Age 65 will then act as the 'pivotal age' for benefit computations.

Figure 5.6 displays the retirement-age-specific adjustments for a worker who has earnings that remain constant after age 60. The graphs relate the retirement income for retirement at age 65 to the retirement income for retirement at earlier or later ages, and compares the implicit adjustments after 1972 with the total adjustments after the 1992 Social Security reform is fully phased in. As references, actuarially fair adjustments at a 3 percent discount rate are shown as well.[1]

According to the 1992 reform, benefits will be reduced by 0.3 percent per month (maximum 10.8 percent) for each year of earlier retirement. The 1992 reform also introduced rewards for later retirement in a systematic way. For each year of retirement postponed past the minimum age indicated in Figure 5.6, the pension is increased by 0.5 percent per month or 6 percent per annum.

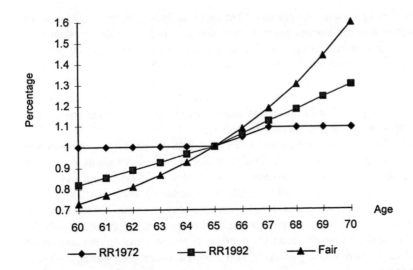

Note: 'RR1972' denotes adjustment factors under the 1972 legislation, and 'RR1992' to those that will eventually be phased in by the 1992 pension reform. 'Fair' refers to actuarially fair adjustment factors at a 3% discount rate.

Source: Börsch-Supan (2000).

Figure 5.6 Adjustment factors to retirement age

Besides old-age pensions, the contributions to the German retirement insurance also finance *disability benefits* to workers of all ages. These are converted into old-age pensions at the latest at age 65. The disability pathway provided a frequently used option into early retirement (besides the flexible retirement option) before the 'pivot age' of 65. A person who was not able to carry on a regular employment received full old-age benefits, the so-called disability pension ('Erwerbsunfähigkeitsrente', EU). A person that could work only half of the time or less compared to a healthy person received two-thirds of old-age benefits ('Berufsunfähigkeitsrente', BU). In the 1970s and early 1980s, the German jurisdiction interpreted both rules very broadly, in particular the applicability of the first rule.

The previous rules governing total and partial disability pensions, as well as the special old-age pension for those aged 60 or over suffering from partial or total disability, were abolished in 2001 based on the 1999 Pension Reform Act. However, generous hardship and other provisions designed to protect confidence in the system mean that the old rules will continue to be effective over a relatively long transitional period (some rules until 2017). After this period, insured beneficiaries are still able to draw pension benefits for partial or full disability until the age of 65 but under different conditions.[2] One main aspect is that the current labor market situation needs not to be taken into account any more.[3] Moreover, if a pension is claimed for disability prior to the age of 63, deductions from benefits similar to those which apply to old-age pensions payable to the long-term insured are phased in until 2004. The pension adjustment factor for each calendar month for which a pension is drawn for a partial or full disability prior to age 63 is –0.3 percent and up to a maximum of –10.8 percent (see Table 5.1).

Besides the above-mentioned retirement pathways *survivor pensions* are paid to wives if the insured husband dies. Survivor pensions are 60 percent of the husband's applicable pension for wives that are age 45 and over or if children are in the household ('große Witwenrente'), otherwise 25 percent ('kleine Witwenrente'). For couples married after the year 2001 a new law has to be applied: survivor pensions are not 60 percent any more but only 55 percent of the husband's disability pension. In return, however, the number of children is now taken positively into account when determining survivor benefits.

Survivor benefits are a large component of the public pension budget and of total pension wealth. Certain earnings tests apply if the widow has her own income, e.g. her own pension. This is only relevant for a very small (below 10 percent) share of widows. Only since recently, are male and female survivors treated equally. Additionally, spouses can choose whether to receive a survivor pension or a newly introduced pension-splitting.

5.3.2 Public Sector Pensions

As opposed to employees, civil servants do not pay explicit contributions for their pensions as the other employees in the private and public sectors do.[4] Instead, the 'gross' wage for civil servants is lower than the gross wage of other public sector employees with a comparable education. The generosity of gross pensions received by civil servants *vis-à-vis* the private sector workers is partially offset by the preferential tax treatment of private sector pensions.

There are three pathways for civil servants: the standard, the early, and the disability retirement option. The standard retirement age is 65. Before 1 July 1997 the early retirement age for civil servants was 62, and thus one year less than the early retirement age in the Social Security system. In 1997 the early retirement age was raised to 63. Adjustment factors for early retirement are phasing in linearly between the years 1998 and 2003, and will reach 0.3 percentage points per month of early retirement, the same as in the private sector.[5]

The average retirement age for civil servants in the year 1999 was 58.9 years and thus almost one year lower than in the private sector. Disability is the most important pathway to retirement for civil servants: 47 percent of those who retired in the year 1999 used disability retirement. Only about 9 percent of civil servants retired at the regular retirement age of 65.[6]

5.4 OPTIONS TO CHANGE RETIREMENT PATTERNS

The complexity of rules described in the previous section shows that there are many mechanisms to change retirement patterns. We consider six possible reform measures. As a reference scenario, we examine the pension reforms already implemented in 1992 and 1999 which, however, will only take effect after a long transitional period. We then examine four reform proposals involving higher actuarial adjustment factors and higher statutory retirement ages. Finally, we consider how retirement probabilities respond to the introduction of an individual pension account system based on the Swedish model. These six reform scenarios are defined in more detail in the following.

The core aspects of the *reference scenario* encompass an increase of the early retirement ages, the introduction of actuarial adjustment factors in the 1992 pension reform described in section 5.3, and the new rules designed to accelerate the implementation of the 1992 reform which took effect in 1999. We will not predict the transition path. Instead, we simulate the long-term impact of the reforms after full implementation. We have modeled the following rules for the reference scenario:

- The adjustment factors for early retirement introduced by the 1992 reform amount to 3.6 percent (not exceeding a maximum of 10.8 percent) for each year of early retirement. The adjustment factors introduced in 1992 only began to be implemented on an incremental basis subsequent to the period covered by our sample and will only take full effect after 2017. A long-term insured employee will then only be able to take retirement, with a maximum deduction of 10.8 percent, at the age of 62.
- Adjustment factors will now also be introduced for each calendar month during which an insured person claims a disability pension prior to the age of 63. These adjustment factors are the same as those for old-age pensions: 0.3 percent per month and a maximum of 10.8 percent.
- Reductions in widow/widower's pensions from 60 percent to 55 percent of the spouse's partial disability pension.[7]

- 'Child-raising pension' and unemployment pensions are no longer effective. The only channels now open to all claimants are those of early retirement for the long-term insured, the partially or severely disabled.

This reference scenario describes the retirement probabilities generated if the statutory status quo in 2003 remains unchanged and no new reform measures are passed.

We then compare these outcomes with five reform elements. To begin with we wish to examine the effects which higher *actuarial adjustment factors* have on retirement decisions:

- *Reform option 1: Increase adjustment factors to 4.5 percent:* Compared with the reference scenario which provides for deductions of 3.6 percent per annum, this scenario is based on deductions of 4.5 percent per annum, and a maximum of 13.5 percent. All the other rules are identical to those in the reference scenario.
- *Reform option 2: Increase adjustment factors to 6 percent:* This scenario introduces deductions of 6 percent per annum (maximum 18 percent). All other factors remain unchanged.

These actuarial adjustments are highly unpopular, and the recent increase from 0 to 3.6 percent is still not fully phased in, such that little is known about the actual response to this recent reform step.

Next, we examine how a further increase in the *statutory regular retirement age* would affect actual retirement ages. A common rule of thumb states that, in response to a change in the retirement rules, one third of workers retire at the new retirement age, one third continue to retire at the old age of retirement and accept the deductions which this implies, and one third avoid the new rules by claiming benefits for disability. The next two variants examine the validity of this rule of thumb:

- *Reform option 3: Increase age limit by one year:* All the age limits – including those of the disability pathways – reached after the transition period shown in Figure 5.1 are increased by one year. As a result, the standard pension age, for example, is raised from age 65 to 66, and the earliest retirement age for the long-term employed from age 62 to 63, and so on. Only the contributory periods for old-age pensions of partially and fully disabled persons remain unchanged at age 60.
- *Reform option 4: Increase age limit by two years:* Increase in all age limits by two years. All other factors remain unchanged.

Finally, as an alternative to these parametric reforms, we model the transition from the current defined benefit system to a 'notional defined contribution' (NDC) system which, while retaining the essential features of the current public pension system, would be, as its proponents argue, more sustainable, more flexible, and more transparent.[8] Notional defined contributions involve an 'individual pension accounts system' in which pension entitlements would be based on the actual amount of contributions paid in to an otherwise unchanged, that is pay-as-you-go, pension system. Paid contributions would be accumulated on individual pension accounts where they would receive fictitious ('notional') interest based on the rate of return provided by the pay-as-you-go system. As a rule, the interest rate would correspond to the growth rate of the total wage bill, responding to both demographic and employment changes. Assets bearing fictive interest of this type would be converted, on retirement, into a lifelong pension annuity based on actuarial calculations. The level of pension would depend on remaining life expectancy and would therefore respond to demographic factors at least as far as its initial level is concerned.

- *Reform option 5: Introduce fully actuarial NDC system:* In this case we take account of a system which is again based on the 1992 and 1999 legislative reforms. The most significant difference between this and the reference scenario is the change in the actuarial adjustment factors which are implicitly based on the internal rate of interest in the NDC system and remaining life expectancy.

A similar system was introduced in Sweden about ten years ago. Palmer (2000) and Settergren (2001) explain the workings of the Swedish NDC system and the initial experiences since it was introduced. A reform package along these lines was also passed in Italy in 1995 as part of the so-called Dini Reform. The Italian 'new entrants' system' features a very long transition period and will only be relevant for workers who are younger than the baby boom generation. Franco and Sartor (2003) provide a critical evaluation of the planned Italian NDC system.

5.5 METHODOLOGY

Our modeling approach and the estimates are taken from Berkel and Börsch-Supan (2004). Their methodology follows the seminal work by Stock and Wise (1990) who introduced the *option value* as a central incentive variable that captures the impact of pension rules on retirement behavior. Earlier analyses of the German pension system using this option-value framework were carried out by Börsch-Supan (1992), Schmidt (1995), Börsch-Supan and Schmidt (2001), Siddiqui (1997), Börsch-Supan (2000 and 2001) and Börsch-Supan et al. (2004).

The variable to be explained is old-age labor force status. Because Germany has very few part-time employees, we use a binary explanatory variable – fully in labor force and fully retired. The definition of 'retired' is not unambiguous. Retirement definitions commonly employed in the literature include inter alia the retirement status self-reported by the respondent, the fact that there are few work hours, or the receipt of retirement benefits, among other definitions. We use the first concept, which is self-reported status, and include pre-retirement, mainly financed by a mixture of unemployment compensation and severance pay, in our definition of retirement.

As explained in section 5.3, a worker contemplating retirement has several pathways to choose from, ranging from several types of old-age pensions, a disability pension, and various pre-retirement schemes. The choice is restricted since most of these pathways are subject to eligibility criteria. Among those, we distinguish between 'strict eligibility rules' that are tied to objective variables such as age, gender and previous contribution history, and 'soft eligibility rules' that are subject to discretionary decisions, notably the determination of a workers' disability status.[9]

Distinguishing these pathways is important because several explanatory variables (option value, Social Security wealth) are a function of the expected pension benefits which in turn depend on the pathway chosen. In the computation of this expected value, we use the observed frequencies as weights.[10] Let's suppose the observed frequency of disability status at age 59 is 33 percent, and the sample person is not eligible for any other pathway at that age. Then expected benefits at age 59 for this person will be a third of the (common) benefit level. Börsch-Supan (2001) provides an instrumental variables interpretation of this method and explores the sensitivity with respect to a more sophisticated choice of instruments.

Our main explanatory variable is the option value established by Stock and Wise (1990). This variable evaluates all current and future payments of the different retirement pathways less possible contributions that have to be paid, and compares these present values to the utility aspect of leisure when being retired. Hence, this variable captures the option value to postpone retirement and expresses for each retirement age the trade off between retiring now (resulting in a stream of retirement benefits that depends on this retirement age) and keeping all options open for some later retirement date (with associated streams of first labor, then retirement incomes for all possible later retirement ages).

More formally, let $V_S(R)$ denote the expected discounted future utility at age S if the worker retires at age R, specified as follows:

$$V_S(R) = \sum_{t=S}^{R-1} \text{u}(YLAB_t^{NET}) \cdot a_t \cdot \delta^{t-S} + \alpha \sum_{t=R}^{\infty} \text{u}(YRET_t(R)) \cdot a_t \cdot \delta^{t-S}$$

where

S	planning age,
R	retirement age,
$YLAB_t^{NET}$	after-tax labor income at age t, $t = S...R-1$,
$YRET_t(R)$	after-tax pension income at age t, $t \geq R$,
a_t	probability to survive at least until age t given survival until age S,
δ	discount factor $= 1/(1+r)$.
α	relative utility of leisure, to be estimated.

Utility from consumption is represented by an isoelastic utility function in after-tax income, $u(Y) = Y^\gamma$. To capture utility from leisure, utility during retirement is weighted by $\alpha > 1$, where $1/\alpha$ is the marginal disutility of work.

The option value for a specific age is defined as the difference between the maximum attainable consumption utility if the worker postpones retirement to some later year minus the utility of consumption that the worker can afford if the worker would retire now. Let $R*(S)$ denote the optimal retirement age if the worker postpones retirement past age S, that is, argmax$[V_S(r)]$ for $r>S$. With this notation, the option value is

$$G(S) = V_S(R^*(S)) - V_S(S).$$

Since a worker is likely to retire as soon as the utility of the option to postpone retirement becomes smaller than the utility of retiring now, retirement probabilities should depend negatively on the option value.

The option value captures the economic incentives created by the pension system and the labor market because the retirement income $YRET_t(R)$ depends on retirement age according to the adjustment factors in Figure 5.6 and on previous labor income by the benefit computations.[11]

We compute the option value for every person in our sample, using the applicable pension regulations and the imputed earnings histories. We choose the usual discount rate of 3 percent. Conditional survival probabilities are computed from the standard life tables of the German Bureau of the Census ('Statistisches Bundesamt'). The option value depends also on the joint survival probabilities of spouses through survivor pensions.[12] We assume independence of survival of spouses to compute the joint probability. We use a grid search estimate of the relative utility parameter α of 2.8.[13] For simplicity, we choose a curvature parameter γ of 1.0, since earlier maximum likelihood estimates were only insignificantly larger than 1.0.

The option value requires the computation of future contribution rates and pension benefits. In order to enforce internal consistency, they are simulated using the macroeconomic pension model underlying Börsch-Supan et al. (2003). This internal consistency is important. Assume a policy proposal, which reduces the replacement rate by x percent. This immediately lowers the contribution rates by the same x percent if the system is pay-as-you-go and financed through contributions.

In addition, the usual socio-demographic variables such as age, gender and marital status are incorporated in our regression analysis. The complexity of possible age effects is modeled by a set of age-specific dummy variables. Moreover, we include wealth (indicator variables of several financial and real wealth categories) and a self-assessed health measure. We do not use the legal disability status as a measure of health since this is endogenous to the retirement decision. The desire for early retirement may prompt workers to seek disability status, and frequently the employer helps in this process to alleviate restructuring. As noted in section 5.3, disability status was granted for labor market reasons without a link to health until recently.

We link the explanatory variables to the dependent variable by a binary probit model which generates the core output of our model, namely the predicted retirement probabilities under the various alternative retirement rules specified in section 5.4. Detailed estimation results, based on an unbalanced panel of 2 223 individuals with 14 401 observations aged 55 through 70 in the West German Socio-Economic Panel (GSOEP), can be found in Berkel and Börsch-Supan (2004). It suffices to point out that the option value is highly significant and precisely measured.

5.6   RETIREMENT PATTERNS UNDER VARIOUS REFORM OPTIONS

We first simulate the 1992 and 1999 reform as our reference scenario such as if they were already fully implemented.[14] We then simulate the implementation of the five reform options described in section 5.4. We calculate the incentive variables implicit in each reform scenario, that is a new option value and a new Social Security wealth for each of the individuals in our sample. The age indicators in the scenarios involving an increase in retirement age are also increased by one or two years in the forecast as these capture the habitual effect of, for example, the statutory pension age.

Our results are shown in Table 5.1 and Figures 5.7 and 5.8. Table 5.1 summarizes the key data for the distribution of retirement ages, separately for men and women – that is the average retirement age and the percentage of people retiring before the ages of 60, 62 or 65. The overall distribution of new retirees is shown in diagrammatic form in Figures 5.7 and 5.8, again separately for men and women. The graphs on pages 99/101 show the distribution of retirement ages, that is the probability that a person will enter retirement at a specific age. The graphs on pages 100/102 show the accumulated retirement probabilities, that is the probability with which a person of a specified age has retired, for each age. Our calculations include all people retiring between the ages of 54 and 72 who draw an old-age pension or disability benefits.

We first present the results for male workers and then refer to the tables and charts to discuss how the introduction of actuarial adjustment factors and the changes in initial retirement rules impact the number of people entering retirement.

Based on the status quo established by the 1972 reform – that is the main provisions affecting the people in our observation period – the full implementation of the 1992 and 1999 reforms would lift the average male retirement age by almost two years from age 61.2 to 63. The impact on women, as shown below, is much weaker. An increase in the average age of retirement is thus foreseeable in the future on the basis of existing legislation alone.

An upward shift in the entire fabric of age limits by two years increases the average effective retirement age for men by a further nine months from age 63 to 63.7. Figure 5.7 clearly illustrates how the two ages at which most insured persons retire – at age 60 or 65 – increase by two years. However, some people draw benefits for loss of earning capacity or put up with the actuarial deductions attached to earlier retirement rather than going along with this shift in age limits.

The introduction of higher adjustment factors also has a very distinctive impact on retirement decisions. Deductions of 4.5 percent increase the average retirement age by nine months from age 63 to 63.7. Deductions of 6 percent have a considerably stronger incentive effect and even lift the average retirement age up to age 64.9. As shown by Figure 5.7, more people retire at age 65 and fewer at age 60 or 61.

Women respond less strongly than men to a shift in age limits. Under the 1972 pension legislation, the average age of retirement for women is age 61.7 and will only rise by 0.7 years to age 62.4 when all the Riester and 1999 pension reform rules are implemented in full. However, it is important to bear in mind that the estimates summarized in this chapter are based on the behavior of employees and employers from the mid-1980s to 1990s. The future behavior, particularly of female workers, may well change significantly, that is more closely resemble that of male workers, in the period 2005 to 2025 to which the projections in this chapter apply.

Table 5.1 The impact of different reform options on retirement age

	Mean retirement age	Percentage of persons who retire before age 60	Percentage of persons who retire before age 62	Percentage of persons who retire before age 65
Men:				
1972 legislation	61.2*	17.2 %	58.2 %	81.9 %
Pension reforms 1992 + 1999	63.0	4.7 %	42.4 %	51.7 %
plus adjustment costs of 4.5%	63.7	3.2 %	31.3 %	37.4 %
plus adjustment costs of 6%	64.9	2.1 %	18.6 %	20.0 %
plus 'pivotal age' +1 year	63.3	5.8 %	26.0 %	52.6 %
plus 'pivotal age' +2 years	63.7	7.2 %	11.3 %	53.4 %
NDC system	65.3	2.3 %	19.2 %	19.4 %
Women:				
1972 legislation	61.7*	10.8 %	58.6 %	66.9 %
Pension reforms 1992 + 1999	62.4	6.3 %	52.4 %	54.8 %
plus adjustment costs of 4.5%	62.7	5.3 %	48.6 %	50.1 %
plus adjustment costs of 6%	63.2	4.1 %	42.0 %	42.9 %
plus 'pivotal age' +1 year	62.6	6.7 %	42.8 %	55.0 %
plus 'pivotal age' +2 years	62.3	6.9 %	9.4 %	55.1 %
NDC system	63.3	4.2 %	41.8 %	41.8 %

Note: * These values correspond to the mean retirement age calculated from the VDR statistics of 1995, based on old-age pensions and disability entries for all persons aged 54 to 72.

Source: Berkel and Börsch-Supan (2004).

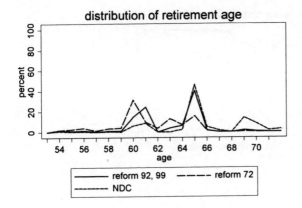

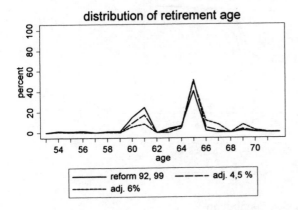

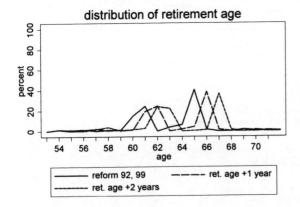

Figure 5.7 Predicted distribution of retirement ages, men

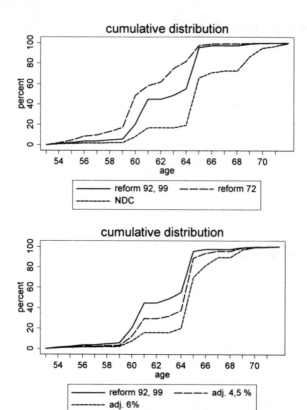

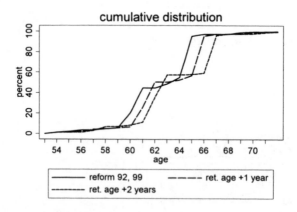

Source: Berkel and Börsch-Supan (2004).

Figure 5.7 (continued)

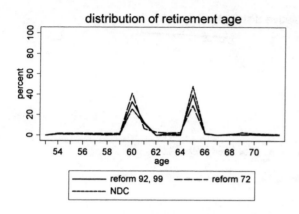

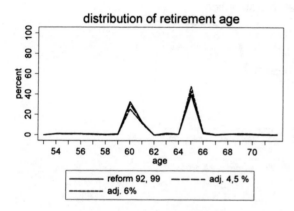

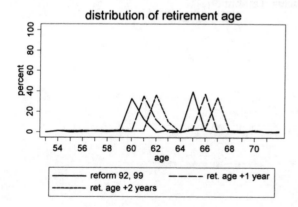

Figure 5.8 Predicted distribution of retirement ages, women

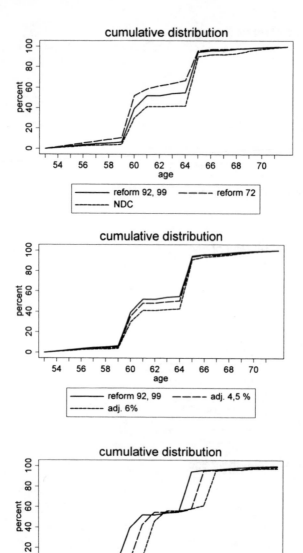

Source: Berkel and Börsch-Supan (2004).

Figure 5.8 (continued)

A shift in the entire fabric of age limits for women by one year produces a postponement of three months and the average age of retirement moves up from age 62.4 to 62.6. A shift of two years is accompanied by a stronger drift towards disability benefits; the average age of retirement in this scenario is only 62.3, and thus remains to all intents and purposes unchanged.

This behavior is very clearly illustrated by Figure 5.8: in the basic scenario, most women retire between the ages of 60 and 65. A shift in the age limits by one (or two) years also postpones the bulk of retirements among women by the same one (or two) year period. However, not everybody retires later; some people claim disability benefits earlier (the second 'peak' flattens out as the age limits are progressively increased, while the first 'peak' rises). This is the primary effect for women.

The incentive effect of higher adjustment factors is also weaker for women: a deduction of 4.5 percent increases the average age of retirement by three months from age 62.4 to 62.7. A deduction of 6 percent increases the average retirement age by six months to age 63.2.

Finally, our simulations demonstrate that the introduction of the NDC system would also have a major impact on the average age of retirement in comparison with the Riester and 1999 reforms (see Table 5.1). The average age of retirement increases by more than two years for men from age 63 to 65.3 and less dramatically by almost one year for women from age 62.4 to 63.3. Of the five reform elements examined, this variant generates the highest average retirement age and, as such, evidently has the most powerful incentive effects. As demonstrated by Figures 5.7 and 5.8, the distribution of new retirements is similar to that in the scenario involving higher adjustment factors. This applies equally to men and women. This is hardly surprising given that the NDC system in fact differs both in technical respects and from the underlying transfer philosophy of the pay-as-you-go system. However, as the earnings points rules embodied in the German PAYG system resemble fairly closely the actuarial principle of equivalence between contributions and benefits, the main difference between the two systems is that the NDC system includes adjustment factors which are actuarially fair and thus considerably higher than in the reference scenario.

5.7 SUMMARY AND CONCLUSIONS

Early retirement was introduced in Germany by the 1972 reform. Using historical data, we showed that this reform was highly influential – it reduced the average retirement age by about 3.5 years. It was also a large success in political terms, contributing to a landslide victory of the then ruling government. Times have changed, however, and the costs of early retirement are plaguing the German economy. Can we turn the clock back and undo the effects of the 1972 reform?

In order to predict retirement patterns under various reform options, we have modeled and estimated the influence of pension legislation on retirement decisions in Germany. Retirement probability is summarized as a function of an incentive variable which encompasses pension legislation and other control variables. As incentive variables we use the option value of postponing retirement by one year. This model is then used to simulate various reforms to the retirement rules. Our calculations show that the introduction of an actuarial adjustment factor of 3.6 percent per annum and other changes to the retirement rules already introduced by the 1992 and 1999 reforms will, over the next few years, increase the average effective retirement age for men by almost two years and that for women by a considerably lower period of almost nine months. A shift in the structure of age limits as a whole by a further two years would postpone the effective retirement age of men by, on average, around nine months and would have little or no effect on the retirement age of women. Alternatively, an increase of the actuarial adjustment factor from 3.6 percent to 6 percent would increase the average age of retirement by almost two years. This effect would be considerably weaker for women; nevertheless, their average age of retirement would increase by around one year.

These results have relevance not only for Germany, but also for the many other European countries which have public pay-as-you-go systems that are not actuarially neutral with respect to retirement age, notably the French, Italian and Spanish public pension systems. Our results illustrate that in particular increased actuarial adjustment factors offer major potential for postponing the effective age of retirement as an important mechanism to regain financial sustainability.

NOTES

*   We thank Anette Reil-Held, Florian Heiss, Christina Wilke and Joachim Winter for their many helpful comments, and the DFG through the Sonderforschungsbereich 504, the National Institute of Aging through the NBER, and the State of Baden-Württemberg and Gesamtverband der deutschen Versicherungswirtschaft (GDV) for co-funding this study. The usual disclaimer applies.
1.   A higher discount rate yields steeper adjustments.
2.   They are now referred to as partial or full 'Erwerbsminderungsrente (EM)'.
3.   Before, persons with bad labor market prospects would be categorized 'disabled' even without any major health problem.
4.   Civil servants are also exempt from unemployment insurance contributions, since civil servants have a lifetime job guarantee. The government pays a certain fraction of health expenses of the civil servant and his or her dependents (ranging from 50 to 80 percent). The rest has to be covered by private insurance.

5. Very specific rules apply to some civil servants. For example, the regular retirement age for police officers is age 60; for soldiers it is even lower and depends on their rank.
6. Cf. 'Zweiter Versorgungsbericht der Bundesregierung', Bundesdrucksache 14/7220, 19.10.2001.
7. As our estimates specify the incentives to retire of married people as a unit, we take account of the survivor's pension rules but not of pension splitting.
8. Börsch-Supan (2003) discusses the economic and political pros and cons of introducing an NDC system.
9. Under the 1972 legislation 'disability' depends on health as well as labor market characteristics.
10. These weights are flow based using VDR data.
11. Benefits are computed on a lifetime contribution basis. They are the product of four elements: (1) the employee's relative wage position, averaged over the entire earnings history, (2) the number of years of service life, (3) several adjustment factors, and (4) the average pension level. For more details see Börsch-Supan et al. (2004).
12. For the significance of this extension, see Coile (1999).
13. Börsch-Supan et al. (2004).
14. We use a version of the so-called weighted exogenous sampling maximum likelihood (WESML) to ascertain that the reference scenario exactly reproduces the 1997 cumulative distribution of retirement ages. We use the stock data of the VDR. All our simulations use the same weights. We therefore predict how this population would behave under a different set of rules, not how a future (possibly different) population would behave. This is important in order to separate program effects from population change effects. The program effect includes both changes in the access to pathways and the generosity of each pathway.

REFERENCES

Berkel, B. and A. Börsch-Supan (2004), 'Pension Reform in Germany: The Impact on Retirement Decisions', *Finanzarchiv*, **60**(3), pp. 393–421.
Börsch-Supan, A. (1992), 'Population Aging, Social Security Design, and Early Retirement', *Journal of Institutional and Theoretical Economics*, **148**, pp. 533–57.
Börsch-Supan, A. (2000), 'Incentive Effects of Social Security on Labor Force Participation: Evidence in Germany and Across Europe', *Journal of Public Economics*, **78**, pp. 25–49.
Börsch-Supan, A. (2001), 'Incentive Effects of Social Security under an Uncertain Disability Option', in D.A. Wise (ed.), *Themes in the Economics of Aging*, Chicago: The University of Chicago Press, pp. 281–311.
Börsch-Supan, A. (2003), 'What are NDC Pension Systems? What do they Bring to Reform Strategies?', MEA-Discussion Paper, MEA, Universität Mannheim, and World Bank Discussion Paper, Social Protection Series, The World Bank, Washington, DC.
Börsch-Supan, A. and P. Schmidt (2001), 'Early Retirement in East and West Germany', in R. Riphahn, D. Snower and K. Zimmermann (eds), *Employment Policy in Transition: The Lessons of German Integration for the Labour Market*, Heidelberg: Springer, pp. 83–102.
Börsch-Supan, A. and R. Schnabel (1998), 'Social Security and Declining Labor Force Participation in Germany', *American Economic Review*, **88**, pp. 173–78.
Börsch-Supan, A. and C. Wilke (2003), 'The German Social Security System: How it Was and How it Will Be', MEA-Discussion Paper 34-03, Universität Mannheim, and MRRC-Discussion Paper, University of Michigan, Ann Arbor.
Börsch-Supan, A., F. Heiss, A. Ludwig and J. Winter (2003), 'Pension Reform,

Capital Markets, and the Rate of Return', *German Economic Review*, **4**(2), pp. 151–81.

Börsch-Supan, A., R. Schnabel, S. Kohnz and G. Mastrobuoni (2004), 'Micro Modelling of Retirement Choices in Germany', in J. Gruber and D. Wise (eds), *Social Security Programs and Retirement Around the World: Micro-Estimation*, Chicago: The University of Chicago Press, pp. 285–343.

Brugiavini, A. (1999), 'Social Security and Retirement in Italy', in J. Gruber and D.A. Wise (eds), *International Social Security Comparisons*, Chicago: The University of Chicago Press.

Coile, C. (1999), 'Retirement Incentives and Couples' Retirement Decisions', Ph.D. Dissertation, MIT.

Cutler, D., and L.M. Sheiner (1998), 'Demographics and Medical Care Spending: Standard and Non-Standard Effects', NBER Working Paper 6866.

Franco, D. and N. Sartor, 'Notional Defined Contribution in Italy: Unsatisfactory Present, Uncertain Future', paper prepared for the Conference on NDC Pensions (Stockholm, 28–30 September 2003).

Gruber, J. and D.A. Wise (eds) (1999), *Social Security and Retirement Around the World*, Chicago: University of Chicago Press.

Palmer, E. (2000), 'The Swedish Pension Reform Model: Framework and Issues', Social Protection Discussion Paper Series No. 0012, World Bank.

Schmidt, P. (1995), *Die Wahl des Rentenalters – Theoretische und empirische Analyse des Rentenzugangsverhaltens in West- und Ostdeutschland*, Frankfurt: P. Lang.

Settergren, O. (2001), 'The Automatic Balance Mechanism of the Swedish Pension System', *Wirtschaftspolitische Blätter*, **4**.

Siddiqui, S. (1997), 'The Pension Incentive to Retire: Empirical Evidence for West Germany', *Journal of Population Economics*, **10**, pp. 463–86.

Stock, J.H. and D.A. Wise (1990), 'The Pension Inducement to Retire: An Option Value Analysis', in D.A. Wise (ed.) *Issues in the Economics of Aging*, Chicago: University of Chicago Press, pp. 205–30.

Verband deutscher Rentenversicherungsträger (VDR) (1995–2002), 'Die Rentenversicherung in Zeitreihen', Frankfurt am Main.

Zweiter Versorgungsbericht der Bundesregierung, Bundesdrucksache 14/7220, 19 October 2001.

6. Assessing the impact of pensions policy reform in Ireland: the case of increasing the pension age*

Cathal O'Donoghue

6.1 INTRODUCTION

Ireland, as in many other countries, has a set of regulations and customs that result in a large proportion of the population retiring from the labour market on or before a set retirement age, in Ireland's case 65 or 66, with 15 per cent of males and 3 per cent of females aged 65+ participating in the labour market after this point.[1] Added to this, participation in the labour market has declined for younger age groups, with only just over 50 per cent of males in the 60–65 age group participating in the labour market in 2002, down from over 70 per cent 20 years previously. At the same time life expectancy has been rising by about two years (life expectancy at birth) for both males and females in the 10-year period 1985–95 and at levels below the EU average, is expected to continue to rise into the future.[2] Earlier retirement and longer life expectancy results in longer periods in retirement. Longer retirement will therefore clearly result in increased demands on support mechanisms such as public pensions and assistance for the elderly and for health and social care.

In addition to the current and future expected lengthening of the retirement period, demographic changes will result in a larger elderly population relative to the working age population, resulting in greater numbers of people in retirement, placing further pressures on public support mechanisms for the elderly.

At present, unlike many other countries in Western Europe, Ireland currently still has a relatively young population, with about 40 per cent of the population aged 25 or under and only about 12 per cent of the population aged 65 or over. The proportion of elderly has remained relatively constant at about 10 per cent over the whole twentieth century. Despite historically high birth rates, high levels of emigration have tended to offset this effect to keep the population constant or in fact falling over the period.

However, the elderly, as a percentage of the population, are expected to increase in the future. Life expectancy at birth has risen by on average two years a decade for men and three for women since WWII. Official population projections assume that life expectancy will increase by about 1.5 years per decade into the middle of this century, with life expectancy projected to rise to 77.8 in 2031 for males and to 83.8 for females.

Fertility rates also have fallen significantly over time from a total fertility rate (TFR) peak of 4 in the mid-1960s to 1.89 in the mid-1990s. Although there has been a slight rise in fertility rates during the late 1990s' economic boom, fertility rates in Ireland are high by EU standards and so are likely to fall, or at least remain constant over time. The effect of this decline is to reduce the size of future working age cohorts and so combined with increasing life expectancy, this will increase the size of the elderly population relative to the working age population, posing further public finance pressures.

Counterbalancing the rising old-age dependency ratio due to the changes in life expectancy and fertility, rising immigration will tend to lower the dependency ratio. However, this effect is unlikely to be sufficient to stem the rising elderly dependency ratio.

Figure 6.1 describes the distribution of the Irish population by age group for 1961, 2002 and a forecast for 2050. The result of these assumptions is that the population will gradually rise by nearly 25 per cent between 2002 and 2045, declining thereafter. Although fertility rates are below the long-term replacement rate, the number of births will rise as the large birth cohorts of the 1970s and 1980s have children. Forecasted immigration levels will also increase the population. However, after this period the population will fall due to the lower fertility rate. The large dip in the 20–30 age group in 1961, deviating from what one would expect to be a relatively concave curve, reflects the very high emigration levels of the 1950s which gave Ireland the highest old-age dependency ratio in Europe in 1960. Conversely it is one of the reasons for such a small retirement age cohort in 2000. Emigration has been less important for succeeding generations, resulting in higher working age cohorts. Although significant improvements have been made in the child and young adult mortality rates, improvements in mortality amongst the elderly have not matched that in other countries and thus longevity has not had much of an impact on the demographic structure thus far (Fahey and Fitzgerald, 1997).

Over the 1990s and into 2000, the elderly dependency ratio looks positive (see Figure 6.2). This is due to a number of factors. Firstly, the high emigration levels of the 1920s/30s birth cohort means that the generation entering retirement was small. Over the period 2000–2050 however, the picture is expected to change, with the proportion aged 65+ expected to more

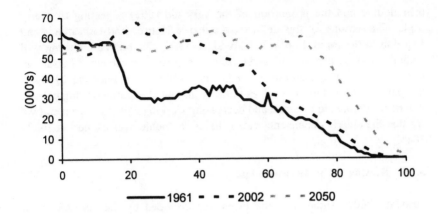

Notes:
Projection assumptions:
1. Birth rate remains constant at 1.75.
2. Life expectancy for males rises to 77.8 and for females to 84 in 2031.
3. Net immigration of 15 000 is assumed 2001–2005, 10 000 per annum 2006–2010 and 5 000 per annum 2011–2031.

Source: Census 1961, 2002 and author's calculations.

Figure 6.1 Age distribution of Irish population, 1961, 2002 and 2050

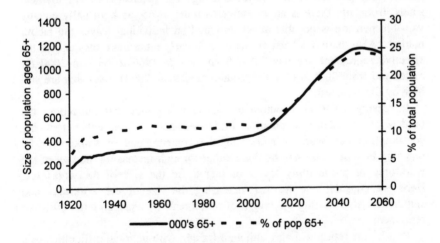

Note: Projection assumptions as per Figure 6.1.

Source: Census (various years) and author's calculations.

Figure 6.2 Number of people aged 65+, 1922–2060

than double and the proportion of the very old (80+) expecting to nearly triple. The reasons for this lie in factors that influence short-term trends and also due to the rapid drop in fertility since 1980. The numbers retiring will naturally rise as a result of larger cohorts reaching retirement. In addition, this is coupled with the dramatic reduction in birth rates since the 1970s. If this pattern of low birth rates does in fact continue, then large retiring cohorts will be accompanied by small and decreasing working cohorts. As a result we see that the elderly dependency rate is likely to double over the period 2000–2045.

6.1.1 Raising the Retirement Age

Pestieau (2003) argues that the incentives provided by the tax and social protection systems in OECD countries have created incentives to retire early. The higher the level of tax, the lower the marginal benefit of working is, increasing the incentive to retire. At the same time benefits typically do not vary with retirement age and so retiring later does not increase the value of the benefit. Social security and tax systems will therefore tend to distort retirement ages downwards. Rising incomes and the spread of private pension plans over time also create an income effect to retire early.

In Ireland, the official retirement age was 70 in 1961 falling to 65/66 in the period of the early 1970s and has remained at this level since. The old-age contributory pension is now payable at age 66, regardless of employment status. Ironically there is an incentive to retire at 65, as a virtually equally valuable pension is payable at 65 provided an individual leaves the labour market.[3] Also there has been an increase in early retirement rates and so the effective retirement age has fallen from 68.1 in 1960 to 63.4 in 2000 for males and from 70.8 to 60.1 for females (Pestieau, 2003); rates that are still high by EU standards.

Increasing the level of output of society is a policy that can reduce the burden of an ageing population that does not involve either reducing consumption per head by increasing the contributions of workers or by reducing benefits. This can be done either through increasing the size of the workforce or productivity levels or increasing the size of the workforce. Here, we consider one way of increasing the size of the workforce and simultaneously reducing the length of retirement, by increasing the effective retirement age.

Raising the retirement age, although fraught with political difficulties, is a policy frequently advocated to reduce the impact of the ageing of the population and earlier retirement ages. The impact of funding longer periods in retirement represents an increasing burden on workers. Barr (2001) argues that raising the state pension age should embody an endogenous retirement age, where the retirement age responds to changes in the life expectancy.

Implementing policies that increase the actual retirement age has a number of effects. Raising the retirement age, provided the increased potential workforce can be converted into an increased *actual workforce*, simultaneously reduces the number of pensioners and increases the number of workers, and imposes some of the cost of longevity on pensioners rather than workers. It improves the public finance position, increases economic growth because of a larger workforce and is also likely to reduce income inequality and poverty.

Policies that can be used to increase the effective retirement age include the following:

- Raising the official retirement age itself seems the most logical first step. It increases the age at which pensions are paid. However, across the OECD, there are not many examples of increasing the retirement age for men, other than bringing the retirement age above 60. The US will increase the pension age from 65 to 67 over 25 years. A number of Nordic countries currently have retirement ages at 67. Mainly, however, policies that have been implemented have been aimed at equalizing retirement ages between men and women. Policies that increase the incentive for pensions to be deferred, and thus receiving an increased pension, may also help to increase the effective retirement age. While many of the countries have a limit at which pensions can be deferred of age 70, Finland, Sweden and the UK have removed, or will remove, this age limit.

Even if the official retirement age were increased, there is no guarantee that participation rates would increase very much as even at present, the participation rate of those below the existing retirement age has decreased over time. Therefore, any attempt to increase the effective retirement age would have to focus on policies that discourage early retirement.

- Reduce incentives provided by the public pension system to retire early by removing early-retirement provisions from the social security code. For example many Central and Eastern European countries have raised the age at which people can receive early retirement benefits. Italy and Germany have raised the number of contributions that need to have been paid before someone is entitled to these benefits, while Sweden has introduced actuarially based payment adjustments. Denmark has increased the use of active labour market policies, so that opportunities for training and rehabilitation are considered before entitlement to early retirement benefits is considered. In Ireland, possible reform may include the elimination of benefits such as the pre-retirement allowance and may include more stringent work tests and eligibility requirements for invalidity benefits.

- From an equity perspective, one may want to compare policies that increase the incentive to retire later across all groups in the population. Those with private pension plans will be more able to afford to retire earlier, so that later retirement may shift to those who cannot afford to retire early. Spreading the burden across the population may require reducing the incentives to retire early provided by private pensions by adjusting the tax favoured status of private pension plans to decrease these incentives.

- A parallel strand to reducing the pull factor from benefits and pensions to retire early is to increase the incentive to work itself by targeting work incentive policies at older workers. Examples include the use of in-work benefits/refundable tax-credits as in the UK, which increase the in-work incomes of low wage older workers, who may face high work disincentives.

- Employers may be reluctant to hire older workers or to have early retirement schemes because of the perception that their skills may be obsolete and thus have lower productivity (OECD, 1996). Other measures that may increase the productivity of older workers, increasing their return from work, include enhancing their skill levels by increasing active labour market and re-education/training policies for the older age groups to improve their abilities to participate in the labour market and improve their chances of being employed.

- Promote the use of productivity based wage increases rather than seniority rules in wage negotiation/bargaining processes. The use of seniority rules may result in older workers having wages higher than productivity levels, giving an incentive for organizations to employ younger workers.

- Use labour market legislation to remove labour market age discrimination and to increase the ease of flexible retirement and part-time work for older workers who may not wish to work full-time, but where custom and practice may prevent them from working part-time.

- Pay state pensions and pensions to civil servants at a later age. Significant proportions of employees work for the public sector, generally with generous pension schemes, often with earlier retirement ages than the official pension age. Hence the ageing of the population also has a public finance effect through the public sector pension bill. The same arguments that apply to public pensions for workers in all sectors apply to public sector workers.

- A potential policy solution to changing the retirement age is to give workers the choice of retirement age, varying social insurance contributions, so as to allow workers to select higher contribution rates to be able to retire earlier. Given their discount rates, more individuals may choose to consume more in the short term, have lower social contribution rates and retire later.

If policies that aim to increase effective retirement were to be implemented then notice would have to be given well in advance. This is because individuals and firms need time to adjust their investment/savings behaviour in the spheres of education/training, saving/pension accumulation, house purchase and so on. In the US the transition to increase the retirement age will take 25 years.

OECD (1988) presents a number of potential problems with raising the state retirement age. If labour market conditions are more difficult for older workers perhaps because of the perceived gap between pay and productivity, then changing the official retirement age may not have much of a labour market outcome. Instead older individuals may move from being pensioners to being unemployed, with little impact on fiscal pressures. Improved training may increase their employment prospects. They also highlight the fact that although individuals are living longer, it is not clear as to the extent to which they are staying healthy for longer. In this case raising the state pension age may result in a shift from pension to disability benefits. Raising the state pension age will affect the poorest more as they will be less likely to have other savings or occupational pensions, resulting in these groups working longer. Simply raising the state pension age may therefore not increase the effective retirement age by much. Fields and Mitchell (1984) argue that raising the retirement age by two years may only result in a rise in the effective retirement age by two months.

In this chapter, we consider trends in labour participation by older age groups and consider the implications for the state system for old-age support through pensions and means tested benefits in Ireland. Utilizing a microsimulation model we evaluate the cost and distributional implications of a change to the state retirement age. The chapter is designed as follows. The next section describes the Irish public and private systems of support for the elderly. Section 6.3 describes the main trends in the labour market. Section 6.4 presents an overview of the main methodology used in this chapter, dynamic microsimulation. In Section 6.5, we report the results of our baseline simulation, while in section 6.6 we simulate the impact of increasing the effective retirement age. Section 6.7 concludes.

6.2   THE IRISH PENSION SYSTEM

The Irish pension system is in many respects typical of the Anglo-liberal style of welfare state, with a relatively insignificant social insurance system, where means testing and progressive income taxes are more important. Public pensions and benefits are in general Pay-As-You-Go (PAYG). There are a number of important differences between the UK and Irish tax–benefit systems. Firstly means testing tends to be more important (see Evans et al., 2000). Social insurance is less well developed than in the UK, with flat rate benefits and with no earnings related components. Flat rate benefits tend to be of higher value than in the UK. Having a larger self-employed population, the coverage of social insurance also tends to be lower.

6.2.1   Old-Age Insurance Pensions

The state insurance system for the elderly was established in 1961 and provides for three main pensions for the elderly: the old-age contributory pension, the retirement pension and the survivor's pension. Combined, these instruments are the most important public pension/benefits both for the elderly and for the population as a whole.

Each pension is similar in design with payments being related to the number of (pay-related) contributions paid. Each has a personal rate, additional payments for any dependent children under 18 and a living alone allowance as well as an age allowance for the over 80s. The first two also have additional payments for dependent adults.

A single person entitled to the maximum pension, on the average wage faced a replacement rate in 2002 of 33.1 per cent, while a married couple faced a net replacement rate of 66.2 per cent (O'Donoghue, 2004a). Surviving spouses can receive a similar benefit called survivor's pension. Individuals without sufficient contributions paid before retirement at 65 who had been in receipt of the invalidity pensions continue to receive this.

Old-age contributory pensions were originally paid to those who were 70 years old or over. Between 1973 and 1977 this age limit was reduced to 66. It requires an average of 20 weekly contributions per year to get the minimum pension and for contributions to have begun before age 55. The retirement pension has similar conditions but is available to the insured over 65 who have retired from full-time work. About two thirds of recipients receive the maximum rate.

Survivors' contributory benefits are paid to survivors after their spouse's death if either spouse is insured. Again the pension depends upon the number of years of contribution, however, 90 per cent of recipients get the maximum pensions.

6.2.2 Social Insurance Contributions

The coverage of the social insurance system has expanded substantially since the 1950s (see O'Donoghue, 2004a). Initially full coverage was limited only to full-time private sector employees, with partial coverage of public sector workers. In addition until the 1970s, non-manual workers earning more than the contribution ceiling were excluded from membership of the social insurance scheme. This resulted in 1955 in a situation with coverage for only about 60 per cent of the workforce, with full coverage for just over half (Hughes, 1985). Over time, the proportion of the workforce in private sector non-self-employed employment has increased, resulting in a gradual increase in the insured population. By 1973, 73 per cent of the population were covered. A number of further structural reforms have resulted in increased coverage. In 1974, the contribution limit was lifted for non-manual workers, increasing total coverage to nearly 85 per cent in 1975. The main effect of this reform was to nearly double the coverage for partial benefits within the public sector. Recent structural reforms have further increased coverage, including the extension of partial cover to the self-employed with earnings over a threshold in 1988. Part-time workers were included in the system in 1991. New public sector workers from 1995 are covered for all benefits. In recent years, the dominant force in the expansion in the numbers covered by the social insurance system has been demographic and economic as both the working age population and the labour force has increased dramatically in size. This is witnessed by the doubling of the insured population in the years 1980–98, and the continued increase to 2002.

Despite these reforms, until recently there had been a number of significant gaps in coverage. In 1998, only 75 per cent of those covered were covered for all benefits, with the rest being made up of self-employed, low-wage workers and existing public sector workers. Also there had been a number of groups completely excluded from coverage. Those within the labour market excluded from membership include those earning less than the contributory threshold, the self-employed in receipt of unemployment assistance, some participants on social employment programmes and relatives assisting the self-employed.

Contributions are credited automatically for claimants of unemployment, disability and maternity benefits and invalidity and retirement pensions. Recipients of unemployment assistance, pre-retirement allowance, injury benefit, careers allowance, while participating in a back to education programme or on a state training courses must have worked and paid at least one Pay-Related Social Insurance (PRSI) contribution in either of the previous two complete income tax years before making the claim. Students who have paid insurance contributions before entering university will also now receive contribution for periods in education.

Contributions have moved from flat rate payments, which existed until 1978, to first a partially earnings related system in 1974, then to a wholly earnings related contributory system in 1979, Pay-Related Social Insurance (PRSI). Total contributions are divided between employee and employer contributions that are paid into the social insurance fund and income levies paid into general taxation. PRSI is paid by workers on earnings up to a ceiling subject to an allowance that varies for different types of workers. Income over the ceiling faces a marginal rate of zero. Employer contributions (ERSIC) for employees have a similar structure except for employees with earnings below the ERSIC reduced rate limit who face a lower ERSIC rate. Flat rate health contribution levies, education and training levies are also paid by individuals who have earnings above an exemption limit. This movement from flat rate benefits and contributions to flat rate benefits and earnings related contributions, combined with a limited linkage between contributions and benefits, has resulted in a social insurance pension system which is highly redistributive, reducing the pure insurance element of the system.

6.2.3 Means Tested Social Assistance Benefits[4]

For those ineligible for contributory pensions, there are corresponding means tested benefits available. These benefits are typically lower valued than the contributory based instruments, and in 2002 a single person entitled to the maximum pension, on the average wage faced a replacement rate of 27.2 per cent, while a married couple faced a net replacement rate of 53.4 per cent (O'Donoghue, 2004a). The pre-retirement allowance is paid to those aged 55 or over, who had been in receipt of unemployment benefits for 15 months and who retire from the labour market.

6.2.4 Indexation

Figure 6.3 describes the trend in the net replacement rate from 1955–2002. For single persons, replacement rates in general are quite low by European standards, with the replacement rate never reaching 40 per cent, and with the lowest replacement rate being just over 10 per cent in 1955. From 1955–65, we observe a fall in the replacement rate. This is because single person benefits in general fell with respect to net average earnings. The replacement ratio rose from 1965 to 1987, and is partly due to rising benefit levels and partly due to higher taxation, which reduces the denominator, net average earnings.

Since 1987, falling taxation and benefit levels have resulted in higher denominators and lower numerators, pushing replacement rates down. During this period, resources were used to narrow the differential between benefit rates, so that the lowest benefit rates such as short-term unemployment benefits were increased in value relative to the more generous old-age benefits. Because of this and also because of the general indexation policy, benefits between 1987 and 1998 have fallen further behind earnings, despite rapid economic growth. Between 1998 and 2002, this trend has largely reversed, improving the replacement ratio, however with indexation being at the discretion of the government and thus strongly dependent upon the state of the public finances, in the periods of lower growth, benefit replacement rates may fall further.

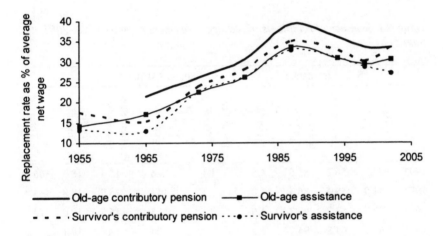

——— Old-age contributory pension   —■— Old-age assistance

- - - · Survivor's contributory pension · · · • · · · Survivor's assistance

Notes:
1. Net replacement rate is defined as net out-of-work income divided by net in-work income at the average wage.
2. Net out-of-work income: benefits – out-of-work taxes – out-of-work social insurance contributions.
3. Net in-work income: average earnings + in-work benefits – in-work taxes – in-work social insurance contributions.

Source: O'Donoghue (2004a).

Figure 6.3 Net replacement rate for old-age, early retirement and survivor's benefits, 1955–2002

6.2.5 Number of Recipients of Public Pensions

In Table 6.1, we report the number of recipients of the different public pensions available in Ireland. While for much of the period, the old-age non-contributory (means tested) pension has the highest number of recipients, it disguises the fact that most recipients get social insurance based pensions, rising from about 60 per cent of all recipients in 1992 to 71 per cent in 2001 as a result of the increase in the size of the insured population. Although remaining relatively constant as a percentage of all benefits, the proportion of recipients of the survivor's contributory pension has the highest level of receipt by 2001. The means tested old-age non-contributory pension has the biggest fall in percentage of recipients, falling from 31 per cent to 22.2 per cent. This is explained by the fact that more elderly people are becoming eligible for insurance pensions, as witnessed by the fact that the biggest increase in recipients occurs in the contributory old-age and retirement pensions which rose from 35 per cent of recipients in 1992 to 44 per cent in 2001.

Table 6.1 Number of recipients of old-age/retirement benefits 1992–2001 (000's)

	Social Insurance				Social Assistance				
Year	Old-Age Contrib.	Retirement	Survivor's Contrib.	Invalidity	Disability Pension	Old-Age Non-Contrib.	Pre-Retirement Survivors	Non-Contrib.	Total
1992	72.7	55.2	85.5	4.5	1.1	113.6	15.4	18.6	366.6
1993	71.9	58.4	86.4	4.8	1	111	15.9	18.8	368.2
1994	70.8	62.2	90.7	4.9	1	108.3	15.3	19.0	372.2
1995	69.2	65.8	94.7	5.2	1	103	15	19.1	373.0
1996	68	69.7	96.1	5.3	1	101.6	14.2	19.0	374.9
1997	70	71.8	97.3	5.3	1	98.8	13.6	18.8	376.6
1998	71.7	75.3	98.5	5.5	1	95.9	13.9	18.4	380.2
1999	76.2	78.9	99.8	5.7	1	93	13.1	18.0	385.7
2000	86.2	78.4	100.4	6	1.1	90.7	12.5	17.4	392.7
2001	94.9	80.3	101.3	6.2	1.2	89.1	11.8	16.8	401.6

Source: Statistical Information on Social Welfare Services (2001).

6.2.6 Cost of State Pensions

In Figure 6.4, we report trends and projections of old-age and survivor's insurance and assistance benefit expenditure, 1955–2060. The demographic assumptions underlying the projections are the same as in Figure 6.5. Three alternative indexing assumptions are made. The first scenario assumes that all incomes rise at the rate of productivity growth.[5] The second set of assumptions is based upon indexing assumptions from a long-term forecasting paper of the Department of Finance outlined in Box 6.1. The third assumption corresponds to a proposal of the Working Group on Benchmarking and Indexation that the lowest valued benefits should increase to 27 per cent of the Gross Average Industrial Wage (27 per cent GAIW), equivalent to a percentage increase in 2000 of 20 per cent, and that other benefits be increased proportionally. Thereafter it is assumed that benefits increase at the rate of productivity growth.

BOX 6.1 DEPARTMENT OF FINANCE (DOF) PROJECTION ASSUMPTIONS

- Social Insurance Contributions increase at 80 per cent of the rate of productivity growth. As a result, revenues will tend to fall slightly relative to average income over time.
- Social Welfare benefits per recipient will rise at 1 per cent above the rate of inflation. As this is below the growth rate, it will have the effect of a falling replacement rate over time and as a result will cause benefits to fall relative to earnings.
- All other incomes increase at the rate of productivity growth.

Source: Department of Finance (1998).

We see that over the early years of the state, expenditure grew relatively slowly from about 1.5 per cent of GNP in 1922 to 2.5 per cent in 1960. After this period however, old-age support as a percentage of GNP rose to a peak of 6 per cent in 1987. Although as we saw in Figure 6.2, the percentage of the population aged 65+ rose only slightly (in fact the elderly dependency rate fell – Figure 6.5), we see in Figure 6.3 that the introduction of insurance pensions and rapid rise of the replacement rate had the biggest influence on the rise in expenditure. Between 1987 and 2000, expenditure fell to 3 per cent. Part of the reason is the decline in elderly dependency rate that resulted from a relatively small retirement cohort (Figure 6.5) and also due to the decline in the replacement rate seen in Figure 6.3.

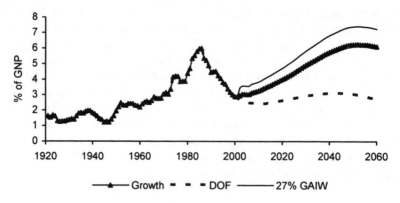

—▲—Growth - - - DOF ———27% GAIW

Notes:
1. Growth assumption is based on the assumption that benefit rates grow at the rate of productivity growth.
2. Department of Finance (DOF) projections, see Box 6.1.
3. 27 per cent GAIW refers to the assumption that increases the lowest valued benefits to 27 per cent of the Average Industrial Wage (Gross), and that thereafter the growth scenario is followed.

Source: O'Donoghue (2004a).

Figure 6.4 Historical and projected old-age and survivor's benefit expenditure, 1920–2060

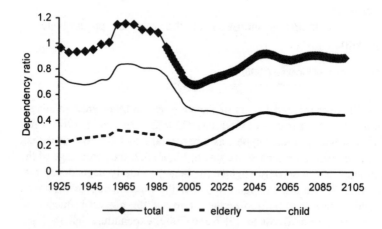

—♦—total - - - elderly ———child

Note: Projection assumptions as per Figure 6.1.

Source: Census (various years) and author's calculations.

Figure 6.5 Child, elderly and total dependency ratios, 1925–2100

6.2.7　Reform Issues: Public Pensions

Reforms to the public pensions system over the late 1990s to the early twenty-first century have focused on widening coverage, introducing a funded element to the system and reducing the disincentives to save within the system.

Participation rates, especially for women because of home responsibilities, and young people as a result of participation in the labour market, are relatively low. Until 1994, unlike in countries such as Britain and Germany, their contribution to society was not recognized within the social insurance system, However since 1994, carers of children aged under six and since 1995 aged under 12 or incapacitated, have the number of contributory years required to be eligible for a pension, reduced by up to a maximum of 20 years when calculating long-term benefits. This policy is similar to Home Responsibilities Protection (HRP) in the UK.[6]

Because of the concerns raised above about the future increase in public pension expenditures, the National Pensions Reserve Fund Act 2000 established a national pensions fund to help finance both public pensions and public service occupational pensions. Each year, at least 1 per cent of GNP will be deposited in the fund between 2001 and 2055. From 2025 the exchequer will be able to draw down monies from the fund to finance expenditures on public pensions and on the occupational pensions of public sector workers.

Recent policies have also focused on disincentives to save within the means tested component of the system. The system now allows substantially higher levels of assets to be exempt from means testing and has restructured the imputed interest rate on assets.

A proposed policy, although as yet not implemented, is the abolition of the requirement to retire to receive the retirement pension at 65. There are no current plans to allow for deferred rights.

6.2.8　Private Provision

Ireland, like other Anglo-liberal countries such as the UK, New Zealand and Australia places an important emphasis on private provision in supporting pensioners in retirement. Private provision consists of two types of pension, occupational pension plans that are usually linked to employment in a particular industry or employer, and personal pension plans that are tied to an individual.

Occupational pension schemes can be broken up into two types, those that are guaranteed by the state, covering employees in the public sectors and those provided by firms in the private sector. The public sector schemes were the first to evolve and cover occupations such as civil servants, police, armed services, teachers, health workers and also employees of state enterprises such as electricity and transport workers and so on. These schemes have virtually universal coverage across the civil service. Private sector pension schemes on the other hand are much newer, with only 6 per cent of current schemes existing in 1960, and have a relatively lower coverage (Keogh and Whelan, 1986).

After a period of increasing coverage of occupational pensions, ESRI surveys in 1995 found that 52 per cent of the employed workforce was covered by occupational schemes, down from 54.4 per cent 1985, but up from 35.6 per cent in 1974. Recent Statistical Office figures indicate that the percentage of employees with an occupation pension has fallen to about 46.9 per cent. The numbers in employment are however much larger, and so more of the population are covered.

Firm-level pensions tend to be defined benefit, with contributions being actuarially calculated to meet the liabilities of the scheme. Firms usually pay all or some of the contributions. Defined benefit pensions have the advantage of giving workers stable expectations of their retirement earnings and are concentrated amongst full-time workers, especially in public service. In 1992, about 12 per cent of occupational pension members were covered by defined contribution pension schemes (National Pensions Board, 1993). By 1995 this percentage had increased to 17 per cent as employers shifted pension risk to their employees (Hughes and Whelan, 1996).

Personal pensions are similar to defined contribution schemes in that the pension risk is held by the individual. These are usually held by the self-employed or by individuals whose firm does not have an occupational scheme. Increasingly as the labour market becomes more flexible, more employees are saving in personal pension plans. They have the advantage of being mobile in that in moving between jobs, individuals can easily bring their pension with them. In addition ownership of the fund is unambiguous and individuals can set their own retirement age. Like defined contribution schemes, pension risk is held by the individual.

In Table 6.2, we describe the coverage of occupational and personal pension coverage in the Irish labour market in 2002. The table reports the percentage of each age group in the different categories employee/self-employed, with occupational pensions/personal and occupational pensions/no pensions. For men the coverage rate of any type of pension rises to a peak of 67 per cent in the 45–55 age group, while for women, indicating the relative later expansion of women's employment, the peak is lower, being at 52 per cent in the 35–45 age group. Coverage is higher for males than females, 56 per cent of males in the labour force aged 20–65 having some form of pension compared with 44 per cent of females. Coverage rates are higher for employees than the self-employed with 59 per cent (56 per cent) of male (female) employees covered by pensions, compared with 48 per cent (31 per cent) of the self-employed. As a result the total coverage rate for the labour market including both employees and the self-employed is 55.8 per cent of males and 44.3 per cent of females, 51 per cent in total.

Table 6.2 Private and occupational pension coverage 2002 (as percentage of age group)

Age Group	20	25	35	45	55	65+	Total 20–65
Males							
Self-employed with employment pension	0.6	6.9	15.2	18.9	19.8	19.7	12.3
Employees with an employer's pension only	21.7	36.2	40.2	38.6	29.7	7.4	35.1
Employees with a personal pension only	1.3	5.5	6.6	4.8	5.0	2.2	5.0
Employees with both employer's and personal pension	0.7	2.8	4.3	5.1	3.2	1.1	3.4
Employees with no pension	71.7	37.9	19.6	16.5	18.6	16.8	30.8
Self-employed with no pension	3.8	10.7	14.0	16.0	23.7	52.8	13.3
Total	100.0	100.0	100.0	100.0	100.0	100.0	100.0
Females							
Self-employed with employment pension	0.0	1.5	3.3	4.3	4.3	6.3	2.4
Employees with an employer's pension only	22.5	40.1	42.8	35.6	27.4	11.5	36.2
Employees with a personal pension only	0.8	3.6	3.9	4.9	4.9	6.0	3.6
Employees with both employer's and personal pension	1.0	2.3	2.4	2.8	1.9	0.0	2.2
Employees with no pension	74.7	48.2	41.7	45.0	48.2	50.8	50.2
Self-employed with no pension	1.0	4.3	5.9	7.4	13.3	25.3	5.4
Total	100.0	100.0	100.0	100.0	100.0	100.0	100.0

Note: Self-employed include assisting relatives.

Source: Quarterly National Household Survey 2002.

6.2.9   Reform Issues: Private Pensions

Recent reform of private pensions has attempted to increase the coverage of personal pensions, and encourage saving by increasing tax relief.

An initiative designed to increase the coverage of private pensions was the introduction in 2002 of the Personal Retirement Savings Accounts (PRSA). These are individual pension savings accounts with the same tax favoured status as occupational pensions. They are fully portable and so can facilitate ease of movement between different employments, and are regulated, so that firms must offer them to employees, fees are limited to 5 per cent of contributions or 1 per cent of assets, and transfers between funds are not penalized.

Because individuals on average take up private pensions plans relatively late in life, the tax system has been adjusted to provide an incentive to invest more in pensions at later ages. From a position where 15 per cent of earnings could benefit from tax relief for all ages, now the percentage of earnings that attracts tax relief has increased to 20 per cent for the 30–39 age group, 25 per cent for the 40–49 age group and 30 per cent of earnings for the 50+ age group.

6.3   TRENDS IN THE IRISH LABOUR MARKET

In this section, we describe the changing labour market situation in Ireland. Figure 6.6 reports the labour force participation rate by gender and age group during the period 1975–2002. While prime age male participation rates have fallen slightly over the period, participation rates of older males (55+) have fallen substantially. The participation rate of the 55–59 age group has fallen by 15 per cent, that of the 60–64 age group has fallen 30 per cent and for the 65+ age group, the fall has been nearly 50 per cent over the period. For women, there has been a very different trend. Employment rates for younger women have converged rapidly towards male levels. The trend exhibits cohort effects as the rise in age-specific participation rates started for younger ages before that of older ages.

We notice that for both males and females, there is a large difference in the employment rates of 60–64 and 65+ age groups. The large fall in the participation rate indicates that although the decline in the participation rate before the official retirement age is important, the official retirement age still has an effect.

Males

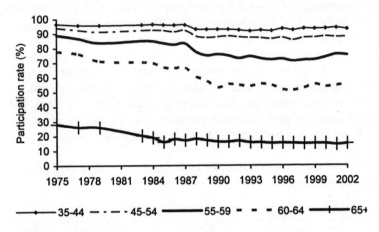

Females

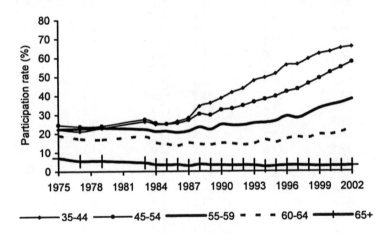

Source: Labour Force Survey 1975–97, Quarterly National Household Survey 1998–2002.

Figure 6.6 Labour force participation by age 1975–2002

This can be seen in more detail if we examine the participation rate for single age years. In order to highlight the impact of the official retirement age on retirement, we compare the participation rates of employees with the self-employed for single year age groups. Table 6.3 reports the participation rate as a percentage of the age group of (a) those in work, (b) those in employment and (c) those in self-employment for those aged 54–74. We notice that the decline with age in the percentage of individuals who are self-employed is much flatter than for the decline for employees. In the case of males, the percentage of 74-year-olds self-employed at age 74 is 55 per cent of the rate at 54, while for employees it is about 6 per cent. The biggest proportional year-on-year fall in the employment rate is the year after the old-age pension age at 66, where the percentage of 66-year-olds in employment is nearly 60 per cent less than the percentage of 65-year-olds. The percentage of those in self-employment actually increases at this age. Before this age, the decline is much more accentuated for employees than for the self-employed, with the percentage of 65-year-olds in employment being only 40 per cent of the rate of 54-year-olds, compared to 98 per cent for the self-employed.

Table 6.3 In-work, employment and self-employment rates aged 54–74 (as percentage of age group)

Age	Male			Female		
	In-work	Employee	Self-employed	In-work	Employee	Self-employed
54	85.3	45.6	39.7	28.3	8.8	6.4
55	85.6	48.9	36.8	29.5	9.4	5.9
56	84.0	44.2	39.8	25.2	4.5	5.7
57	81.1	38.9	42.2	23.6	6.0	6.0
58	76.4	36.9	39.5	24.3	5.4	7.3
59	72.9	37.8	35.2	23.0	5.7	6.2
60	68.7	32.6	36.1	21.6	4.9	6.3
61	64.9	26.2	38.7	19.3	5.1	6.2
62	67.4	23.6	43.8	17.3	3.5	4.7
63	59.7	23.9	35.8	14.0	4.3	4.9
64	60.8	20.2	40.6	12.7	1.9	5.5
65	57.5	18.6	38.9	12.0	1.1	5.4
66	47.6	7.7	39.9	6.4	0.0	2.3
67	39.1	6.2	32.9	5.9	0.0	2.7
68	34.6	4.1	30.5	4.2	0.0	3.4
69	33.7	5.5	28.2	6.5	0.0	4.1
70	34.2	6.2	28.0	6.2	0.0	3.8
71	31.3	3.4	27.9	4.7	0.0	3.8
72	31.1	4.6	26.4	5.1	0.0	4.0
73	31.1	5.0	26.1	5.8	0.0	4.9
74	24.7	2.9	21.8	5.4	0.0	4.3

Notes:
1. In-work: if an individual has income from work.
2. Employee: an individual who has income from employment and where employee income is at least as important as any self-employment income.
3. Full-time: employee and works at least 30 hours per week.
4. Self-employed: an individual who has income from self-employment and where self employed income is more important than any employee income.

Source: Based on pooled European Community Household Panel (ECHP) data 1994–2000.

There are a number of factors that might explain this differential decline. The self-employed are more likely to be able to choose when they retire than employees, and will have more control over their retirement decision than employees, who may have to retire at set retirement ages. Also, the self-employed are not eligible for the state retirement pension at 65, which requires an individual to retire from work, rather they only become eligible for the old-age pension at 66, which has no retirement requirement. Therefore this may provide some evidence that individuals who have more power over the retirement age such as the self-employed, may retire later than if facing the constraints that employees may face.

However, this may merely be a selection issue and those who are more likely to retire later are more likely to be self-employed. Also the self-employed are less likely to have private pension provision and so are less likely to be able to retire earlier. We see in Table 6.2 that for both employees and the self-employed, the peak age for holding private pensions is in the 45–55 age group. While about 75 per cent of employees hold private pensions at this age, only about 55 per cent of the self-employed hold them. For both male employees and the self-employed, this rate declines by about 10–15 per cent for the 55–64 age group and by about 40 per cent more for the 65+ group. This indicates that those with pensions are more likely to retire early than those without pensions. This may also indicate that the likelihood of retiring early or at the retirement age for both employees and the self-employed is similar, conditional on holding a pension.

6.4   METHODOLOGY

6.4.1   Dynamic Microsimulation

In this chapter we are interested in examining the impact of a change in retirement ages. In particular we are interested in the impact of this change on public pensions. In order to assess the impact of a policy change, we need information about pensions before and after the policy change. For this reason the policy has to be simulated. Because pensions rules are quite complex, it is necessary to use micro-data to simulate these policies. Also because pensions require information about work histories, we need quite long-running panel data. Long-running panel surveys only exist in a small number of countries such as the US, Germany or Sweden. However even these surveys are not sufficiently long-running to simulate pensions. The longest such panel available in Ireland is only eight years long. Therefore in order to analyse the impact of such a policy reform, we need to simulate both the policy reform and the data on which the reform is analysed. We therefore use a dynamic microsimulation model.

Dynamic microsimulation is a method that synthetically simulates panel data and involves simulating over a lifetime or period of time, components that influence the lifetime distribution of income such as mortality, earnings patterns, retirement decisions and so on. See O'Donoghue (2001) for a survey.

6.4.2 Model Description

The model used in this chapter is described in more detail in O'Donoghue (2001) and can be characterized as a dynamic steady state cohort model. The model simulates for a single cohort, a range of life-cycle processes, demographic, labour market, education and occupational pension behaviour. The model also simulates the Irish tax–benefit system in detail.[7]

Labour market behavioural equations are estimated using the 1994 *Living in Ireland Survey*, a 4000 household income survey, part of the European Community Panel Survey, described in Callan et al. (1996). Transitions were estimated using recall data from 1993 and current information from 1994. In the future, access to further waves of the panel will improve the model estimates. Most demographic processes such as mortality, fertility and education are estimated using official statistics.

In order to generate the correct life-cycle distribution of age and births, the main demographic processes, education, fertility, disability, marriage and mortality are simulated. While these characteristics depend primarily on age, marital status and gender, own and parental occupation and education levels are also important determinants. Because of the recent volatility in migration flows we assume no migration in the current model. Marriage is simulated by first selecting individuals in the model to marry and then by utilizing a matching algorithm, potential partners are selected from the population. Readers interested in the impact on the composition of the population due to these demographic behavioural assumptions are referred to O'Donoghue (2001).

The labour market process is hierarchical. Firstly those who are in education or become disabled are excluded from labour market participation. Secondly, a decision is made as to whether an individual retires from the labour market. This process is influenced by whether an individual suffers long-term illness or periods of long-term unemployment late in life and membership of a private pension plan. A simulation is then carried out on the remaining group to determine whether they will enter the labour market or not.[8] As long periods out of work will reduce the chances of entering work, duration variables are included. Likewise, lack of formal child care support and lone parenthood in Ireland will have an impact on the decision.

Even when one includes these influences on the decision to work, there is a great deal of heterogeneity and thus the model is likely to produce too much career mobility. To partially limit the effect of this, we construct the notion of those in regular and marginal employment (see Atkinson and Micklewright, 1991). Membership of a pension plan or public sector employment, together with an individual's labour market position in the previous period and a generated measure of permanence[9] is used to determine regular/marginal employment.

If an individual is determined as being in work in a period, the model then simulates whether that individual becomes an employee or opts for self-employment. Employees have a choice between two discrete labour supply states, part-time or full-time work. The self-employed have the choice between agricultural and non-agricultural employment. Individuals' employment decisions in the past have a strong bearing on their current decision.

The model incorporates in a relatively simple way the influence of the tax–benefit system on labour market behaviour. Individuals optimize behaviour based on tax–benefit outcomes when deciding to work or not, when deciding to work full-time or part-time, when deciding to become self-employed and when choosing to seek work if out of work. We must note that this behaviour does not incorporate a life-cycle dimension and so changes in future pension entitlement due to the retirement age changes will not be captured in the decision-making. We therefore have to make assumptions about likely changes in behaviour.

It would be desirable to simulate a model of savings and consumption behaviour with wealth accumulation and investment returns. Because of data problems, however, we instead employ a simpler model where only investment, property income and consumption are simulated.[10] Lastly, taxes and benefits are simulated using the EUROMOD tax–benefit model (see Immervoll and O'Donoghue, 2001), which contains detailed rules of the Irish tax–benefit system together with additional modules for social insurance benefits.

A method known as alignment is used to calibrate aggregates simulated by the model with external control totals. This allows macroeconomic conditions to be incorporated exogenously in the model and thus alignment contains the forecast assumptions for the simulations. A validation of the model is described in O'Donoghue (2004b). The distribution of income and employment is consistent with that observed in the 1994 data.

6.4.3   Cohort to Cross-Section

The dynamic microsimulation model simulates a single cohort of the population with behaviour as characterized by the population in the mid-1990s. In order to assess the impact of a change in retirement age, we would ideally like to consider what happens to a representative sample of the population over time. In essence we would ideally use a dynamic population microsimulation model, a model that represents cross-sections of the population. However, as such a model is being developed at the moment and not available for policy analysis, we try to adapt our existing model to suit our purposes.

We use the model to simulate alternative cohorts one by one. As in the case of dynamic population models, we make the assumption that behavioural characteristics of each cohort are similar. In other words we assume that the only difference in behaviour between cohorts is compositional. We allow cohorts to vary compositionally in a number of ways:

i.   Size. Different birth cohorts have different sizes. This difference is incorporated through re-weighting.
ii. Education. Generations retiring in the period before 2045 will largely have completed their education. Therefore we allow different cohorts to have different levels of educational attainment as observed in the distribution educational achievement observed for different cohorts in 2000. In this exercise we focus on the period to 2050, making the assumption that later cohorts have the same education participation rates as recent school leaving cohorts. This is not an unreasonable assumption as although school completion and university attendance rates have increased in the period to 1995, they have remained relatively constant since then. Assuming that education levels remain constant after the early 1920s however assumes that life-long learning policies don't change. If this were to happen then education composition would change in the future.
iii. Mortality. Life expectancy as we have shown has increased over time. We assume later birth cohorts have a rising life expectancy.

This method results in cross-sections with comparable age distributions to those produced by aggregate projections. Incorporating changes in the level of educational attainment, the cross-sections over time capture the rise in education levels amongst older age groups as recent, more highly educated cohorts age. Current patterns of family formation, dissolution and fertility are maintained within cohort–age–education groups. One issue which is maybe regarded as questionable is the assumption of constant returns to scale in education. We do not make the assumption that returns to education decline as the proportion of more highly educated workers rises. Recent media reports of OECD research, however, have highlighted the validity of this assumption.

As we have shown in the validation exercise, differences in the education composition can explain a large degree of inter-cohort variability of incomes. Therefore we can be hopeful that this relationship holds into the future.

The policy environment that has been simulated is 1998. Between 1998 and 2003, there have been relatively minor changes to the structure of the tax–benefit system. Also as the current pension system was introduced in 1961, most of the retired population will be covered by the current legislation. One potential problem area is the fact that we are assuming the social insurance contribution policy has been the same for all retirees. The system moved from a flat-rate system in the 1970s to a pay-related one. However, as pensions require only the number of weeks of contributions and not the value of them or when they were paid, it is less of an issue. We are likely to overestimate coverage by the system of retired civil servants and self-employed, who are less likely to be members of the social insurance system than new retirees. However the reform looks at the implication of a delayed retirement age for new retirees, so this is less of an issue.

6.5   RESULTS – BASELINE SIMULATION

In this section we report the results of our baseline simulations. We have a number of alternative scenarios, defined as follows:

1.   Public expenditure and taxes rise at the rate of growth of productivity.
2.   Department of Finance Assumptions. This scenario takes the Department of Finance assumptions given in Box 6.1 above.
3.   27 per cent GAIW increasing the lowest valued benefits to 27 per cent of the Average Industrial Wage (Gross), described above.
4.   Price Linked Social Security Increments. This scenario assumes that social security benefits increase at the rate of prices rather than productivity growth and so fall 4 per cent per annum below the assumption in scenario 1 to 2010, and 2 per cent per annum after this.

We show in Table 6.4, trends in the different components of disposable income over time. We consider trends for each of the projection scenarios. The table reports trends due to the upward compositional shifts in the education attainment of the population, by discounting by the productivity growth rate. We abstract from changes in the population size over time, by reporting per capita income components.

Considering disposable income first, we see that the upwards shift in educational attainment results in a rise in per capita disposable incomes by 33 per cent between 2000 and 2050. The alternative scenarios report different assumptions about the growth rate in benefit expenditures. The DOF assumption assumes a lower growth rate in pensions than that of productivity growth and so disposable incomes grow at a lower rate. Price indexation of social security benefits results in a lower trend again, while meeting the 27 per cent of GAIW results in a higher growth path in disposable incomes.

Table 6.4 Growth of income components per capita due to compositional changes, 2000–2050 (discount rate equals growth rate)

Year	2000	2010	2020	2030	2040	2050
Disposable Income						
Growth	100	111	118	125	130	133
DOF	100	109	115	120	125	126
Price indexation	100	104	112	116	119	120
27% GAIW	104	114	121	128	134	137
Social Insurance Benefits						
Growth	100	104	127	163	203	236
DOF	100	94	104	121	136	143
Price indexation	100	71	85	90	92	88
27% GAIW	120	125	152	196	244	282
Social Assistance Benefits						
Growth	100	91	86	82	77	74
DOF	100	82	70	61	52	45
Price indexation	100	61	58	45	35	28
27% GAIW	120	109	103	98	93	89
Growth Scenario						
Market incomes	100	116	126	135	140	144
Income taxation	100	120	135	147	156	164
Social insurance contributions	100	117	125	130	132	131

Source: Life-cycle Income Analysis Module (LIAM).

We observe for both social insurance and social assistance benefits that the alternative scenarios push results in the same direction as they did for disposable income. Social insurance benefits which are largely driven by pension age individuals, rise by 140 per cent over the period under the growth assumption and by about 40 per cent for the DOF assumption. Under the price indexation of benefits, expenditure per capita falls 12 per cent, while for the 27 per cent of GAIW assumption, expenditures rise 180 per cent. Therefore relatively small differences in indexation can cause relatively large differences in expenditure over time.

Social assistance benefits exhibit a different trend. These benefits are paid primarily to working age individuals. The impact of the rise in educational attainment in this model is to increase the labour supply and wage rates of individuals reducing the demand for working age assistance benefits. Therefore we notice that under the growth assumption social assistance benefits fall by 25 per cent over the period, with proportional adjustments due to the other scenarios.

As the alternative scenarios relate primarily to benefit expenditure levels, we report only the results for the growth scenario for the other income components. Because of the trend in educational composition, market incomes including employment, capital and private pension income rise by 45 per cent. Income taxation being progressive increases at a faster rate by 65 per cent, while regressive social insurance contributions rise at a lower rate.

We must note that the model merely considers the impact of demographic shifts on current policy. No attempt is made to maintain a balanced budget assumption, which would require other public expenditure sectors to be modelled. Nor is any attempt made to include feedbacks from changes in the structure of the population, labour market or alternative expenditure scenarios. We assume that labour supply and demand are in a similar level of equilibrium as in the mid-1990s and that alternative expenditure scenarios do not interact with economic growth rates or employment levels. For this we would need to interact the dynamic microsimulation model with a macroeconomic model, a science that is still in its infancy. Therefore simulations produced by the model represent a picture of the pressures that influence behaviour without interacting with the rest of the economy or the budget. Nevertheless this first round analysis still has a use as it helps to highlight general directions of trends.

An advantage of a dynamic microsimulation model is that in addition to aggregate trends, the model can also simulate changes to distributions. In Table 6.5, we consider trends in both income inequality as measured by the Gini coefficient and in poverty rates. We note that the unit of analysis of the model is the family and so as highlighted in Table 6.5, the results are not directly comparable with household based measures. We therefore report results relative to the baseline figure in 2000 as trends are more relevant than levels.

Table 6.5 Trends in cross-sectional income inequality and poverty headcount, 2000–2050

	2000	2010	2020	2030	2040	2050
Gini						
Growth	100.0	99.2	98.7	98.5	98.1	97.5
DOF	100.0	102.3	104.6	106.7	108.9	110.2
Price indexation	100.0	109.9	109.3	113.2	116.8	119.1
27% GAIW	94.1	93.9	93.5	93.3	93.0	92.7
Poverty Rate						
Growth	100.0	102.8	105.3	106.5	106.9	108.6
DOF	99.9	105.6	108.7	109.7	111.3	112.6
Price indexation	100.0	110.9	113.2	112.1	113.2	114.6
27% GAIW	93.2	95.0	96.9	95.4	98.2	98.2

Notes:
1. Both measures are based upon equivalized disposable income (EDI), where the equivalence scale used is head 1, other adults 0.7, children 0.5.
2. Poverty headcount utilizes a poverty line of 60% of median EDI.

Source: LIAM.

We see that the greater the level of increase in benefits, the greater the impact on inequality. Due to rising education and income levels, income inequality falls most under 27 per cent GAIW assumption and less so under the growth assumption. Under the DOF and price indexation scenarios, inequality rises as the value of benefits falls relative to other incomes.

Turning to poverty, we see that the impact of the compositional shift is to have a rising trend in relative poverty over time. Although average incomes are rising, the incomes of the poorest are rising at a lower rate, therefore more individuals fall into poverty. Also, although benefits rise at the rate of productivity growth, because of the composition shift in the population, the average disposable income rises at a faster rate and so the poverty line (60 per cent of median equivalized disposable income poverty line) rises at a faster rate than benefits. As a result more of the poorest fall into poverty. The initial increase in benefits in the 27 per cent GAIW scenario means that poverty rates are lowest for this scenario, while the lower the rate of price indexing, the greater the poverty rate.

6.6 RESULTS OF POLICY REFORM – INCREASED RETIREMENT AGE

We now consider the impact of a policy reform, increasing the retirement age by five years from 65 to 70. While simply increasing the retirement age by five years may not necessarily lead to increased participation rates, we consider also the case where complementary policies described in section 6.1, are introduced so that the participation rates of those in the age group 65–70 increase. The objectives of this reform are two-fold. Firstly, increasing the retirement age would shorten the retirement period and so ease public finance pressures and secondly, increased participation rates are likely to result in a substitution of work income for pension income, which is likely to increase the incomes of individuals and reduce poverty levels. Of course the impact of reform is strongly influenced by the labour participation impact. The greater the impact of the labour market policies, the more powerful the retirement policy will be in achieving its objectives.

Without a structural model of retirement behaviour, we have to make an assumption about the new retirement path. In particular, we make the assumption that employment rates at 55 are the same and that the participation rate at 70 after the introduction of these policies will be the same as it currently is at 65. This is a strong assumption to make and it may be regarded as an upper bound, with the lower bound being that of no change.[11] We assume that the decline in participation observed between 55 and 65 is 'stretched', so that although we will have the same participation rate at 70 after the reform as at 65 before, the decline in participation is flatter. Without using a structural model of retirement behaviour it is difficult to tell what the compositional impact of this reform would be on participation rates. For the purposes of the analysis, we make the assumption that the effect is random, which is an oversimplified assumption.

In Table 6.6 we consider the impact of the reform on income components. Looking at disposable income first, we see that the lower the level of benefit indexation in the scenario, the greater the impact of the policy.

This is because the forecasted baseline poverty rate due to lower benefit indexation is higher and so the employment effect of the reforms would achieve a greater reduction in poverty.[12]

For the population as a whole, disposable incomes rise by about 1 per cent per annum for the growth scenario, and by 1.5 per cent to 2.5 per cent for the price indexation scenario. As the reform affects the 55+ age group exclusively, we consider the impact on the incomes of this group separately. The impact on incomes of the 55+ group is about 1.5 to 4 times higher than that of the whole population.

Table 6.6 Impact of raising retirement age on income components (percentage change income)

	2000	2010	2020	2030	2040	2050
Population						
Disposable income						
Growth	0.0	0.4	0.8	0.7	1.0	0.6
DOF	0.0	0.4	1.2	1.1	2.1	1.7
Price indexation	0.0	0.0	1.7	1.5	2.6	2.2
27% GAIW	0.0	0.4	0.4	0.3	0.6	0.3
Other income Components[a]						
Market income	0.0	0.7	3.2	2.9	3.8	3.4
Social insurance benefits	0.0	−2.6	−29.3	−30.8	−28.1	−26.5
Social assistance benefits	0.0	1.2	0.8	2.7	2.8	3.4
Income taxation	0.0	0.9	2.3	2.1	2.6	1.0
Social insurance contributions	0.0	4.1	5.8	6.0	7.7	8.4
Tax–benefit system	0.0	−0.4	−3.1	−3.0	−3.6	−3.6
Aged 55+[a]						
Disposable income	0.0	1.1	3.3	1.1	2.5	1.5
Market income	0.0	21.9	26.2	25.8	27.0	28.9
Social insurance benefits	0.0	−3.2	−31.4	−32.8	−29.4	−27.4
Social assistance benefits	0.0	5.1	1.4	9.3	8.0	10.7
Income taxation	0.0	3.7	8.1	6.4	6.6	3.8
Social insurance contributions	0.0	21.9	26.2	25.8	27.0	28.9

Note: [a] Growth scenario is used for these measures.

Source: LIAM.

While simulation suggests that market incomes rise by about 3–4 per cent for the population as a whole, because market incomes are relatively less important for the 55+ age group, we see that the impact of the reform is to increase these incomes by about 25 per cent for this age group. Because of the increase in the retirement age and because of the concentration of social insurance benefits amongst the 55+ age group, we see that social insurance benefit expenditures fall substantially by between 25 per cent and 33 per cent in the post-2020 period. In the early years of the reform, the affect is lower as most of the retirees retired at the old retirement age. Social assistance benefits rise, as individuals who are out of work below the retirement age are more likely to receive these benefits. Thus there is a transfer from contribution based to means tested instruments. However, the increase in assistance benefits is more than compensated by the decrease in insurance benefits. As market incomes rise, social insurance contributions and income taxation also rise. The net impact on public finances is relatively small over the transition, but as the effective retirement age increases by five years, the combined effect of all the tax–benefit instruments is simulated to be about a 3–3.5 per cent reduction in net expenditure as a percentage of household disposable income, a figure varying from about 30 per cent to 50 per cent of the expenditure on social insurance pensions. Therefore the policy potentially makes substantial public finance impacts.

In Table 6.7, we report the impact of the policy reform on poverty and inequality. Under the growth assumption, overall poverty rates (60 per cent of median equivalized disposable income poverty line) are assumed to decline by 3–4 per cent. For the 65+ age group the poverty rate rises initially as those out of work in the 65–69 age group move from higher valued retirement benefits to lower valued working age benefits. As incomes rise as the full impact of the reform takes effect, the poverty rate for this group falls in 2020 by 7 per cent; however, as the poverty line rises, although the incomes of this group, including those of the poor rise, they rise at a slower rate than the rise in the poverty line and so the impact on the reform on the headcount poverty line has less of an effect. However, it reduces the poverty gap and so the poor are less poor as a result of the reform. Initially, the fall in poverty of the 55–64 age group is counter-balanced by the initial rise in poverty of the 65–69 age group, however in most of the post-2020 period, the decline of the poverty rate of the 55+ age group is greater than for the 65+. Income inequality widens initially as the value of benefits falls, but then falls over time as the incomes of the poorest rise.

Table 6.7 Impact of raising retirement age on income inequality and poverty headcount 2000–2050

	2000	2010	2020	2030	2040	2050
Population	0.0	−1.7	−3.3	−4.1	−3.4	−2.4
Aged 65+	0.0	4.0	−7.3	−6.5	−4.1	−2.6
Aged 55+	0.0	0.0	−10.5	−7.9	−3.1	−0.6
Gini	0.0	0.5	−0.1	0.0	−0.5	−0.8

Notes:
1. Both measures are based upon equivalized disposable income (EDI), where the equivalence scale used is head 1, other adults 0.7, children 0.5.
2. Poverty headcount utilizes a poverty line of 60 per cent of median EDI.

Source: LIAM.

6.7   CONCLUSIONS

As in many other western countries, the average length of retirement has been increasing as the effective retirement age has fallen due to early retirement and life expectancy increases. Over the course of the 1970s the official retirement age at which insurance pensions were paid fell from 70 to 65/66. Continuing current trends in the ratio of elderly people to those of working age, the dependency rate is likely to double over the first half of the century. This double directed effect is likely to put pressures on the Irish public pension system both through lower revenues from a smaller workforce and greater welfare costs due to longer retirement. The objective of this chapter was to assess the potential impact of an increase in the official and effective retirement ages in Ireland.

We highlight how Ireland has a public pension system with a primarily anti-poverty focus supplanted by a largely funded private pensions system. Due to the structure of the Irish public pensions, which are flat rate, it is likely to face less of a fiscal crisis than other countries.

The main analysis of this chapter was to examine the impact of raising the official retirement age to 70, and at the same time raising the effective retirement age through complementary labour market policies.

In making our projections to 2050, we considered four alternative forecast scenarios, each with alternative benefit indexation assumptions. The principal driving force in our projections is the shift in the educational composition as the proportion of the adult population with upper-secondary or higher level qualifications rises from 42 per cent in 2000 to 74 per cent in 2050. The resulting higher employment and wage rates are forecasted to increase market incomes by about 44 per cent more than the increase in average productivity. Progressive income taxation results in a higher proportionate increase in income taxation.

Increasing employment and wage rates amongst working age people due to the educational compositional shift is likely to lead to a decline in the working age social assistance benefits. Increasing insurance coverage and elderly dependency rates is, however, likely to lead to significantly higher social insurance pensions.

As a microsimulation model, it is possible to consider distributional issues. The main influence on the trend in the income inequality under the assumptions we have modelled is the level of benefit indexation. Indexation lower than the rate of productivity growth is likely to increase inequality. Because of the educational shift in the population, the growth in incomes and thus the poverty line (using a relative poverty line) is likely to grow faster than benefits unless benefits are increased at a faster rate than economic growth. Because most state pensions provide incomes below the poverty line at present, poverty rates are expected to increase as the income of those solely in receipt of pensions falls relative to the population as a whole and as the size of the pensioner population rises.

The impact of increasing the retirement age under the assumptions we make varies from 1–2 per cent of household disposable income per capita depending upon the benefit indexation assumption used. The lower the level of indexation, the greater the impact of the policy change, because of the greater gap between in-work income from retiring later and the public pensions one would receive on retiring earlier. One notable impact in driving the increase in disposable incomes is the fall by about 30 per cent of social insurance benefits per annum. In addition, taxes and social insurance contributions rise, combining to result in an improved public finance position, reducing net expenditures. Increasing the effective retirement age would also reduce income inequality, but in particular it would help to reduce poverty rates. Therefore this policy is likely to simultaneously reduce public finance pressures and reduce poverty rates.

One needs to be cautious about the numerical estimates produced by such a modelling framework. Firstly the results are based upon a prototype model under development and so results are likely to alter as the model specifications improve. Secondly the model does not contain any feedbacks with the rest of the economy, and therefore policies that may reduce or increase public deficits have no influence on growth or employment rates. Lastly the model does not attempt to balance the public budget and therefore in reality large imbalances may not be allowed to continue indefinitely. The method, although not containing these interactions, is valuable for highlighting broad impacts of policy, demographic and economic changes. One can view the results as being potential pressures, signalling the general directions of the impacts rather than a forecast as to what will happen. Dynamic microsimulation modelling as a science needs to improve to incorporate these interactions, linking micro results to macroeconomic models and CGE models. In addition, behaviour, especially in this case, that of the retirement decision, could be modelled in a more structural fashion, allowing us to produce a better prediction of the likely responses of policy change on the actual date of retirement.

Overall, economic ageing is less of an issue in Ireland than in many other EU countries. According to EC (2002), Ireland, although it has a higher elderly dependency ratio than at present, will have amongst the lowest elderly dependency ratio in the EU, at about 85 per cent of the average rate across the EU. Combined with a relatively cost effective public pensions policy, this is likely to result in less serious public finance pressures. In addition the policy levers exist to alleviate any build-up in these pressures. Pre-funding of the pension fund will reduce these pressures, while the absence of an official indexation policy allows the government, as it has done in the past, to have lower pension increases during more difficult financial periods. Therefore the argument on public finance grounds for the introduction of a policy to increase the effective retirement age is less strong than in other EU countries.

Ireland, however, has above average poverty rates in the EU. In addition, the elderly in 2000 have a higher poverty risk[13] of 43.3 per cent compared with 16.9 per cent of the working age population (DSFA, 2002). This is because the elderly have not been able to benefit to the same extent from the economic boom as working age people. When one utilizes the official measure of poverty used by the National Anti-Poverty Strategy, as defined by a combination of deprivation indicators and financial poverty, the gap is lower. The level of measured poverty is also much lower. However, even if the extent of people living on very poor incomes is not captured by the official measure it is fair to say that 43.3 per cent of the elderly population living on incomes of less than 60 per cent of median income raises concerns.

As the elderly population rises and if indexation of pensions does not keep pace with earnings growth, then the position is likely to get worse. Therefore it may be necessary to increase pension amounts by a greater amount than the indexation levels considered here to alleviate poverty. If that is the case, the public finance pressures will be greater. Raising the effective retirement age, however, is a potential mechanism for reducing poverty, both by reducing poverty levels through more people working and by raising extra resources due to a larger labour force which can pay for further poverty alleviation policies. It will also shift the intergenerational burden of providing resources to maintain the elderly from younger generations to the older generations themselves.

NOTES

* The author gratefully acknowledges financial assistance from the Postgraduate Fellowship of the Economic and Social Research Institute, Dublin. The chapter uses data from the 1994 *Living in Ireland Survey*, made available by the Economic and Social Research Institute, Dublin. The chapter was written while a SAGE Visiting Fellow at the London School of Economics. The author acknowledges the hospitality shown. I am grateful to my supervisor Jane Falkingham for detailed comments on my work, on my colleagues Herwig Immervoll, Jamie Coventry and Paul Kattuman for their advice. The author is responsible for all remaining errors.

1. CSO Statistical Year Book, 2003.
2. CSO Irish Life Table No. 13.
3. There is a commitment by the present government to abolish this anomaly.
4. There are additional benefits which elderly individuals can claim. All individuals over the age of 66 receive free travel. Those who live alone or with dependants and who are reliant on social welfare payments, are entitled to free television licences, allowances for free telephone rental, free electricity and fuel, up to a maximum limit. Poor households can also claim means tested assistance with their housing costs.
5. Per capita productivity growth rates are forecasted to average 4 per cent until 2010 and 2 per cent thereafter.
6. HRP is however more generous in that carers can get credited contributions as long as they are in receipt of child benefit payable to families with children aged 16 or under, or in secondary education up to the age of 18.
7. Because there are several hundred behavioural equations, we do not report these results here. (See O'Donoghue, 2001.)
8. On leaving school, a separate process to the main labour market module is used to determine whether an individual enters the labour market. This is because transitions at this stage in the life cycle tend to be different from those of other people entering the labour market after non-participation.
9. This measure is generated from information in the *Living in Ireland Survey* regarding the proportion of time since leaving education spent out of work.
10. Blomquist (1981) argues that as capital income is a return on savings, one should not include this in the lifetime income concept. However, as a source of income it is important to consider when comparing standards of living.
11. Given the tightness of the Irish labour market in recent years with falling unemployment rates, despite large-scale immigration and increased participation rates, it is reasonable to assume increased participation rates of older cohorts while that of younger cohorts remain the same.
12. Although each scenario has the same in-work income, each has lower benefits to replace and so the denominator is smaller, the lower the level of indexation, and so the greater the impact of the reform.
13. Using a 60 per cent of median equivalized disposable income poverty line.

REFERENCES

Atkinson, A.B. and J. Micklewright (1991), 'Unemployment Compensation and Labour Market Transitions; A Critical Review', *Journal of Economic Literature*, 29(4), pp. 1679–1727.

Barr, N. (2001), *The Welfare State as Piggy Bank*, Oxford: Oxford University Press.

Blomquist, S. (1981), 'A Comparison of Distributions of Annual and Lifetime Income: Sweden Around 1970', *The Review of Income and Wealth*, **22**, pp. 243–64.

Callan, T., B. Nolan, B.J. Whelan, C.T. Whelan and J. Williams (1996), *Poverty in the 1990s, Evidence from the 1994 Living in Ireland Survey*, Dublin: Oak Tree Press.

Department of Finance (1998), *Long term Issues Group Paper*; report by the Department of Finance, Ireland, mimeo.

Department of Social and Family Affairs (DSFA, 2002), *Sustainable and Adequate Pension Provision for an Ageing Population*, Ireland's National Strategy Report to the EU Commission on its Pension System, Dublin.

EC (2002), *Special Feature on Pension Funds – Data 1997–2000*, Luxembourg, Office for Official Publications of the European Communities.

Evans, M., C. O'Donoghue and P. Vizard (2000), 'Means Testing and Poverty in 5 European Countries' in V. Atella (ed.) *Le Politiche Sociali in Italia ed in Europa Coerenza e Convergenza nelle Azioni 1997–1999*, Bologna: Il Mulino.

Fahey, T. and J. Fitzgerald (1997), *Welfare Implications of Demographic Trends*, Dublin: Oak Tree Press.

Falkingham, J. and J. Hills (1995), *The Dynamic of Welfare*, Hemel Hempstead: Prentice Hall/Harvester Wheatsheaf.

Fields, G.S. and O. Mitchell (1984) 'The Effects of Social Security Reforms on Retirement Ages and Retirement Incomes', *Journal of Public Economics*, **25**, pp. 143–59.

Hughes, G. (1985), 'Payroll Tax Incidence, The Direct Tax Burden and the Rate of Return on State Pension Contributions in Ireland', General Research Series Paper, 120, The Economic and Social Research Institute, Dublin.

Hughes, G. and B. Whelan (1996), *Occupational and Personal Pension Coverage 1995*, ESRI, Dublin.

Immervoll, H. and C. O'Donoghue (2001), 'Towards a Multi-Purpose Framework for Tax–Benefit Microsimulation: A Discussion by Reference to EUROMOD, a European Tax–Benefit Model', EUROMOD Working Paper no. 2/01, Department of Applied Economics, University of Cambridge.

Jenkins, S. (1995), 'Accounting for Inequality Trends: Decomposition Analyses for the UK, 1971–86', *Economica*, **62**, pp. 26–63.

Kalisch, D.W. and T. Aman, 'Retirement Income Systems: The Reform Process across OECD Countries', OECD Ageing Working Paper 3.4.

Keogh, G. and B. Whelan (1986), *National Survey of Occupational Pension Schemes*, ESRI, Dublin.

National Pensions Board (1993), *Developing the National Pension System*, Final Report of the National Pensions Board, Dublin, The Stationery Office.

O'Donoghue, C. (2000a), 'A Dynamic Microsimulation Model for Ireland: A Study of a Flexible Dynamic Modelling Framework', paper presented to the 6th Nordic Workshop on Microsimulation, Copenhagen, June.

O'Donoghue, C. (2001), 'Redistribution in the Irish Tax–Benefit System', unpublished PhD dissertation, London School of Economics.

O'Donoghue, C. (2002a), 'Redistribution over the Lifetime in the Irish Tax–Benefit System: An Application of a Prototype Dynamic Microsimulation Model for Ireland', *Economic and Social Review*, **32**(3), pp. 191–216.

O'Donoghue, C. (2002b), 'The Generation Game: All Gain No Pain? Ageing, Intergenerational Equity and Generational Accounts', *Journal of the Statistical and Social Inquiry Society of Ireland*, **30**, pp. 65–106.

O'Donoghue, C. (2004a), 'Redistributive Forces in the Irish Tax–Benefit System', NUI Galway, Department of Economics Working Paper.

O'Donoghue, C. (2004b), 'Assessing the Impact of Pensions Policy Reform in Ireland: The Case of Increasing the Pension Age', NUI Galway, Department of Economics Working Paper.

OECD (1988), *Reforming Public Pensions*, Social Policy Studies, 5, Paris.

OECD (1994a), *New Orientations for Social Policy*, Social Policy Studies, 12, Paris.

OECD (1996), *Ageing in OECD Countries: A Critical Policy Challenge*, Social Policy Studies, 20, Paris.

Pestieau, P. (2003), 'Are We Retiring Too Early?', in O. Castellino and E. Fornero (eds), *Pension Policy in an Integrating Europe*, Cheltenham, UK and Northampton, MA, USA: Edward Elgar.

7. Retirement age rules and pension reforms in Italy*

Angelo Marano and Paolo Sestito

7.1 INTRODUCTION

Among the OECD countries, Italy stands out for a swift population ageing and for the sizeable dimension of its public pension expenditure, which, at 14.9 per cent of GDP, is among the highest in the EU-15 and accounts for about two-thirds of the overall social protection expenditure – which is, in contrast, below the EU-15 average.

Quite understandably, the prospective financial sustainability issues have so far dominated the policy debate and the many actual interventions carried out. The three pension reforms of the 1990s have remarkably tackled the longer-term financial sustainability, as the introduction of a notional defined contribution system is going to guarantee an equilibrium between contributions and expenditures irrespective of macroeconomic and demographic trends.

However, those reforms have still left some discontent: the introduction of the new system is going to require a long transition period, while a small increase in pension expenditure is still expected over the next 30 years, before a gradual decline takes place. This additional rise and the current high level of expenditure actually leave little room of *manoeuvre* for the policy maker (possibly interested in reducing the tax level and/or increasing other components of social protection expenditure). Thus, further measures have been undertaken in 2004 in order to reduce, over the medium run, the financial burden of public pensions.

While concerns about the adequacy of the pensions entitlements of future generations are also rising and the new changes will push up, albeit not immediately, the effective age of retirement, the complex web of different rules created by the overlapping of all pension reforms with inequalities across generations and different frameworks governing the retirement decisions are issues still relatively unexplored in the policy debate.

This justifies the focus of this chapter on retirement age rules and elderly employment. Section 7.2 presents the Italian pension system and the reforms of the 1990s, which introduced a notional defined contribution system. Section 7.3 discusses the 2004 reform and the associated debate, mostly related to the goal of raising the retirement age. The situation of the elderly in the labour market is analysed in section 7.4, while section 7.5 concludes. Appendix 7.A reviews some of the data that better describe the size of the ageing problem in Italy, while Appendix 7.B summarizes the different legal ages of retirement.

7.2   THE PENSION REFORMS OF THE 1990s AND THE NEW NOTIONAL DEFINED CONTRIBUTION SYSTEM

The Italian social security pension system is composed of a compulsory pay-as-you-go public system for all workers and a Defined Contribution (DC) voluntary private second pillar, fully-funded, organized and managed on an individual or collective basis. Means tested social assistance pensions (*assegni sociali* and *pensioni sociali*) and supplements to the social security pensions (*integrazioni al minimo*) guarantee a minimum income level beyond 65 years of age.

Total expenditure amounts to 14.9 per cent of GDP (2002), almost entirely attributable to the public system. We refer here to the Eurostat (SESSPROS) definition of *expenditure on pensions* which includes 'disability pensions, early-retirement benefits due to reduced capacity to work, old-age pensions, partial pensions, survivors' pensions and early-retirement benefits for labour market reasons' (Eurostat, 2003). Notice that such an aggregate does not coincide with the Eurostat definition of *expenditure for old-age and survivors*[1] (15.5 per cent of GDP in 2002), as it includes benefits not considered in the old-age function, while excluding non-pension related items included in the old-age function. The most important discrepancy arises from the *Trattamento di Fine Rapporto* (TFR), a sort of deferred wage that applies to all private employees (a similar system, working along pay-as-you-go lines, also operates in the public sector), which is not considered as pension expenditure, although it is included (as *other cash benefits*) in the old-age function. Under the TFR system, each year firms accumulate as book reserves about a month's worth of salary for each worker (6.91 per cent of payroll on average), which is paid back at the end of the working relationship (because of retirement, resignation or layoff) but also can be accessed when needed for funding some occasional expenses (most often for buying a house). From the TFR funds the employer pays employees a rather low but safe return (1.5 per cent per year plus three-quarters of the inflation rate).[2]

The supplements to the social security pensions mentioned above are not classified by Eurostat as means tested, as, although the supplements themselves are means tested, the pensions which they augment are not. It follows that the overall expenditure is mostly classified as *non-means tested*. However, if these means-tested top-ups were reclassified, the overall *means tested expenditure* in the pensions domain would climb up by 1.3 per cent of GDP (almost one-tenth of the total), exposing a quite unnoticed feature of the Italian welfare system: the rare use of means testing within the non-pension-related schemes and a sizeable means tested safety net for over 65-year-olds.[3]

For what concerns the first pillar, although there remain many different schemes along job-category lines, most of them are administered by the social security institution for the private sector (INPS) which accounts for two-thirds of the expenditure and insures the majority of private sector employees and the self-employed. Public sector pensions are administered by a separate institution (INPDAP). Some categories of professionals have their own institutions dealing with first pillar pensions, in any case supervised by the Ministry of Labour and Social Policies (MLSP) and classified as part of the public administration under the ESA95 accounting standard.

Compulsory pension expenditure is monitored by the *Nucleo di Valutazione della Spesa Previdenziale*, which publishes an *Annual Report*, while medium and long-term projections of pension expenditure are updated every year by the Department of General Accounting of the Ministry of the Economy.[4] Statistical accounts of pensioners and pensions are published jointly by ISTAT and INPS.[5] Private pension funds are supervised by COVIP, an independent authority which also publishes, on a regular basis, data on membership and performances.

The present system has been thoroughly restructured by three major reforms that took place in 1992 (Amato reform), 1995 (Dini reform) and 1997 (Prodi reform), which introduced several changes that are already fully operational and others that are building a new system to be gradually phased in. There have been subsequently minor adjustments, while a new reform has been approved by the Parliament in 2004 (see section 7.3).

Before 1992, the Italian pension system was highly fragmented and based upon a defined benefit (DB), 'earnings-related', rule. Generally pension entitlements were computed on the basis of a (2 per cent) * (pensionable earnings) * (contribution years) formula, the latter up to a maximum of 40 years. While the precise definition of 'pensionable earnings' was very different among job categories and schemes, reference was generally made to the average of the individual's last years' earnings.

Access to pensions was conditional upon either age – in the case of the standard old-age pensions (*pensioni di vecchiaia*) for which the minimum age was 60 years (55 years for females) – or years of contributions – for the seniority pensions (*pensioni di anzianità*). There were widespread differences across job categories both in the eligibility rules and the exact computation of the contribution years, which were often defined in a very lax way and included many periods of non-employment. Pensions benefits enjoyed real wage indexation, as their amount, after retirement, was indexed to both consumer prices and real wage rises (of the corresponding job category).

In 1992, the difficult public finance conditions led to a pension reform of a parametric nature. The age requirement for the old-age pension was progressively increased (to 65 years for males, 60 years for females), the access to seniority pensions temporarily blocked and the lax eligibility rules for public employees tightened. Moreover, the definition of pensionable earnings was modified to take into account a longer working period and gradually the entire working life, the indexation of pensions to real wages was abolished and the indexation to prices was reduced for pensioners receiving benefits greater than three times the minimum pension.

In 1995, the Dini reform brought a change in the very structure of the pension system. The new system, while still being financed on a pay-as-you-go basis, shifted from a DB to a DC rule. More precisely, a 'Notional Defined Contribution' (NDC) method of calculation, uniform (and neutral) across the different job categories, was introduced. Pensions are now computed as the product of total pension contributions, capitalized at the (five-years moving average of the) annual GDP growth rate, and age-at-retirement specific coefficients, calculated on the basis of the (average across sexes) life expectancy at retirement.[6] The coefficients are actuarially adjusted every ten years, thus the first update should take place in 2005.

Embedded in the new NDC system is an intrinsic *financial sustainability* feature, as expenditure would tend to evolve in line with contribution receipts, being insulated (even if with a lag) from demographic and macroeconomic shocks. Moreover, the NDC system allows *flexibility* as far as retirement is concerned. Individuals are allowed to choose whether to retire at an earlier age (beyond a minimum of 57 years) with lower entitlements, or to postpone retirement (up to 65 years of age) so incrementing future pension entitlements through three channels: the accumulation of more contributions, the further capitalization of past contributions and the actuarial adjustment of the coefficients described above (we will come back to these points in section 7.3). As such, DC schemes (funded or unfunded like the one described here), embedding actuarial adjustment rules, lead to a neutral incentives structure and allow flexibility at the individual level. Such flexibility could even include the possibility to cumulate pension and work income without the need to introduce difficult-to-enforce ad hoc measures.

The NDC system is not yet the one relevant for individuals now contemplating whether to retire. Workers with at least 18 contribution years at the end of 1995 (that is retiring up to around 2015) continue to have their pensions calculated using the old DB formula, as modified by the 1992 reform. Thus, although they do not benefit from real wage indexation and are subject to the tightening of the access thresholds to seniority and old-age pensions, they experience only a limited cut in the value of their pension at retirement, due to the less favourable computation of pensionable earnings introduced in 1992 (and such a change penalizes them less than the following cohorts). A discontinuity, with a significant reduction of entitlements, will affect the next cohorts of retirees, mostly due to the application of the new formula: workers having some contribution prior to 1995 will have their entitlements computed by a mix of the old and new formulas (the new formula is applied 'pro rata', that is only for the working life after 1995), while people who have entered the labour market since 1995 will have their entire pension based on the new system.

The reduction of future pension entitlements is illustrated well in Figure 7.1, which shows the change of the replacement rate (that is the pension to the last work income) between 2003 and 2050 in the four cases of an employee and a self-employed person retiring at 60 or 65, with 35 or 40 years of seniority respectively. The graph shows a constant pension replacement rate for the current decade, when retirees' entitlements would still be fully governed by the previous DB system, and a sharp discontinuity in the 2010–2030 decades. Some further reductions (for given age and seniority) are expected even after 2030, because of the adjustment of the coefficients used in the calculations related to the lengthening of life expectancy.[7]

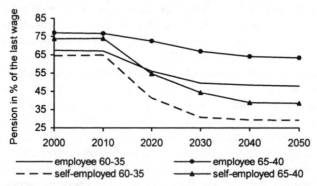

Note: Pension coefficients are updated in line with the increase in life expectancy assumed in the Eurostat central scenario.

Source: Elaboration on data presented in the 'Statistical Appendix' to MLSP (2002a).

Figure 7.1   Italy – replacement rates of the public pension system for different types of workers, different ages of retirement and career lengths

The decline in the pension replacement rate at retirement, coupled with the lack of real wage indexation, leads to a sizeable reduction in unitary pensions, such a decline being the most important factor contrasting the demographic trends' impact upon aggregate pension expenditure (Tables 7.1 and 7.2).[8] By itself, the rise in the demographic dependency ratio (the ratio of the elderly to the working age population, see Appendix 7.A) would imply an increase of public pension expenditure by 9.5 points of GDP between 2000 and 2050, the third highest in the EU-15, as shown in the second column of Table 7.1. Such a potential increase would be almost fully absorbed by the forecasted employment gains (reducing expenditure by 3.1 points), by stricter eligibility requirements (amounting to 1.4 points) and, more importantly, by the above-mentioned decrease in unitary benefits (amounting to 4.9 points). Within the EU-15, Italy would be so characterized by the second lowest increase in pension expenditure, both with respect to the period 2000–2050 and to the period 2000–*peak of expenditure*, a peak which is expected in Italy around 2030, as a by-product of both the lengthy phasing in of the reforms and the timing of the ageing process itself. The increase of two percentage points would nevertheless not be negligible, particularly as it would add up to the relatively high current levels (Table 7.2).

While the lack of real wage indexation applies to the whole stock of pensions – this being an element through which currently retired persons also participate in the financial adjustment process – the reduction of the replacement rate at retirement shown in Figure 7.1 will apply only to the inflow of new retirees. Thus, even in 2050 the stock of pensions calculated (fully or partially) according to the old defined benefit rules will remain around 45 per cent (Table 7.3).

Incidentally, notice that, besides the discontinuity in the formula used to calculate entitlements described above, the Dini reform is characterized by another source of discontinuity over time. As seen, the updating of the coefficients used in order to implement the actuarial adjustment is due at ten-year intervals. Such a discontinuity may imply differences in the entitlements granted to (otherwise) identical individuals having to decide whether to retire immediately before, or immediately after, the updating itself. There may arise inequities and incentives to anticipate the retirement in order to avoid a drastic drop in entitlements, and the enforcement of updating that is likely to reduce benefits may become highly sensitive politically. Indeed, equity, efficiency and political economy feasibility considerations would suggest there should be more frequent updatings.

While the 'structural character' of the Dini reform shows its effect only in the medium and long term, some of the measures introduced in 1995 also intervened on more short-term issues, further reinforcing what had already been done in 1992. The 1997 Prodi reform operated along the same lines. In

Country Experiences

particular, the two reforms further tightened the requirements for seniority pensions; as a result, the access requirements to seniority pension have been gradually raised to 38 (40 since 2008) years of contribution (at any age), or 35 years of contribution (upon reaching 57 years of age for employees and 58 years for the self-employed). These measures, as well as the non-indexation of pensions to real wages discussed above, are the main factors behind the stabilization of expenditure as a percentage of GDP attained in the most recent years. These measures are also those most relevant in order to explain the recent inversion in the trends concerning the actual age of retirement (see section 7.3).

Table 7.1 The four factors driving the change in public pension spending between 2000 and 2050: 2001 EPC projections[a]

	Dependency	Employment	Eligibility	Benefit	Total	Residual
B	5.2	−0.9	0.9	−2.0	3.3	0.0
DK	4.1	−0.2	0.9	−1.7	2.7	0.1
D	6.2	−0.7	2.0	−2.7	4.8	0.2
GR	9.9	−3.6	1.4	4.0	11.7	0.5
E	8.2	−2.4	2.0	−0.3	7.5	0.5
F[b]	7.7	−0.9	0.7	−3.6	3.9	−0.1
IRL	4.5	−0.9	1.4	−0.7	4.3	0.1
I	9.5	−3.1	−1.4	−4.9	0.2	0.0
L[c]						
NL	5.4	−0.6	0.5	0.2	5.5	0.2
A	10.5	−2.2	−3.0	−2.9	2.4	0.1
P	6.7	−1.1	−2.4	0.1	3.5	0.1
FIN	6.6	−0.1	−1.3	−0.1	5.0	−0.3
S	3.9	−0.5	0.8	−2.6	1.7	0.0
UK	2.4	0.0	−0.1	−3.4	−1.0	−0.1
EU-15	6.4	−1.1	0.6	−2.8	3.1	−0.2

Notes:
(a) The figure for the EU-15 is the weighted average for countries reporting results. The decomposition is based on the following identity:

$$\frac{\text{Pensexp}}{\text{GDP}} = \frac{\text{over 55}}{\text{pop 15}-64} * \frac{\text{pop 15}-64}{\text{employment}} * \frac{\#\text{ pensions}}{\text{over 55}} * \frac{\text{ave pension}}{\text{ave lab productivity}}$$

The growth rate until 2050 of the l.h.s. is roughly (due to the discrete time approximation) equal to the sum of the growth rate of the four components of the r.h.s. Multiplying the growth rates by the pension expenditure to GDP ratio in 2000 one obtains the data in the table.
(b) For France the projection stops in 2040 instead of 2050.
(c) Luxembourg emerged as an outlier in the EPC report because of the assumption of a large increase in cross-border workers. Thus data were not reported.

Source: Economic Policy Committee (2001).

Table 7.2 Public pension expenditure as a percentage of GDP: 2001 EPC projections [a]

	2000	2010	2020	2030	2040	2050	Peak change
B	10	9.9	11.4	13.3	13.7	13.3	*3.7*
DK	10.5	12.5	13.8	14.5	14	13.3	*4.1*
D	11.8	11.2	12.6	15.5	16.6	16.9	*5*
GR	12.6	12.6	15.4	19.6	23.8	24.8	*12.2*
E	9.4	8.9	9.9	12.6	16	17.3	*7.9*
F[b]	12.1	13.1	15	16	15.8		*4*
IRL	4.6	5	6.7	7.6	8.3	9	*4.4*
I 2000	13.8	13.9	14.8	15.7	15.7	14.1	*2.1*
I 2002 (c)	14.1	14	14.7	15.8	15.6	14.1	*2*
L	7.4	7.5	8.2	9.2	9.5	9.3	*2.2*
NL	7.9	9.1	11.1	13.1	14.1	13.6	*6.2*
A	14.5	14.9	16	18.1	18.3	17	*4.2*
P	9.8	11.8	13.1	13.6	13.8	13.2	*4.1*
FIN	11.3	11.6	12.9	14.9	16	15.9	*4.7*
S	9	9.6	10.7	11.4	11.4	10.7	*2.6*
UK	5.5	5.1	4.9	5.2	5	4.4	*–1.1*
EU-15	10.4	10.4	11.5	13	13.6	13.3	*3.2*

Notes:
(a) Not taking into account pension reforms introduced after 2000.
(b) For France the projection stops in 2040.
(c) Source: Ministry of the Economy (2004) using the same EPC scenario.

Source: Economic Policy Committee (2001).

Table 7.3 Distribution of the stock of pensions at the end of the year on the basis of the formula used (at retirement) to calculate the pension

Year	Formula used to calculate pensions			
	Old (earning based) formula	Mixed system	New (contribution based) formula	Total
2002	98.4%	1.6%	0.0%	100%
2005	96.6%	3.4%	0.0%	100%
2010	92.0%	7.7%	0.3%	100%
2020	71.1%	27.2%	1.7%	100%
2030	40.0%	51.9%	8.1%	100%
2040	17.9%	54.4%	27.7%	100%
2050	4.9%	41.4%	53.7%	100%

Source: Statistical Appendix to MLSP (2002a).

In the period following the Prodi reform, three lines of intervention have been pursued. Firstly, there have been some increases in the minimum values of social security and social assistance pensions. Secondly, a scheme of incentives to postpone retirement for those workers who have reached the seniority pension access minimum threshold has been introduced, a scheme, however, rather unused and which the government has now strengthened (see next section). Thirdly (and interacting with the previous line of intervention), a gradual easing of the norms allowing work and pension earnings to be accumulated has been pursued: after the changes enacted in 2000 and in 2002, pensioners in the DB and intermediate systems may cumulate their pension with work income if they retired above 58 years of age and with a contribution period of at least 37 years. This possibility on one hand provides an incentive to postpone retirement beyond the current minimum requirements, on the other hand it displaces any incentive to postpone the collection of seniority pensions beyond such thresholds.[9]

To complete the picture, one has to come briefly to the role of private pension funds. One of the common goals of all Italian pension reforms has been to boost the development of private pension funds. Indeed, an idea generally shared in the Italian debate since the early 1990s is that the above depicted decline in unitary benefits had to be tackled by the insurgence of a mixed system, in which elderly people get their income from both a pay-as-you-go public system (with the intrinsic financial stability features described above) and a fully-funded supplementary pillar.[10] Also the gradualism of the reforms concerning the first pillar reforms, besides being driven by socio-political feasibility considerations, was meant to distinguish between the current cohorts of the elderly, who had not the time to accumulate such funded schemes, and the young, who would have had such an opportunity.

The first regulatory intervention on private pension funds dates therefore back to 1993, when, to the *pre-existing* (and of little relevance) pension funds, two new types were added: the first based on collective agreements (*contractual*, or *closed-end funds*), mostly targeted at employees, and the second (*open pension funds*) aimed at supplying supplementary pensions to the self-employed and to employees working in sectors where no contractual funds have been set. Both are based on the DC principle. Other normative interventions followed the first, setting a framework that brought the first pension funds to become operative in 1997. Pension fund contributions receive a fiscal advantage, and overall the fiscal system is a hybrid ETT, where, to avoid double taxation, only part of the pension is subject to personal income taxation, so that the system roughly approaches an EET.[11] In addition, in 2001 some individual pension plans managed by insurance companies (*Piani Individuali Pensionistici* – PIPs) were given the same fiscal advantage, so that the second and third pillars now comprise four types of funds: the pre-existing pension funds, the contractual ones, the open ones and the PIPs.

However, because of the delays in setting up the funds, notably in the public sector, only 2 million people, about 10 per cent of total employment, are currently members of a fund. The participants tend to be individuals in their 40s or 50s, working in sectors characterized by relatively high wages or with a strong Union presence. Thus, it seems that membership is concentrated on the people who have less need of the supplementary pillar in order to further their overall future pensions entitlements. The reasons for this are often related to the tax advantages to be reaped and to the possibility of differentiating one's own saving choices. Among the non-members, besides lacking information about their future pensions entitlements,[12] it appears that the young and low income people are less ready to accumulate further pensions rights, possibly because of liquidity constraints or because they just do not feel rich enough to insure themselves. Moreover, there has been a strong 'revealed preference' towards the old TFR system which, while also related to inertial behaviour and lack of information, is partly attributable to the desire to preserve the income-cushion role of the TFR and the fact that it allows people to safely obtain a sizeable capital when retiring (or even earlier).

7.3   THE 2004 PENSION REFORM

Further interventions in the pension field are currently under way. The government proposed a new pension package in 2001, which has been modified several times and finally approved by Parliament in July 2004 (Law n. 243/2004). The new law is an enabling bill, thus the government is now drafting the detailed legislative decrees which will make effective the measures envisaged by the reform.

With respect to the initial plans, the government has renounced a reduction of pension contributions for newly hired workers (*decontribuzione*), which would have actually worsened the pensions deficit (both in the present and in the future, unless coupled by a further reduction of unitary benefits on top of those already shown in Figure 7.1). As for the development of supplementary pension, the original plan of making the diversion of TFR to pension funds compulsory has been softened into a silent-consent clause, that should start operating during 2005. More importantly, from the viewpoint of this chapter, the original intention of leaving access rules unchanged has been reversed, as the government has started to look for budgetary savings to balance the increase in expenditure forecasted for the next decades. These savings, peaking at about 0.8 per cent of GDP around 2015, would be produced by further raising the minimum age thresholds for the seniority pensions; this is planned to be implemented abruptly on 1 January 2008 and later on more gradually.[13] In the period up to 2008, instead, the key intervention will be the strengthening of the incentives to postpone retirement for those workers who have reached the seniority pension thresholds, so maintaining the intentions, stated already in 2001, of avoiding immediate restrictive measures on this type of pension.

In this section we concentrate upon the three sets of interventions concerning the pension access rules. The first two measures concern seniority pensions in the old DB system and are, up to 2008, the above-mentioned incentives to postpone retirement after reaching the current minimum thresholds; later on, the abrupt rise of such thresholds themselves. The third measure concerns the rise of the minimum retirement age in the new NDC system, which, because of the way the system operates, produces somewhat different results.

As will be clear from the following, the effect of the first measure on pension expenditure is uncertain and in any case deemed to be small and actually neglected by the official estimates focusing upon aggregate expenditure. More substantive savings, which appear as the interventions' ultimate target, would come from the two other sets of measures instead (Figure 7.2).

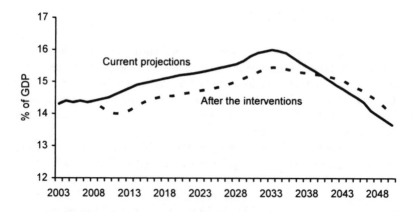

Source: Technical annex to the 2004 pension reform (Law 243/2004).

Figure 7.2 Pension expenditure: current projections (pre-2004 reform) and projections taking account of the measures contained in the 2004 reform

7.3.1 The Incentives to Postpone Retirement in the Period up to 2008[14]

The first measure, which the government has made effective in October 2004, gives the option of claiming exemption from pension contributions to private employees who could get a seniority pension, but instead continue working without claiming their pension. Such an incentive scheme will operate at least until 2008 and the saving on contributions (as said, currently at 32.7 per cent of the payroll) will be entirely cashed by the worker, on a tax-exempt basis. On the other hand, the accrued pension will be frozen (in real terms) from when the decision is made, while the right to retire will be certified, regardless of any future change in the minimum requirements, so as to avoid anticipated retirement flows induced by fears of future tightenings as those discussed in sections 7.3.2 and 7.3.3. On the basis of the incentive scheme, the worker's current net income can rise by more than 50 per cent, depending on the individual's tax rate and earning level (Table 7.4). However, this is not enough to conclude that the new scheme will really be effective.[15]

Table 7.4 The effect of the incentive on the payroll

Gross earnings (€)	Personal tax rates		Increase % of net earnings with tax exemption of the incentive
	Average	Marginal	
12 500	11.9%	23%	40.7%
25 000	22.6%	29%	46.4%
50 000	30.8%	39%	51.9%
75 000	33.9%	45%	54.3%

Source: Author's own calculations.

A similar measure had already been introduced in 2001, but in a much weaker form, so that few people made use of it and we can neglect it.[16] As a matter of fact, currently about 50–60 per cent of employees[17] retire having just reached the requirements for seniority pensions. A few others retire with seniority and age just above the minimum requirements. The remaining ones retire gradually later on, with peaks in the retirement flows on reaching 40 years of seniority or at 60 (females) and 65 (males) years of age, needed for the old-age pension. Thus, to assess the efficacy of the new incentives, one has to consider both the movement of people from retirement to postponement and people simply opting to use the new scheme, but who would have postponed anyway.

This is also relevant in evaluating the effects of the incentives on the public budget. The current savings for the public purse include only the reduced pension flows due to those who would not have postponed retirement otherwise, while both groups would contribute a reduction in the contributions flow and must be taken into account on the cost side. Given the relative size of pension entitlements upon reaching the seniority threshold and the contribution rates, the scheme would finance itself if the former group accounted for approximately one half of the population actually using the scheme.[18,19]

Thus, we have to consider: a) which people, in the current environment, that is with no incentive scheme, are likely to postpone their retirement, and which tend to retire as soon as possible; b) how the incentive scheme is affecting the former and the latter.

From a worker's perspective, the postponement choice is today preferred by people with relatively low work disutility and, for a given degree of work disutility, by those with very low discount rates (not discounting at all the increase of pension entitlements obtained while continuing to work[20]), or those who have the capacity for further increasing their future pension entitlements (because they are going to experience sharp wage increases and/or because they are a long way from the maximum pensions ceiling). On the other hand, people heavily discounting the future or with little opportunity to increase their pension entitlements (because they are high income workers whose entitlements are already close to or above the maximum pensions ceiling, or because they are going to experience a wage decline due to unemployment or health reasons) are those who, for a given degree of work disutility, choose the immediate retirement option.

Indeed, it has to be remembered that the DB system, linking pensions to final wages, systematically favours non-manual and highly-skilled workers capable of maintaining a steep wage profile at the very end of their working life. Symmetrically, the least employable among the elderly, provided they have accumulated enough seniority rights, could find withdrawing from the labour market financially more profitable than accepting a low wage offer, the latter having a sizeable negative impact upon future pension entitlements.

Clearly the labour market options and opportunities for elderly workers are more complex than are here described. Just to state a few of the issues not covered here, consider that we are assuming that work disutility may be simply expressed in money terms, and we are ignoring factors such as the presence of the TFR stock, which also might induce workers with liquidity problems (and a large inherited TFR) to opt for retirement. More importantly, the above discussion assumes that the postponement option is freely available to the worker, so it does not take explicitly into account the 'employability' and demand-side factors (see section 7.4). However, the sketched profile of who currently chooses the retirement option is quite robust. Actually, the demand-side considerations may somehow be included in the picture considering them among the determinants of the future wage developments – a worker at risk of being dismissed and/or unlikely to find a new 'good job' being characterized, in the above picture, by an expected wage cut and thus being induced to 'choose' the retirement option also because of the induced reduction in his or her future pension entitlements.

So we may conclude that – besides those with high work disutility – the people opting for retirement are those with high discount rates, dismal work prospects and/or whose future pension entitlements may not rise because of institutional constraints (that is high income people).

How will the incentive scheme affect this differentiated bunch of people?

It is unlikely that people with very high disutility of work will adhere to the new scheme. At the same time, there will be some people who would have chosen to postpone anyway – because of a low work disutility and a low discount rate – and who, because of their relatively high current work income and tax rate, greatly appreciate the incentive scheme and simply use it instead of the previously available postponement option. Such a group of people would, however, represent a deadweight loss for the scheme. On the other hand, there may be individuals induced by the new scheme to postpone retirement while in the previous framework opting for retirement because of dismal wage prospects, large enough work disutility, lack of space for substantial further pension improvements (because their entitlements were already capped) or a high discount rate.[21] Among these more differentiated bunch of people – made up of less employable people appreciating the freeze in future pension entitlements and high income people very much appreciating the tax favoured regime of the new scheme – the scheme might induce genuine postponement choices.

Table 7.5 offers a partial picture of how all such dimensions interact in determining individuals' convenience. It considers the increase in pension wealth derived from postponing retirement for two years in the alternative cases of using or not using the new incentives. The dimensions taken into consideration are the work disutility, the discount rate, the current wage and the pension replacement rate. It is shown that some people who will use the new scheme would have postponed retirement anyway (data in italics): the new scheme dominates the retirement option by more than the postponement without use of the incentives was already doing. Others, instead (data in bold), are induced by the new scheme to postpone, but it appears that such situations crucially depend on all factors considered.

Such a brief description makes clear that it is difficult to identify to what extent the incentives may be effective. *Ex-ante* evaluations would require us to know much more in detail the characteristics of who already postpones retirement and who retires as soon as possible. Furthermore, the picture is even more complex as the postponement option will be dominated by the opportunity to cumulate work and pension income, which is now allowed with no penalties even before reaching the old-age pension age thresholds of 37 years of seniority and 58 years of age. Also, it is unclear what are the implications of granting the individual worker the right to postpone his or her retirement in a world in which retirements are often induced by firms pushing away their senior workers. In practice, the analysis suggests extreme caution regarding the possible effectiveness of the incentives, while enlightening some possible redistributive effects, amplified from the tax exempt treatment of the pension contributions cashed in by the worker.

Table 7.5 The effects of the new incentives: change in pension wealth postponing retirement for two years

Increments are expressed in % of earnings in the last year of work.[a]
Italics shaded: individuals who would postpone retirement anyway, but choose to use the new incentives. **Bold shaded:** individuals who choose to postpone thanks to the new incentives.

Seniority 35 years, individual income yearly growth rate 0.55%		Discount rate	Replacement rate [c]	Change in pension wealth postponing retirement for two years at different degrees of disutility of labour [d]			
				0%	33%	67%	100%
With incentives	Work income = 25 000 [b]	1.0%	70%	92.1%	44.5%	−3.2%	−50.9%
		3.0%		*89.4%*	*43.2%*	−3.1%	−49.4%
		5.0%		*86.9%*	*41.9%*	−3.0%	−48.0%
	Work income = 50 000 [b]	1.0%	64%	*96.6%*	*54.4%*	*12.1%*	−30.1%
		3.0%		*93.8%*	*52.8%*	**11.8%**	−29.2%
		5.0%		*91.2%*	*51.3%*	**11.4%**	−28.4%
Without incentives	Work income = 25 000 [b]	1.0%	70%	96.9%	49.2%	1.5%	−46.1%
		3.0%		81.2%	34.9%	−11.4%	−57.7%
		5.0%		69.5%	24.5%	−20.5%	−65.5%
	Work income = 50 000 [b]	1.0%	64%	88.9%	46.7%	4.4%	−37.8%
		3.0%		75.7%	34.7%	−6.3%	−47.3%
		5.0%		65.9%	26.0%	−13.8%	−53.7%

Notes:
(a) Using an individual with 35 years of seniority and 57 years of age. The year of the choice of whether to prolong work or not is 2004.
(b) Work income refers to the last year of work before the choice.
(c) The replacement rate refers to the moment of the choice.
(d) Expressed in percentage of net work income.

Source: Author's own calculations.

7.3.2   The Increase of the Minimum Requirements for the Seniority Pension

More substantial results, on both the retirement age and the pension expenditure sides, are expected from the second measure, the jump of the minimum age requirements for seniority pensions in 2008.

Overall (see Appendix 7.B), also considering the postponement of the retirement exit 'windows', from 2008 the new law raises the minimum age by more than three years, from 57 and 4.5 months to 60 years and nine months for employees, and from 58 and 7.5 months to 62 years and three months for the self-employed. Such thresholds would be increased by one further year in 2010 and again in 2014. In practice, seniority pensions would virtually disappear for women, while the opportunity would also gradually fade away for males, who could eventually get a seniority pension only two years and three months (employees) and nine months (self-employed) before the old-age threshold. Only people with 40 years of seniority, or women accepting a sharp reduction of entitlements (opting for an integral application of NDC entitlements rules), could continue retiring at the current ages; these cases, however, tend not to be very relevant in practice.[22]

The measure is expected to be effective, although rather abrupt. According to official estimates, 330 000 workers belonging to three consecutive cohorts would be forbidden to leave work for more than three years by 2010, rising to 460 000 by 2013. Over the following years the effectiveness of the measure should be further strengthened by demographic factors, as the relevant cohorts would progressively be those of the mid-1960s baby boom.

Even the effects on expenditure will be substantial and will build rapidly. As shown in Figure 7.2, savings would rapidly rise, peaking at 0.8 per cent of GDP in 2015 with respect to the scenario based upon the previous legislative frame, an effect of both the lower pension expenditure in absolute value and the higher GDP associated with the labour supply boost caused by the new seniority requirements. Notice that until around 2025 almost all the savings will originate from this intervention, as only few of the individuals who will then retire will be affected by the measures concerning the NDC system (see section 7.3.3).

Over time, however, the effect upon expenditure of the reduced retirees' inflow will increasingly be counterbalanced by the fact that people obliged to postpone retirement accumulate higher seniority and thus higher pension entitlements. As new retirees would be increasingly subject to the new NDC system and thus less and less affected by such a measure, this effect on benefits would be more and more relevant, while the demographic wave of the cohorts born around the mid-1960s would gradually fade away.

At a certain moment the savings due to such a measure per se would disappear and pension expenditure would surpass the current baseline: after 2025–2030 the rise in the seniority pension access rules would end up affecting none of the new retirees, while most of the individuals affected during the previous years would be still alive and, as said, receiving higher pensions because of the higher seniority they had been forced to mature. To some extent the third set of measures discussed in section 7.3.3 has been motivated precisely by the need to avoid such an increase in aggregate expenditure around 2030, which is exactly the period when pension expenditure is deemed to peak.

Before dealing with the third set of measures, two further points of the planned interventions have to be stressed: the *abruptness* and *timing* of the change.

The sharpness of the raising of the age threshold for the seniority pensions would produce further inequalities across cohorts into a system in which the reforms of the 1990s, while generally leading to a more equitable system across job categories, had already produced sharp differences across cohorts. In any case, as the intervention would be very much concentrated upon workers relatively close to their planned retirement age and who have few opportunities to adjust their choices and behaviour, the welfare effect upon them might be substantial.[23] Furthermore, the sharpness of the change would imply a sizeable, even if somehow announced and therefore expected, labour supply shock to be accommodated by the labour market.

Whatever the political roots of the timing chosen, it has to be admitted that the interventions start binding when the large cohorts of the baby boomers enter their retirement decision period and during a period in which the reduction in the working age population is likely to have already induced the firms to change their attitudes towards elderly workers. However, as said, the financial impact of the intervention would be reversed precisely when the expenditure is expected to peak.

All in all, it is doubtless that a more gradual increase in the seniority requirements, while delaying the savings path, would allow more equity, leaving the labour market more room for an adjustment; provided the gradualism does not nullify the effectiveness of the new thresholds upon the baby boom cohorts, it would also shift the expenditure savings in a period closer to the peak of overall expenditure.

7.3.3 The Increase of the Minimum Retirement Age in the New NDC System

Whatever the precise timing over the next 20–25 years of the effects that the intervention in seniority pensions will have on expenditure, its efficacy regarding increasing the retirement age and the effect on pension expenditure crucially depend upon a second intervention related to the minimum retirement ages, to extend the same age thresholds to the NDC system. This will modify the 57–65 years range allowed for by the NDC system in the following ways:

a. The seniority requirement to retire before 65 for males and 60 for females would increase from five to 35 years.
b. The minimum retirement age would rise by more than three years in 2008, reaching for females 60 years and for males 60/61 years (employees/self-employed), further rising to 62/63 in the following years.
c. The mechanism of the exit windows would also be introduced in the new system, implying a further nine or 15 months of work before actual retirement.

The issue that such changes immediately raise is that of the overall coherence of the new system, as the flexibility features of the NDC system would practically fade away.

As said before, when fully implemented, the new NDC system (without the interventions just described) would couple *intrinsic financial sustainability* features – as expenditure would tend to evolve in line with contribution receipts, being insulated (even if with a lag) from demographic and macroeconomic shocks – with *flexibility in the age of retirement* within a given age range. More specifically, trends in the average lifespan after retirement would not alter the expenditure path, as the increase in the number of pensions to be paid would be compensated by the cuts in unitary entitlements (assuming a constant age of retirement). As a mirror image of the above, for given contribution rates the postponement of the effective age of retirement would increase unitary entitlements, the aggregate expenditure remaining relatively unaffected as the total number of retirees at each time *t* would decrease, so contributing more to the adequacy of pensions than to the containment of expenditure.[24]

Therefore why also intervene in the new NDC system? There appear to be two, not necessarily alternative, rationales for this.

A first reason is that the NDC system, when fully implemented, would guarantee the financial sustainability but not necessarily the social adequacy of pension entitlements. As already shown in the previous section, the expected decline in the replacement rate (for a given retirement age) is quite sizeable. In this framework the squeeze in the retirement age range provoked by the new intervention would force an increase in unitary pensions.

Notice that this would overlap with three other mechanisms built into the NDC system that would have already induced a postponement of retirement.

Firstly, the decline of the generosity of the system by itself should push people, through a standard labour supply 'income effect', to postpone retirement. Secondly, the flexibility features of the NDC by themselves significantly increase (with respect to the current situation) the marginal incentive to postpone retirement: by postponing retirement (up to 65 years of age) people would increment future pension entitlements through the accumulation of further contributions, the capitalization of past contributions for further years and the application of higher actuarially neutral transformation coefficients (which capture the different life expectancy at each age), which would provide for a neutral retirement incentive structure.[25] Finally, the requirement to have minimum accrued benefits of at least 1.2 times the social assistance pension to retire before 65 years of age, while guaranteeing pension adequacy standards, would impede some people from retiring too early.

A second reason is due to the complex timing of the different regimes and to the fact that the other measures discussed in section 7.3.2 would have, by themselves, led to an increase in the aggregate expenditure around 2030. At this time nobody would have been affected any more by the reduction in flow of retirees while the unitary pensions of those already retired would have been higher because of the rise in the retirement age. Increasing the retirement age threshold also relevant to the NDC system would 'solve' the problem, as it would permanently reduce the number of pensions. While this would again be counterbalanced by the rise in unitary pensions, such an effect would appear only with a lag, so allowing the peak period to be reached around 2030.

Later on the differentiated impact upon the number of pensions – which would decrease with respect to the previous legislation baseline – and their unitary amounts – which would rise – would start having an impact upon aggregate expenditure. At a certain moment total expenditure would even exceed the expenditure expected by pre-reform projections. Such a reversal, however, as shown in Figure 7.2, would now happen when the overall pension expenditure was already on a downward path. More importantly, Figure 7.1 reminds us that the 'forced' increase in unitary pensions due to the measures shown in section 7.3.2 would operate upon cohorts of retirees whose pensions would have been relatively high anyway, while the 'forced' increase operating later on would act upon cohorts for whom pension adequacy would have become the key issue.

The rationales above presented actually do not imply any optimality features of the interventions themselves. Alternative routes – for instance gradually lifting the whole age range envisaged by the NDC system and/or strengthening the minimum benefits requirements constraint relevant within that age range – could have better preserved the overall coherence and flexibility of the NDC system while still forcing up the retirement age.

7.4   THE ELDERLY IN THE ITALIAN LABOUR MARKET

The pensions reforms described in the previous two sections have great implications for the labour market chances and behaviour of elderly workers. At the same time, it is quite clear that the overall financial sustainability and social adequacy of pensions depend upon aggregate employment performance, an important component of which is the elderly segment.

From a worker's perspective, in the previous section we have already shown the relevance of age and seniority thresholds – particularly in the DB regime, still relevant for people now contemplating whether to retire – and financial incentives – by themselves more powerful in the NDC system – in determining elderly labour supply. In this section we broaden the view, trying to characterize the whole labour market situation for elderly workers. The focus is upon the cohorts currently over 50 years of age, while some characterization of past and (possible) future trends is also briefly introduced.

Besides being demographically on the rise, during the 1990s elderly workers have experienced an acceleration in the more secular decline in their employment rate. Only over the most recent years has such a negative trend been halted.

Both the previous sharp fall and the most recent timid rise are more marked among males and in the Centre-North (Figure 7.3).[26] Among females, a positive trend has prevailed throughout the whole decade, such a positive trend being larger in the Centre-North and up to 60 years of age. The recent gains are actually most significant in the 50–54 year age bracket, being still limited in the 55–60 year bracket, while in the 60–64 year bracket there is no positive signal yet. So, among the 55–64 year group Italy remains very a long way from the 50 per cent excellence target for 2010 established in the 2001 Stockholm EU summit, having just started to experience a slight rise (from 27.7 per cent in 2000 to around 30 per cent in 2003).

Focusing upon the age profile of the employment rate, it appears that, while there are groups who are characterized by low employment across the board (females, the Mezzogiorno regions and least educated people), there are groups with high employment when 50 years old but retiring relatively soon (males in the Centre-North, particularly, but not only, those least educated). Figure 7.4a shows that among males the employment rate in the South overtakes that in the Centre-North at around 53 years of age.[27] While low education attainments are always associated with low employment rates, even among males (also in the Centre-North, only four-fifths of the 50–54-

year-old less educated males are employed *vis-à-vis* a 92 per cent employment rate of the most educated), the gap between most and least educated people increases (in absolute terms) when considering people at a later stage of their life cycle.

Centre-North

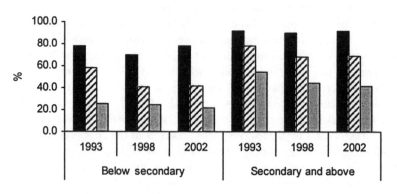

South

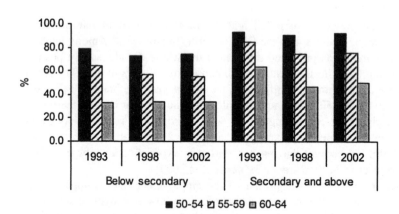

Source: MLSP (2003a), based upon ISTAT LFS data.

Figure 7.3a Employment rate in 1993, 1998, 2002 by sex, area, age group and educational attainment: males

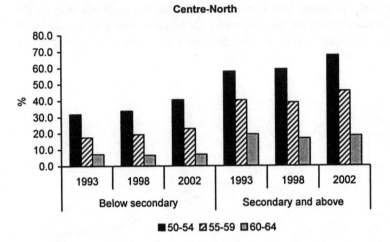

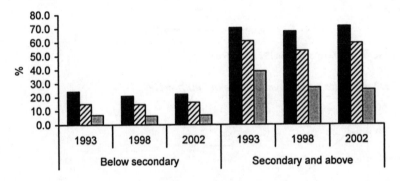

Source: MLSP (2003a), based upon ISTAT LFS data.

*Figure 7.3b Employment rate in 1993, 1998, 2002 by sex, area, age group
and educational attainment: females*

Figure 7.5 shows a well known pattern of the Italian case: the relatively
low relevance of the statutory age of retirement of 65 for males and 60 for
females (see Appendix 7.B). The yearly probability of retirement[28] of a male
worker in the Centre-North already has a peak around 15 per cent at 59 years
of age; such a pattern is clearly related to the presence of seniority pensions
(see sections 7.2 and 7.3). Providing a mirror image of what has already been
noticed with respect to the age pattern of the employment rate, the graph also

shows how the males' exit rate is higher in the Centre-North than in the South, precisely because the opportunity for Southern workers to access such a scheme is much lower, because they have generally accumulated fewer seniority rights granting access to that scheme.

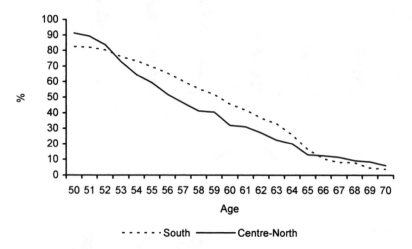

Source: Sestito (2002) based upon ISTAT LFS data.

Figure 7.4a Elderly employment rate in 2000: males

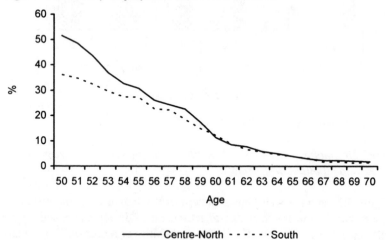

Source: Sestito (2002) based upon ISTAT LFS data.

Figure 7.4b Elderly employment rate in 2000: females

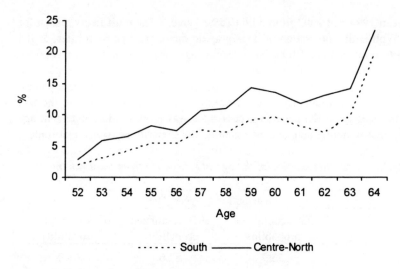

Source: Sestito (2002) based upon ISTAT LFS data.

Figure 7.5a Exit rate from employment – 2000: males

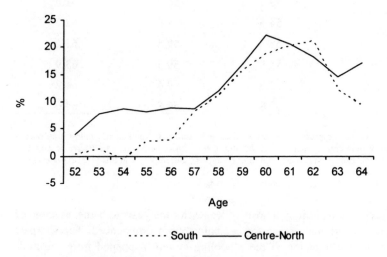

Source: Sestito (2002) based upon ISTAT LFS data.

Figure 7.5b Exit rate from employment – 2000: females

However, as said, some positive trend in the retirement pattern is already developing. Table 7.6 shows that the 50 per cent cumulated probability retirement age (of a 50-year-old individual in employment) increased between 1994 and 2002 from 57.6 to 59.8 years.[29] The most likely reason for this trend is the interaction of demographic factors and pension rules, as the cohorts now in their fifties have increasingly accumulated fewer years of work seniority[30] and face more stringent retirement rules. The table also shows that much of the shift towards a postponement in the retirement pattern has happened at relatively younger ages. This is probably linked to the fact that the change in the pension access rules was more binding over that age range, that is among people contemplating the seniority pensions' exit route.

Table 7.6 Different quartiles of the age of retirement from employment

	Distribution by year [a]		
	25% cumulated probability	50% cumulated probability	75% cumulated probability
1994	53.9	57.6	61.0
1995	53.5	57.2	60.9
1996	54.3	58.7	62.8
1997	53.5	56.7	61.0
1998	54.5	58.6	62.7
1999	55.3	59.5	63.4
2000	55.8	59.3	63.9
2001	55.9	59.5	64.2
2002	55.8	59.8	64.6

Note: (a) Each point represents the age at which a 50-year-old hypothetical employed individual would retire from employment with probability *x* when his or her yearly exit behaviour would be dictated by the age specific yearly exit rates on average currently (i.e. in that year) experienced.

Source: MLSP (2003a), based upon ISTAT LFS data.

As such this will imply a positive legacy for the years to come, as some of the trends mentioned above are becoming more pronounced. The sharpest rises in the participation in the schooling system happened from the mid-1950s to the mid-1970s and youth unemployment was particularly high during the 1970s and the 1980s, both factors reducing the accumulated seniority rights of the cohorts progressively ageing.

The low employment of elderly people in Italy does not translate into high open unemployment. The unemployment rate remains around 4 per cent among 55–64-year-old-people – *vis-à-vis* the 7.5 per cent overall rate – and less than 4 per cent of the overall pool of job-seekers is accounted for by them (the share of the elderly in the job-seekers pool is less than 12 per cent, adding in the 45–54-year-old-people). The weight of elderly people in the total pool of the unemployed is a bit more relevant in the Centre-North (more than 9 percentage points and less than 5 percentage points respectively for the 45–54 and 54–64 age groups), where, however, open unemployment is rather low in absolute terms.

Nevertheless, it should be noticed that elderly unemployment, when measured relative to the total, has been increasing over time. The unemployment rate, traditionally a strictly decreasing function of age, now appears to have a slight blip passing from ages in the forties to the fifties (see Sestito, 2002, Table 4.5). Particularly over the most recent years, when elderly employment has been on the rise, elderly unemployment has also been rising (in relative terms), confirming what has been said about the importance of the interaction between demographic compositional factors and pensions access rules in explaining those employment trends. Actually jobless elderly people appear to suffer particularly in finding a new job: at least in the Centre-North, when unemployed, elderly people are more often the long-term unemployed.

Indeed, the low overall activity rate of the elderly (low employment and low unemployment) points at the fact that Italy stands out as a country in which pension schemes are often used at relatively young ages in order to solve redundancy problems, not as a country in which unemployment or invalidity schemes are disproportionately and for long intervals used by elderly people. This is basically due to the regulatory framework. Unemployment benefits are underdeveloped and the universal basic scheme pays just 40 per cent of the previous wage and lasts only six months, a prolongation to nine months for individuals more than 50 years old having been enacted since 2001.[31] More generous and long-lasting benefits (up to three years for people over 50 years of age) apply only to firms (with more than 15 employees) in the industrial sector; in some cases these schemes may be allowed to accompany the dismissed worker up to retirement (so extending beyond the three years maximum even if with a special contribution paid by the firm). While being disproportionately used for elderly people – particularly the more generous mobility scheme now described, in which people over 50 years of age account for two-thirds of the beneficiaries – unemployment benefits remain rather underdeveloped in the Italian case: including the early retirement schemes, less and less used over the last decade, the expenditure for passive labour market policies now represents just 0.6 per cent of GDP (one-third of the EU average). Also regarding invalidity benefits, the Italian case stands out as one of the few EU countries in which no increase has been experienced during the last decade, as the restrictive measures undertaken since the mid-1980s had put a halt to the previous widespread use of those benefits in the depressed South.[32] All in all, the low level of unemployment benefits and the underdevelopment of targeted labour market policies have made the rules of the pension system, and in particular the 'seniority pension' scheme, a crucial element explaining the relatively early withdrawal from the labour market.

At the same time, it is important to note the traditional young orientation of the Italian active labour market policies.[33] The policies have left untouched, or have even worsened, the effect of the sizeable human capital gap related to age, due to the fact that Italy is a country which has experienced the expansion of its schooling system relatively late,[34] upon the employability gap of elderly people.

Some more recent interventions have somehow changed the picture, although still to a very limited extent. The so-called 'Biagi law' (the Legislative Decree n. 276 of 2003) has introduced employment schemes with financial incentives for elderly persons attempting to re-enter the labour market (the 'reinsertion contracts'), at the same time, however, extending the coverage of apprenticeship schemes to young people up to 29 years of age, so confirming the traditional youth orientation of the overall policy package.[35] Moreover, the fiscal employment bonus applicable to persons with no permanent employment over the previous two years, originally introduced in 2000 (and later extended to year 2006) has seen the recent introduction of an age differentiation, with a bonus supplement for elderly workers.[36]

Even irrespective of the presence of financial incentives (and the absence of service-oriented policies focused upon individuals who have lost a job), it has to be stressed that many of the regulatory and contractual arrangements introduced in Italy to favour the access to a job have mostly applied to young people. So, while the traditional stringency of the Italian regulatory framework has been eased for young people, the picture has remained broadly the same for the elderly. As a matter of fact, for instance, part-time work is very rare among elderly people; over time, the positive trend which appears for both males and females in the other age groups – even if within a clearly female feature of part-time work – is significant, among 55–64-year-old people, only in the female component.[37] A positive note can be found in that among elderly people voluntary part-time work (that is those cases in which the respondent declares part-time work for personal or family reasons and not because of the inability to find a full-time job) prevails more frequently than in other age groups.

To some extent the future of the age-related human capital gap is also uncertain. While the past history of the Italian schooling system will imply a reduction in the age gap – because of some deceleration in the human capital accumulation trends among the young[38] – the new technologies may imply an increase in the gap because of the difficulties more aged and least educated people have in updating their skills. In this respect, the malfunctioning of training markets and policies is a relevant problem.

The employability gap does not reflect itself into a wage gap. This may be due to institutional features as well as to selectivity mechanisms, which reinforce each other and further contribute to a reduction in elderly employment. Clearly it is impossible to disentangle the different effects. At a descriptive level, the age pattern of wages shows an age premium that is sizeable and, according to Contini and Fornero (2003), increasing over time. The age profile of wages actually does not show the decline after 50 years of age often manifest in other OECD countries, such a feature being possibly also related to institutional factors and to the fact that in the old DB system pension entitlements were generally linked to the last wages (even among people currently contemplating whether or not to retire pension entitlements are based upon the last ten years' wages).

So this apparent 'high quality' of employment among the elderly is not evidence of a strong market position of this age group. It is very likely that selection mechanisms play a big role, as the least employable among the elderly are simply pushed out of the labour market and attracted into retirement as soon as they have reached the relevant age and seniority thresholds.

Whether in this process supply (the attractiveness of pensions *vis-à-vis* work income) or demand factors prevail is difficult to say. As a matter of fact, the still low open unemployment among elderly people does not mean that the retirement process is made uniquely by abrupt transitions from employment to pension. Whatever the features of these transitions, it is also difficult to say to what extent workers' decisions are the essential ingredient.[39]

In any case, however, elderly employment is not driven uniquely by retirement options and opportunities. Actually Italy is a good example of the non-equivalence of a couple of well known policy targets recently stressed in the (Italian and) EU context: the target employment rate for 55–64-year-olds people and the five-year postponement of the average effective retirement age. In the Italian case the two do coincide among males in the Centre-North, who start from relatively satisfactory employment in their late forties, so that increasing the employment rate among the 55–64 age group mostly implies postponing the retirement age. For females and the Southern regions, however, even employment levels in the late forties (and earlier) need to be increased in order to produce a progressively higher employment rate among the 55–64 age group (so as to engineer a rise in the employment rate of this age class even with an unchanged age pattern of retirement).

7.5   SUMMING UP: WORKING LONGER IN THE GENERAL POLICY FRAMEWORK

We now want to put together the different pieces we have been dealing with, summing up how the issue of postponing retirement beds in the general pension policy framework.

The ageing process is particularly sizeable in the Italian case, as a rather subdued fertility pattern adds up to the lengthening of life expectancy and to the legacy of the baby boom. Its effects are already visible in the labour market, as an increasing share of the working age population is accounted for by elderly people.

During the past, the pension expenditure in Italy has substituted for other components of the welfare system. Consequently, the current level of pension expenditure stands quite high and the associated financing burden, together with the general conditions of the public purse, has inhibited the development of other components of the welfare system. While this has contributed to limit the incidence of welfare traps, the access to pensions for people in their fifties has led to relatively important retirement traps and few policy efforts to help the people involved to find new jobs. Moreover, while poverty relief is quite pervasive among elderly people, the social safety net is still underdeveloped and, even within the retirees population, the pension system does not contain measures addressing the special needs of the eldest ones with self-sufficiency problems, who are forecast to become an increasingly relevant issue.

In this framework, the pension reforms of the 1990s have significantly curbed the effect of ageing on pension expenditure, driving it on a path that would imply an increase by just two percentage points of GDP in the next 30 years, an amount much less sizeable than that automatically implied by ageing itself, reverting towards lower levels later on. Demographic effects are actually tackled by the gradual decrease in unitary benefits, such a decline being in part due to the non real-wage indexation of pensions and in part a feature of the application of the new NDC method and of the link, established within such a system, between pension entitlements and life expectancy at retirement. While the relatively infrequent nature of the updates of such a link, at ten-year intervals, may encourage disturbing discontinuities over time in the entitlements – a sizeable discontinuity being also embedded into the delayed phasing in of the reforms of the last decade – the link by itself guarantees the financial sustainability of the system *vis-à-vis* the demographic evolution.

However, the internal composition of the financial achievements granted by the past reforms was, to a large extent, unsatisfactory. Among the three main routes through which the financial soundness of a generic pay-as-you-go system may be pursued in the face of a strong ageing process – cutting unitary entitlements, increasing contribution rates or lengthening working life – there appears an excessive bias towards the first solution.

In these respects, two (non-alternative) routes have been generally identified in the Italian debate in order to avoid all the burden of the adjustments needed to preserve the financial sustainability falling upon unitary entitlements, so jeopardizing the adequacy of the system.

The first is aimed at integrating the public component of the system with a supplementary fully-funded private pillar, which should provide for additional resources to future retirees. Whatever the doubts such an option can fuel (Marano, 2002), the wide support it receives from the relevant actors (governments, employers, trade unions) is a characteristic peculiar to the Italian framework.

The second route pertains to increasing elderly employment and the effective age of retirement, so that an extended working life would accompany an increased life expectancy. In the long run, when the new NDC is fully phased in, this will allow unitary pension entitlements to be preserved while providing for further economic growth opportunities and for an active participation of elderly people in social and economic life. In the near term, when the old DB system remains the relevant one, boosting elderly employment will contribute to ease the pressures upon expenditure deriving from ageing and the gradual phasing in of the new system.

Reaching these two goals is not an easy task, also because of the complexities and discontinuities already created by the overlapping of two different systems, the old DB and the new NDC. Indeed, the issues at stake and the possible policy levers may differ across the two systems. Furthermore, considerations related to the logic of each system, to the labour market functioning, as well as to demographic factors, matter. This is true for both goals, as the passage through the retirement decision period of the baby boom cohorts in the next decades strongly impinges upon the possibility to divert resources for the establishment of a second pillar, as well as upon the need and possibility to handle a significant postponement of retirement.

This chapter has focused upon the second goal, that is on elderly employment, and we now review some of the main points discussed above, firstly concerning the rules of the old and the new pension systems, and then the functioning of the labour market.

As for the rules of the pension system (not considering the 2004 interventions):

- In the near future, the effects on retirement age are expected to be negligible. Three distinct factors contribute to further weaken whatever gain – as embedded in the DB formula or originated by ad hoc measures – an individual could derive from postponing retirement. Firstly, the opportunity, strengthened in the recent years, to cumulate work and pension incomes even for some seniority pension retirees. Secondly, the expanding area of the so-called "non-typical jobs, characterized by more flexibility and a lower payroll tax rate. Thirdly, the still pervasive presence of the hidden economy. So, the positive trend in the average age of exit from the labour market which seems to be materializing anyway is due to the combined effects of the gradual tightening of the seniority thresholds and the beginning of a gradual decline in the actual seniority rights accumulated by the new cohorts of elderly people.[40]

• In the longer run – as the new NDC system will apply – both the reduced generosity of pensions (for given age and seniority) and the marginal incentives for postponement embedded into the actuarial adjustment of the benefit formula should provide for stronger incentives. This could have also compensated for the fact that, before the changes introduced by the 2004 reform, in the NDC system the seniority requirement accompanying the age requirement of 57 years was just five years, against the 35 required in the old DB system; furthermore, also the supplementary constraint dictating that in order to retire before the age of 65 one needs to have pension entitlements at least equal to 1.2 times the minimum old-age allowance was expected to be very binding, at least for low income people.

As already argued, these different pension rules interplay with functioning of the labour market. In the past, and still now, demand-side factors were pushing out of the labour forces and towards early or seniority retirement cohorts of elderly workers characterized by low schooling. The traditional lack of attention paid to elderly people by active labour market policies has been, if anything, worsened by the fact that many of the recently undertaken flexibility enhancing measures were tilted towards easing access to the market for young people, and by the virtual absence of life-long-learning and retraining programmes targeted at elderly workers. In the future, a better functioning labour market and a reduced human capital gap across generations – as implied by the reduced pace of human capital accumulation across generations – should improve elderly workers' chances. Nevertheless, it seems fair to say that further discretionary changes in the policies, paying specific attention to elderly workers' needs and supporting changes in the traditional human resources practices, are needed.

All in all, taking account of both the labour market functioning and the pension rules features, it appears that it would have been extremely difficult to increase actual retirement at least in line with the expected increase in life expectancy. Actually, shifting the actual age of retirement upwards by five years would imply positioning it at the very limit of the 57–65 window envisaged for the NDC system, the incentives embedded in the NDC system only applying up to 65 years of age.

It is against such a picture that the 2004 pension reform has to be analysed. It has focused upon a single instrument, a sharp (although delayed) increase of the minimum age thresholds for seniority pensions, such thresholds also being reinserted as a relevant feature in the future NDC system. While not irrelevant, the incentives to postpone retirement are in any case limited to the period up to 2008 and have net quite uncertain effects.

We have already shown the quantitative, in terms of overall expenditure, and qualitative, in terms of balance between unitary pensions and number of retirees, features of the new law. Here, we briefly revisit two possible sources of problems and inconsistency.

The first concerns the *abruptness*, and *timing* of the change in the seniority requirement.

The sharpness in the tightening of requirements for seniority pensions could produce further inequalities across cohorts and have a substantial welfare effect upon them. Furthermore, the sharpness of the change would imply a sizeable, even if somehow announced and therefore expected, labour supply shock for the labour market.

At the same time, the timing chosen for the intervention tends to produce strong savings in the short and medium terms, when the baby boom cohorts enter into their retirement decision period. However, in the long run, due to the higher seniority and thus higher pension entitlements that workers will be forced to mature, the financial impact will be limited precisely when the expenditure is expected to peak. All in all, while the concentration of the effort around the envisaged period is quite sensible, the sharpness per se appears quite problematic and, within the same approach focused upon raising the seniority threshold, one wonders whether a more gradual approach and the introduction of some flexibility *vis-à-vis* individuals' choices would have possibly enhanced both efficiency and equity. In any case, other sources of inequalities embedded in the last decade's reforms would also deserve some fine tuning.

The second problem concerns the lack of consistency with the NDC system and the loss of some of its flexibility features. While the action upon the minimum age threshold for retirement may be beneficial as it boosts labour supply and increases unitary entitlements, the latter being potentially quite an important issue in the longer run, the practical disappearance of the retirement age window, which was a particular feature of the new NDC system, implies that the greatest source of flexibility of that system will be lost.

In such a framework it may be worth concluding by emphasizing on one side the positive features that would be associated with a timely but gradual and continuous – so as to avoid the many discontinuities and inequities across cohorts generated by the overlapping of different regimes – transition to an NDC system in which financial sustainability at the macro level and flexible individuals' choices at the micro level are combined. On the other side there is a need to guarantee that such a passage does not undermine pension adequacy, which requires for all individuals the accumulation of sizeable pension contributions during their adult life, that is adequate contribution rates paid over a longer contribution period. This points to the overall need for increasing both the average seniority at retirement and the average retirement age.

7.A APPENDIX: THE AGEING CHALLENGES IN A NUTSHELL

Among the OECD countries, Italy stands out for the swiftness of its ageing process. Ageing is the result of three distinct factors: an increasing life expectancy, the age structure of the current working age population, as produced by the baby-boom-baby-bust of 40 years ago, and a subdued fertility rate.

The basic facts are illustrated in Table 7.A1, which shows the demographic dependency ratio of old people (ratio of the population aged 65 and over to the population aged 15–64) and some data regarding life expectancy at birth and at retirement underlying the national 'central scenario' developed by ISTAT.

The ISTAT scenario assumes an increase in life expectancy at birth of 5.2 years for males and 5.5 years for females between 2000 and 2050, a net flow of immigrants of 110–20 thousand units per year and a slight recovery in the (cross-sectional) total fertility rate from 1.26 in 2000 to 1.41 in 2020 and thereafter. All the expected rise in life expectancy is forecasted over the 2000–2030 period and a large part is concentrated at later ages, so that life expectancy at 60, which is now around 20 years for males and 24 years for females, should increase by about four years by 2030. As for fertility, the forecasted rise is mostly 'technical': the above-mentioned 1.26 current fertility rate is assessed transversally, cumulating different age-specific fertility rates, and is therefore negatively – although transitorily – affected by the shift in the age of first birth of subsequent cohorts. When this effect dies out (the timing of this being forecasted around 2020), the aggregate fertility rate will *naturally* rise to a level of 1.41.

Table 7.A1 Demographic indicators

ISTAT central scenario	2000	2010	2020	2030	2040	2050
Demographic dependency ratio (65+/15–64)	26.6	31.5	37.2	46.4	60.1	63.5
Life expectancy at birth:						
Male	76.2	77.9	79.6	81.4	81.4	81.4
Female	82.6	84.4	86.2	88.1	88.1	88.1
Life expectancy at retirement:						
Male aged 65	16.2	17	18.3	19.6	19.6	19.6
Male aged 60	19.9	21	22.3	23.7	23.7	23.7
Female aged 65	20.2	21.5	22.9	24.5	24.5	24.5
Female aged 60	24.6	25.9	27.5	29.1	29.1	29.1

Source: 'Statistical Appendix' to MLSP (2002a).

By itself, the lengthening of life expectancy has permanent effects on the age structure of the population (as measured by the demographic dependency ratio). On top of that, the past baby boom will produce sizeable effects over the next 25 years' retirement flows,[41] while the more recent subdued fertility will produce a shrinking of the working age population at first, and of the overall population later on, the working age population already experiencing an ageing trend. All in all, the overall population is expected to fall from 57.7 millions to 52.2 millions between 2000 and 2050 and the demographic dependency ratio will more than double by 2040, further rising to about 2/3 in 2050, as against a value around 1/2 as the EU average.[42]

These processes could only partly and temporarily be dampened by more sustained immigration flows, as in the long run it is likely that immigrants will adapt their fertility and mortality patterns to those prevailing in the host country. Furthermore, the underlying trends could not be avoided by a recovery of fertility to the level guaranteeing the stability of the population: the working age population would react to fertility only with a substantial time-lag, the massive retirement flows going to occur over the next 25 years (assuming an unchanged retirement pattern) remaining unchallenged. Even in the longer run, the implications of the lengthening of life expectancy would remain operating.

7.B APPENDIX: THE LEGAL AGE OF RETIREMENT

Currently, three different sets of retirement ages have to be considered in the Italian case. Two refer to the old system – which allows for both old-age (*pensione di vecchiaia*) and seniority pensions (*pensione di anzianità*) and one to the new system, which allows only for the old-age pension.

The 1992 Amato reform raised the age for the *old-age pension* from 60 to 65 years for men and from 55 to 60 years for women, along with a minimum contribution period of 20 years. As upper limits, these retirement ages are very effective, as cumulation of work and pension income is possible, while employers are not required to keep the work relationship any longer. However, females have been given the right to continue working until the upper limit that applies to males, and, since, 1992, public employees have the option to work until 67; since 2004 they may also ask to remain until 70.

The reforms of the 1990s also increased the age and seniority requirements for *seniority pensions*: gradually, the contribution requirement has been brought up to 38 years (39 and 40 years starting in 2006 and 2008) regardless of age, or 35 years upon reaching 57 years of age (58 years for the self-employed). To this, 4.5 months on average (7.5 for the self-employed) must be added, because there is an extra time lag between the moment the right matures and the actual retirement (one says the worker needs to await her/his exit *window*). Notice that seniority pensions must not be confused with – much less important now than in the past – early retirements (*pensionamenti anticipati*). Early retirement refers to the situation where retirement before reaching the minimum requirements is allowed in force of norms specifically designed to smooth a firm's or sector's restructuring, thereby avoiding layoffs (see Ministry of Economy, various years, vol III, Tables PS23 and PS24).

The reforms of the 1990s set the *age of retirement in the new NDC system* in a range from 57 to 65, but to retire before 65 workers need at least five years of contributions and accrued benefits of at least 1.2 times the minimum old-age allowance (*assegno sociale*). As stated in the text, the flexibility of the retirement age is allowed by the actuarial correction of the pension formula, which is neutral with respect to the retirement choices: younger pensioners will spread the same capital over more years, thus receiving a proportionally lower pension.

The 2004 pension reform (see section 7.3) increases, from 2008, the minimum age limits for both seniority pensions and the retirement in the new system.

For seniority pensions the access upon reaching 40 years' seniority will be maintained, while the age requirement of 57–58 years together with at least 35 years of contributions will be raised to 60–61 years and further in the following years, also doubling the extra time the worker needs to wait for the opening of the exit window to nine months (15 months for the self-employed). Thus, starting in 2014 male employees will be allowed to retire no younger than 62 and nine months (64 and three months for the self-employed). For females, seniority pensions will be de facto abolished. An exception will only hold until 2015, allowing women accepting a pension entirely calculated using the DC formula, with substantial cuts in their entitlements, to retire at the current seniority pension age thresholds.

For what concerns the NDC system, the government has substituted the current 57–65 years range with the same requirements for seniority and old-age pensions. This implies, with respect to the current situation, not only a rise in the minimum age, but also in the seniority requirements (from five to 35 years) and the introduction of the mechanism of exit windows to retire before 60 (females) and 65 (males).

NOTES

* In the last few years we have discussed several points dealt with here with Raffaele Tangorra, whom we want to thank sincerely; Rocco Aprile and Gianna Barbieri helped us respectively in understanding the many features of the Italian pension system and in handling some of the statistical information. Nonetheless, the opinions expressed are our own and cannot be attributed to the institutions we belong to. This chapter builds upon a lengthier paper presenting further descriptive elements about the Italian pension system and its labour market: Marano and Sestito (2004). With respect to it, however, this version has been updated in order to take into account the pension reform approved by the Parliament in July 2004. Although we worked together at each part, Angelo Marano concentrated particularly on sections 7.2, 7.3.1 and 7.3.2, while Paolo Sestito worked on sections 7.3.3, 7.4 and the two appendices. Section 7.5 contains our common conclusions.

1. Which is sometimes also – although incorrectly – labelled *pension expenditure* (see, for example, International Monetary Fund, 2003).

2. In practice, most workers use at least part of their TFR before retirement. Even workers above 50, who naturally have the highest seniority among age groups, only have in average about 10–11 years of TFR worth, which means that the rest has been used long before retirement (see Statistical Appendix to MLSP, 2002a). In this regard, even the Eurostat's inclusion of the TFR in the *old-age expenditure* is debatable. Also debatable is the widespread practice of classifying it as severance pay, given that the TFR is due regardless of layoff. Nonetheless it should be noted that in the event of dismissal the TFR may constitute a useful cushion during the unemployment spell, particularly appreciated given the Italian underdeveloped unemployment benefits system; the need for the firm to substitute the low cost TFR with other funding sources also acts as an additional drawback when firing employees.

3. See on this MLSP (2003a, chapter 7).

4. The updates are included in the *Documento di Programmazione Economica e Finanziaria* (DPEF) released by the government each July. For the most recent description of the model and its underlying data see Ministry of Economy (2004). Official data on pension expenditure can also be found in a 2001 report on pension expenditure (*Verifica del sistema previdenziale al sensi della legge 335/95* – known as 'Rapporto Brambilla') and in the Statistical Appendix to MLSP (2002a). All official documents and reports referred to here and below are available on the respective ministry's or institution's website.

5. There are two joint periodical publications, based on INPS statistical archives, which contain data on 25 million individual positions and 15.2 million current pensions: *I beneficiari delle prestazioni pensionistiche* and *Le prestazioni pensionistiche*. Some geographical details as well as data on length of contributions and level and type of benefits disaggregations can be found on the INPS website. Further data can be found in Ministry of

the Economy (various years), while data on public employee's pensions can be found in INPDAP (various years).

6.   In practice, the age-at-retirement specific coefficients not only take into account pensioners' life expectancy, but also the probability and life expectancy of survivors, as well as a positive internal return rate. Currently, for a retirement at 60 years of age the coefficient is 5.163 per cent, while at 65 years it rises to 6.136 per cent, regardless of gender. For the exact calculation formula, see Box 5 of the Normative Appendix to MLSP (2002a). The use of coefficients adjusted only for age-at-retirement implies a redistribution in favour of those with greater longevity, which are (definitely) women and (most likely) the more rich. Such an advantage is, however, counterbalanced by the lack of real wage indexation after retirement and the maintenance of some explicit redistributive components, like the income ceilings above which price indexation is not full, and the means tested top-ups before discussed. While no proper examination of the distributional features of the new NDC system as opposed to the previous DB system has been carried out yet, the former is deemed to be more equitable and (in any case) more transparent than the latter, which was systematically favouring those (mostly highly-skilled) people having a steeper wage profile towards the end of their working life. Apart from the intrinsic characteristics of the two systems, the gradual phasing in of the new system further complicates the picture over the forthcoming decades as several intergenerational sources of inequalities are also present.

7.   Figure 7.1 is based on the Eurostat demographic projections, which, contrary to national forecasts, assume that life expectancy will continue to rise during the entire period 2000–2050 (see Appendix 7.A). The decline appears particularly important for the self-employed, whose entitlements will practically halve even when retiring at 65 with a 40-year seniority. This is the effect of the new DC formula and of the lower pension contributions paid by the self-employed: while employees pay a contribution rate of 32.7 per cent of payroll, of which 8.89 per cent is paid by the worker and the rest by the employer (the pension accrual rate being set slightly above, at 33 per cent), for the self-employed the contribution rate is around 17–17.5 per cent, gradually rising to 19 per cent (with an accrual rate of 20 per cent). Indeed, while in the DB system only seniority mattered, and pension entitlements were unaffected by the amount of lifetime contributions and by the age at retirement, in the DC system the opposite holds; seniority by itself plays no role, so that entitlements are determined by lifetime contributions and age of retirement. However, note that for the self-employed both contributions and pension benefits are expressed as a percentage of gross income (that is including the contributions themselves), so that differences in entitlements expressed, as in this case, in terms of gross replacement rates overstate those on a net income base.

8.   Tables 7.1 and 7.2, as well as Figure 7.2 in section 7.3, refer to a narrower definition of pension expenditure than that used before, which excludes about 0.7 points of GDP due to invalidity pensions and early retirement benefits for labour market reasons. Furthermore, Tables 7.1 and 7.2 refer to an EU-15 wide exercise, producing results slightly different from the national scenario shown in Figure 7.2. This scenario, however, is useful because it shows the expected effects on expenditure of the new pension reform (see section 7.3).

9.   In this respect, the current law penalizes individuals subject to the NDC system, which can cumulate pension and work income, as they only receive reduced benefits and, in any case, not before 63 if wishing to work as employees.

10. In Marano (2002) strong reservations about such a reliance on pension funds have been expressed.

11. Of course, 'E' refers to 'exempt', 'T' to 'taxed'.

12. According to some polls, most workers either believe that they will still be treated along the old DB rules, something already legislated out, or that they will get very low benefits, so implicitly expecting further cuts to the entitlements granted by the public system. In these respects, Italy dramatically differs from Sweden, the other country which introduced an NDC system during the last decade, as no systematic information about the likely future entitlements is provided to the workers.

13. However, the pension reform contains a clause that allows the government to define alternative measures on the retirement age and seniority thresholds (or on the timing of the

changes from 2008), subject to the condition that these alternative measures must increase the retirement age and produce the same budgetary savings as the ones currently envisaged.

14. For a more detailed analysis see Box 1 in MLSP (2003b).

15. According to the reform, another ad hoc scheme should also be introduced in order to give people an incentive to opt for a part-time work instead of a seniority pension. While such an alternative route is potentially quite relevant, in that part-time work is particularly underrepresented among elderly workers, in what follows we concentrate upon the general scheme, which has already been finalized.

16. The incentives introduced in 2001 had the savings on contributions shared by both the employee and the employer (respectively 1/3 and 2/3 of the total savings) with no tax advantage. Moreover, both the employer and the employee had to agree upon the postponement, having to sign a new temporary contract lasting at least two years.

17. For the self-employed the situation is somehow different as it has been relatively easy for them to continue working (in the shadow economy) even in cases where the law did not allow them to cumulate pension and work earnings. Given that the option to cumulate work and pension incomes clearly dominates all alternatives, most self-employed people tend to cash their pensions entitlements immediately. Some change in their behaviour could be induced by the new norms on cumulation described in section 7.2, but it is still too early to assess the effects.

18. Neglecting, for the sake of simplicity, the tax implications, on one side, and the possible effects upon aggregate employment and GDP of the people additionally postponing retirement, on the other side, two individuals with work earnings w and using the incentives will imply lower contribution revenues amounting to $(2 \cdot 32.7\% \cdot w)$. The resulting (65.4% $\cdot$ w) is quite close to the typical replacement rate of an individual facing such an option.

19. On an intertemporal perspective, the second group of people – the ones adhering to the incentive, and who would have postponed retirement in any case – would also contribute to some savings, as they will be paid lower pensions.

20. The discount rate may also take into account the role of the subjective probability of death, a parameter we do not deal with explicitly.

21. In the comparison between retirement and opting to use the new scheme the discount rate is (approximately) irrelevant as in both cases the future pension will be the same. Instead, the relevant factors are, on the individual's revenue side, the current work gross income (which determines the size of the incentive) and, on the cost side, the net pension (which is higher the steeper was the previous wage career, provided the individual did not reach the pension ceiling). The discount rate matters only in identifying whether the individual was choosing the retirement option in the no-incentives environment.

22. Currently, also taking into account old-age retirees, the average seniority at retirement is 27.1 years for females and 33.8 for males (Social Protection Committee, 2004).

23. In comparison with their planned retirement pattern they would end up being too 'income rich' and 'leisure poor'.

24. Such a claim is valid only as first approximation and assuming that the changes happen within the 57–65 age window, within which the actuarial adjustment operates. In the NDC system, if everybody worked for one further year, unitary pensions would rise by 3–4 per cent, depending on the exact age of retirement, because of the application of a higher age-specific coefficient and by about 3 per cent because of the increase in the value of total accrued contributions. However, the stock of pensioners at each moment would fall, roughly by the same amount, each individual receiving a pension transfer for one year less and life expectancy at retirement being currently between 16.2 years (males aged 65) and 24.6 years (females aged 60). See Table 7.A1 for this data, which has to be corrected to take into account probability and life expectancy of survivors as well as the size of different cohorts and the different mortality rates at each age. Note also that total pension contribution revenues would rise, while the improvement of unitary pensions would be associated with a higher GDP, as employment would be (at least partly) increased by the enlarged labour supply pool.

25. Incentives to late retirement built-in in a system are generally evaluated (as done in Figure 7.5) in terms of changes in pension wealth originating from one or more years of further

work, or other related concepts. NDC systems tend to show an 'actuarial neutrality' feature in this regard. This suggests some scepticism about findings such as in OECD (2002, Table V.3, p. 147), where the Italian NDC system seems to perform poorly with regard to incentives for working longer.

26. Most of the decrease occurred before 1993, which is the first year considered in the graph for availability of detailed and continuous data. Among 50–59-year-old people the employment rate fell by 4 percentage points (to 46.7 per cent) between 1990 and 1995, after a decline from 51.4 to 50.7 per cent in the previous five-year period. The corresponding figures among males in the Centre-North were falls of 10 points in the 1990–95 period (to 65.6 per cent) and 2 points (from 77.8 to 75.5 per cent) in the previous period. For more on the overall picture of the Italian labour market see Sestito (2002).

27. Note that in the 30–49 year age bracket 82 males out of 100 are employed in the South compared with 94 out of 100 in the Centre-North.

28. The retirement probability is computed using a pseudo-panel approach within the LFS sample. So it refers to the exit from employment and not necessarily to the access to a pension scheme. In other words, the exit rate for age x is computed comparing the employment rate of age x in that year with the employment rate of age $x-1$ in the previous year. The use of the employment rate, instead of the absolute number of employed persons, corrects for the mortality pattern upon the assumption that an employed and non-employed person of a given age have the same mortality risk.

29. The indicators considered represent a summary measure of the age pattern of the yearly probability of exit as measured, for year 2000, in Figure 7.5. The focus is upon those age points in which the cumulative probability of exit of a hypothetical individual employed at 50 years of age and replicating over the future the current yearly exit rates of the individuals at later ages would reach 25 per cent, 50 per cent and 75 per cent. So it differs from the average age of the actual exits, which is affected by the actual age composition of employment as produced by demographic factors and the retirement patterns during the previous years. The use of three points in the distribution differs from the use of the 'average' made in the EU context in order to measure the progress towards the postponement of the retirement age, as it provides a much richer characterization of the underlying age pattern of the retirement exit rates as depicted in Figure 7.5. More details about the construction of the data in Table 7.6 and a comparison with the average age of actual exits may be found in MLSP (2003b).

30. Sestito (2002) estimated that in 1999 the 55–64 year age group averaged 6.8 years of completed schooling, against the 5.7 years averaged by the same age group in 1991. Moreover, it has to be considered that unemployment, and particularly youth unemployment related to the uneasy transition from school to work, had historically been on the rise in Italy since the mid-1970s.

31. For details on the effects of such a prolongation (and the increase from 30 to 40 per cent of the replacement rate) see MLSP (2003a, 2003b).

32. In real terms, in Italy the expenditure for invalidity benefits has been constant over the 1990–2000 period, compared with a rise of approximately one half for the EU average.

33. These have been traditionally focusing upon financial incentives favouring newly hired employees, with little relevance of activation and other service-oriented schemes. These financial incentives are relatively untargeted, as they favour broad groups; if anything, young people are traditionally considered a policy target to whom some schemes are applied (universally). As a consequence, while practically all new employments of young people (under 25 years of age) tend to be covered by some financial incentives, only one out of seven new hirings of people over 50 are likewise covered.

34. Sestito (2002) estimated that in 1999 the 55–64 year age group averaged only 6.8 years of completed schooling, against the 10.9 years averaged by the 25–34-year-old group. Also the Italian low participation in post-schooling learning activities does not help; in any case, training activities appear to be very much concentrated among younger age cohorts and the most educated individuals.

35. For more details on the financial implications of the 'legge Biagi', see Sestito (2004).

36. For a complete picture of the (several) changes in the fiscal bonus and its actual use see

MLSP (2003a).

37. See on this Sestito (2002) and MLSP (2000).
38. This may have negative aggregate implications for growth which we are not dealing with in this chapter.
39. According to Contini and Fornero (2003), only the workers employed in large firms are characterized by a stable employment relationship followed by an abrupt transition to retirement. In small and medium firms, only one half of the job separations interesting elderly people (defined as those over 50) lead to an immediate entry into a pension; the remaining people pass through non-employment and unemployment spells as well as short employment spells in other firms before final retirement. Moreover, there are striking regional differences as the abrupt employment-pension process is more important in the Northern regions (it represents one half of the total flows) where only 10 per cent of the flows involve an unemployment spell; in the South instead – where workers have often accumulated fewer years of contributions allowing access to a pension – only 30 per cent of the total job separation flows involves an abrupt employment-pension transition, while 20 per cent involves an unemployment spell.
40. Such a decline mostly originates from the fact that these new cohorts are increasingly made up of those affected by the rise in schooling participation occurring in the 1950s and by the widespread youth unemployment of the 1970s and the 1980s.
41. New births averaged 950 000 per year during 1960–69, after having been 880 000 during 1955–59 and decreased to 890 000 during 1970–74. In the most recent years (1998–2002) they averaged 530 000 per year, with a slight recovery over the previous period.
42. The picture does not change using the Eurostat 'central scenario' instead of ISTAT's. Such a scenario involves a slightly higher fertility rate, but also a slightly lower life expectancy at birth – above all for females – a net flow of immigrants of just 80 000 units per year and an increase of life expectancy distributed during the entire period. In such a scenario the overall population is expected to fall from 57.7 million to 48.1 million between 2000 and 2050 and the demographic dependency ratio would increase to 61.3 per cent in 2050.

REFERENCES

Contini, B. and E. Fornero (eds) (2003), *Scelte Lavorative e di Pensionamento degli Anziani in Italia*, research report by CeRP, LABORatorio R. Revelli and R&P Ricerche e Progetti for the Ministry of Labour and Social Policies.

Economic Policy Committee (2001), *Budgetary Challenges Posed by Ageing Population*, EPC/ECFIN/655/01- Brussels: European Union.

Eurostat (2003), *Statistic in Focus*, Theme 3, September.

INPDAP (various years), *Annual Report on the Welfare State*, Rome.

International Monetary Fund (2003), *Italy – Selected Issues*, Washington, DC.

Marano, A. (2002), *Avremo mai la pensione?*, Milan: Feltrinelli.

Marano, A. and P. Sestito (2004), 'Older Workers and Pensioners: The Challenge of Ageing on the Italian Public Pension System and Labour Market', CeRP Working Paper 32/04.

Ministry of Economy (various years), *Relazione Generale sulla Situazione Economica del Paese*, Rome.

Ministry of Economy (2004), 'Le tendenze di medio-lungo periodo del sistema pensionistico e sanitario. Le previsioni del Dipartimento della Ragioneria Generale dello Stato aggiornate al 2003', Temi di finanza pubblica e protezione sociale, Quaderno N. 5, Rome.

MLSP (Ministry of Labour and Social Policies) (various years), *Rapporto annuale del Nucleo di Valutazione della Spesa Previdenziale*, Rome.

MLSP (2000), *Rapporto di Monitoraggio sulle politiche occupazionali e del lavoro*, N. 2-2000, Rome.

MLSP (2001), *Rapporto di Monitoraggio sulle politiche occupazionali e del lavoro*, N. 1-2001, Rome.

MLSP (2002a), *National Strategy Report on Pensions*, Rome.

MLSP (2002b), *Employment National Action Plan*, Rome.

MLSP (2003a), *Rapporto di Monitoraggio sulle politiche occupazionali e del lavoro 2003*, Rome.

MLSP (2003b), *Rapporto di Monitoraggio sulle politiche occupazionali e del lavoro 2003 – Nota di aggiornamento*, Rome.

OECD (2002), 'Increasing Employment: The Role of Later Retirement', *OECD Economic Outlook*, no. 72.

OECD (2004), *Ageing and Employment Policies in Italy*, Paris.

Sestito, P. (2002), *Il mercato del lavoro in Italia. Com'è. Come sta cambiando*, Bari-Rome: Laterza.

Sestito, P. (2004), 'Compatibilità finanziarie ed effetti economici della legge Biagi', in M. Tiraboschi (ed.), *La riforma Biagi del mercato del lavoro*, Milan: Giuffré.

Social Protection Committee (2004), *Current and Prospective Pension Replacement Rates – Progress Report by the Indicators' Sub-Group*, Brussels: European Union.

8. Retirement choices of older workers in Italy*

Michele Belloni, Margherita Borella and Elsa Fornero

8.1 INTRODUCTION

During the 1990s the Italian pension system underwent extensive reform, and is now moving, although through a long transition, from a defined benefit (DB) formula to a notional defined contribution (NDC) one. These reforms were directed at re-establishing the long-run financial equilibrium of the system, both through a less generous computation of benefits, and through an increase of the average retirement age.

In this chapter we study the retirement behaviour of Italian workers both before and during the reform period, respectively in the relatively stable period 1985–91 and during the subsequent reform years; we also simulate future retirement patterns both during the transition and in the new steady state. Our descriptive analysis shows stable patterns, characterized by the typical spikes, in the pre-reform period, and 'anomalies' in the reform period, which appear dominated by the tighter eligibility requirements. We firstly estimate a retirement equation over the pre-reform institutional framework for which we have data (1985–91), and use the estimated parameters to project retirement behaviour under the new pension rules. Our empirical analysis omits important factors, mainly due to limitations in our administrative dataset. This contains rich information about the employment and earnings patterns of the observed worker, but lacks any information on his/her family, assets and employer. Our analysis thus captures important elements of the supply side of the market but is far from complete; moreover, it ignores the demand side. Finally, our study of retirement behaviour does not consider the effect of private pensions, as these were virtually non-existent in the considered period.

It is important to add that, at the time of writing, the Italian Social Security system was based on the so-called 'Dini reform', enacted in 1995. While this book was in print, some radical changes have been introduced by a new law (n. 243, dated 23 August 2004) and will enter into force in January 2008. In a sense, and notwithstanding many criticisms which the new law deserves, it has strongly reinforced, as compared with the 1995 reform, the drive to postpone retirement, thereby implicitly addressing the weaknesses that the present chapter emphasizes. While not modifying the rest of the chapter, which is therefore based on the Dini legal framework, we have added for the printed version a last section briefly dealing with the new 2004 developments.

The chapter is therefore organized as follows: in Section 8.2 we review the Italian pension system and its normative evolution, and we provide a descriptive analysis of the retirement patterns over the 1980s and the 1990s. In section 8.3 we perform a micro-econometric analysis, which aims at estimating the retirement decisions as a function of the existing pension rules; section 8.4 provides an evaluation of the effect of the 1995 reform on retirement behaviour. Section 8.5 concludes, while section 8.6 interprets the future rules as a (rough and perhaps unduly severe) remedy against the shortcomings of the Dini reform.

8.2   RETIREMENT IN ITALY: THE NORMATIVE BACKGROUND

Since 1992 the Italian pension system has undergone a series of major changes directed at correcting its main structural defects: a systematic insufficiency of contributions, regardless of the high payroll tax rates,[1] to cover outlays; a pervasive, and often 'perverse', redistribution; and relatively young retirement ages, induced by generous eligibility requirements. Two major reforms were enacted in 1992 and in 1995, followed by two smaller ones in 1997 and in 2004. These reforms have profoundly changed the institutional framework governing the retirement choices of Italian workers.

Essentially, a notional defined contribution (NDC) formula, based on the principle of '*actuarial equivalence*', has been introduced to replace the previous defined benefit (DB) formula in the public PAYG system; eligibility conditions have been accordingly changed. To appreciate the differences compare Figures 8.1 and 8.2. They reproduce the minimum requirements, for both *old-age* and '*seniority*' benefits applying until 1992,[2] for the main pension schemes: private employees, public employees and the self-employed (for simplicity, minor programmes are not considered). Seniority pensions are based only on the length of the working career, quite irrespective of age; old-age pensions are defined as the 'legal' retirement ages and, if not mandatory in a strict sense, represent the limit beyond which employers are entitled to dismiss their employees.

Figure 8.1 illustrates the situation before the 1992 reform.[3] One feature stands out: the heterogeneity of rules across schemes, with participants being allowed (and encouraged) to retire at markedly different combinations of age and seniority (plus, of course, a different generosity of benefits). This diversity of treatment – reflecting political discretion – was undoubtedly favoured by the scarce correspondence between contributions and benefits typical of the DB formula. It is not far-fetched to assert that the variability across occupational categories, gender and type of benefit (old-age *vs* 'seniority' pensions) was less explained by consideration of fairness than by 'exchanges' in the political market, with the more influential groups (such as public employees) obtaining the most favourable conditions.[4] As a second feature, the differentiation of rules was not matched by a high degree of flexibility in the set of choices, with workers being induced to leave either at the earliest or at the legal age (and firms expecting them to).

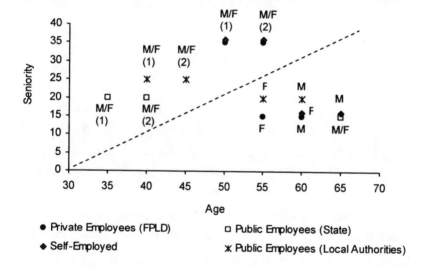

Figure 8.1 Minimum requirements for old-age and 'seniority' pensions, main pension schemes: before 1992 reform

Figure 8.2 refers instead to the NDC regime decreed in 1995. Here the *uniformity of treatment* is made transparent by the actuarial correspondence between contributions and benefits, with exceptions mainly motivated by explicit *ex ante* redistribution in favour of workers whose career is poor and/or intermittent, or more hazardous.[5] The principle reduces the scope for political interference and calls for more autonomy at the individual level. The DC pension is thus complemented by the principle of 'flexible retirement', which implies a much higher degree of freedom for the worker as to when to retire and when to start drawing from her 'accumulated' pension wealth. In practice, the law establishes a *minimum age*, which is 57 years for both men and women; a minimum period of contributions (five years); the condition that the accrued pension benefit is at least equal to 1.2 times the 'social allowance' (if the test is not met, retirement can only take place at age 65, at which age at least the social minimum is paid); adjustment of the transformation coefficients (that is the annuity coefficients to convert the contributions at retirement to the pension level) only up to 65, after which age the worker is allowed to continue, but the coefficient is no longer increased, so that working is effectively penalized. As Figure 8.2 highlights, age will be the main eligibility requirement, while seniority will lose importance.[6]

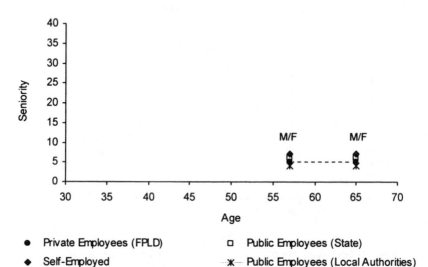

Notes:
a) Exceptions to the minimum age are possible only with 40 years of seniority (not shown in the figure).
b) _ _ _ _ _ A pension of 1.2 times the social allowance (*assegno sociale*) is needed to retire before 65.

Figure 8.2 Minimum requirements for old-age and 'seniority' pensions, main pension schemes: the 1995 NDC regime

Although it represented a strong improvement with respect to past eligibility rules, the new system is not without flaws. An important weakness is that the law does not establish an automatic revision of the minimum age in conformity to changes in longevity patterns: if 57 years could be considered appropriate as the earliest eligibility age in 1995, it will very likely be too low for 2030, not to mention for later dates. While this situation will call for discretionary changes, subject to difficult negotiations with the social parties, having the floor indexed to longevity would have made a much better stabilizer.

A second weakness is in its application. The 1995 law set a very long transition, lasting decades, during which eligibility requirements are envisaged to remain differentiated and quite complex, with changing combinations of age/seniority, with scheduled 'exit-windows' and intermittent stops. On the whole, this is a framework hardly consistent with the European targets, endorsed by the country, concerning the employment rate of older workers and the increase in the average retirement age (not to mention the sustainability problems).

8.2.1 Stylized Facts on Retirement

In a system that has been subject for more than a decade to a sequence of revisions, each one downgrading the preceding one, it is difficult to detect behavioural patterns with respect to retirement. In trying to elucidate the empirical counterpart of the changes in eligibility rules, it is useful to start by considering the yearly distributions by gender and age at retirement over the period 1985–1998. These statistics, computed from the INPS administrative archive (*estratti conto INPS*), are illustrated, for private employees and the self-employed,[7] in Figure 8.3 and in Figure 8.4 for men and women respectively.

The figures suggest a number of considerations.

First, a striking feature of the graphs is the relatively stable pattern of retirement in the 1980s compared to the marked variability of the 1990s. The year 1992 is clearly anomalous and constitutes the watershed between the two sub-periods, given that it opened the reform process, with repeated shrinkage of the previous pension promises.

Second, for men the pre-reform distributions are characterized by the typical spikes at the old-age eligibility – 60 years for employees and 65 for the self-employed. A minor spike is also detectable at 55, compatible with retirement at the (possibly minimal) requirements for a seniority pension (35 years of contributions). In 1992 there seems to be a clear 'anticipation effect': the old-age spikes remain, but the 'hump' at lower ages indicates that workers were trying to take advantage of seniority pensions whenever possible, not just at a 'round' age such as 55.

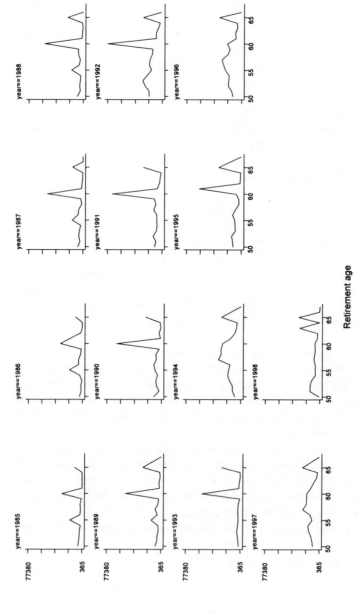

Source: INPS administrative archive (*estratti conto*), authors' own computations.

Figure 8.3 Flows of retirements by age and by year – years 1985–98 – private sector, men, old-age and seniority benefits

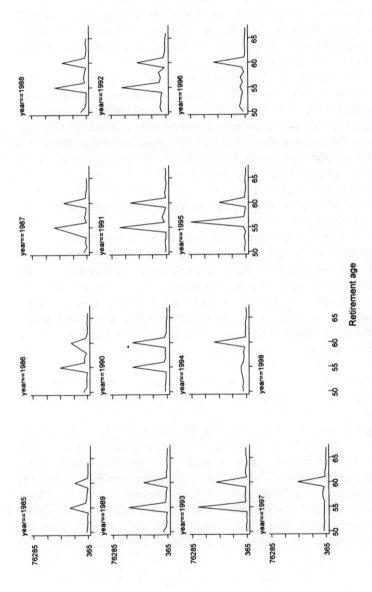

Source: INPS administrative archive (*estratti conto*), authors' own computations.

Figure 8.4 Flows of retirements by age and by year – years 1985–98 – private sector, women, old-age and seniority benefits

Third, the reform period (1993–98) is characterized by a sequence of 'stop' and 'go' intervals dictated by the law: periods when exits were frozen (as in 1993 and 1995), to limit expenditure, followed by 'windows' in which eligible workers could retire (as in 1994 and 1996).[8] Correspondingly, the figures display a less regular pattern: the spikes are less pronounced, as workers tend to anticipate retirement, in fear of new future restrictions, when a window is open. Further, due to the increase in the legal retirement age of dependent workers (which in itself increased the number of workers eligible for a seniority pensions), the spike moves to the right, so that, for example, in 1998 it is detectable at the age of 63 (for the employees), paralleling the other spike at 65 (mainly due to the self-employed).

Fourth, for women the distinction between the pre-reform and reform periods is less noticeable. The spikes in the former correspond to the old-age eligibility, respectively at 55 for the employees and 60 for the self-employed. Women could in fact access seniority pensions with greater difficulty than men because the requirement of 35 years of service was rather stringent – particularly for the cohorts near retirement age in the period under examination – given that women of those generations were unlikely to have enjoyed a continuous working career, if any at all. This also explains why in the reform period the anticipation effect is also less pronounced. On the other hand, the movement of the first spike to the right corresponds, as for men, to the gradual increase in the legal retirement age for private employees.

For both men and women, spikes at 'round' ages (55, 60 and 65) are thus consistent with widespread recourse to the old-age qualifications. As for seniority pensions, it does not seem that people retired as soon as possible, but preferred 'round' ages, which presumably acted as some 'socially shared' behavioural rules. In fact, except for the already mentioned 'anticipation effect', workers' preferences seem to cluster around them (workers retire at 60 much more than at 59, even if they can retire at the latter age, and it would be convenient for them to do so).

To give an order of magnitude, we report in Table 8.1 the exit rates up to these round ages (including age 54, meant to capture pure seniority pensions).[9]

The figures confirm the year 1992 as the demarcation line between two very different periods. The exit rates up to age 54 highlight that exits through the early-retirement provision are more a phenomenon of the reform period, than of the previous years,[10] and are more relevant for men than for women. Indeed, in the second half of the 1980s 'only' around 20 per cent of men retired younger than 55; a very approximate calculation allows us to estimate that these numbers correspond more or less to 50–60 per cent of qualified workers.[11] For women the frequency is much lower, around 12 per cent.

Table 8.1 Exit rates[a] up to the ages 54, 55, 60 and 65, percentage by gender and by year, years 1986–98, private sector

	Up to age 54		Up to age 55[b]		Up to age 60[b]		Up to age 65[b]	
	M	F	M	F	M	F	M	F
1986	15.8	12.5	32.0	55.8	84.2	92.4	100.0	99.6
1987	21.6	9.7	29.3	52.9	84.1	93.1	99.5	100.0
1988	17.8	12.1	27.2	52.1	80.1	92.5	99.1	100.0
1989	19.0	11.9	25.7	58.5	75.5	92.2	99.8	98.5
1990	19.9	7.9	24.0	45.3	81.4	92.9	99.8	99.7
1991	22.1	4.6	26.7	48.7	79.4	91.7	99.8	97.6
1992	*35.6*	*20.0*	*40.9*	*54.6*	*82.7*	*94.8*	*99.4*	*99.6*
1993	15.9	2.9	19.5	53.8	73.2	90.0	98.8	95.5
1994	21.5	27.5	27.1	34.6	75.9	93.0	99.6	99.0
1995	25.7	6.6	30.4	8.9	51.8	94.0	99.7	99.0
1996	27.3	24.9	35.0	31.7	75.8	92.8	99.4	98.0
1997	23.8	17.8	31.0	22.1	73.3	88.7	99.1	97.8
1998	28.6	9.0	33.1	13.5	57.9	95.2	98.7	97.9

Notes:
(a) Cumulative flows of exits up to age out of total exits of the year.
(b) The area in grey corresponds to cases satisfying the requisites for old-age benefits.

Source: INPS administrative archive (*estratti conto*), authors' own computations.

In 1992 the data show a jump in the cumulative exit rates for both men and women, which persists up to age 55 and, to a lesser extent, up to age 60. In the following years, cumulative exit rates reflect the 'stop and go' mechanism already highlighted by Figures 8.3 and 8.4, that is 'big escapes' in 1994 and 1996, respectively following the almost generalized freeze in 1993 and 1995. It is also worth noting, for men, the decreases of cumulative exit rates up to the age of 60 and, although on a much smaller scale, 65; for women, the rates decrease at a much slower pace.[12]

To summarize, the overall impact of the reforms on retirement behaviour is difficult to quantify,[13] and these difficulties become even stronger if we look at the *average retirement age*. According to the National Strategic Report on pensions (MSLP, 2002), the period 1994–2001 is indeed characterized, for private sector workers, by an increase in the average effective retirement age of 1.2 years (from 56.9 to 58.1).

The increase was not uniform across categories of workers, but concerned mainly some of them (Table 8.2 contains detailed information). Looking first at gender differences – in particular at the time path of female exits up to age 55 and of male exits up to age 60 – we see different exit patterns for the two genders, caused by disparities both in the careers and the legislation. As already mentioned, women have a more fragmented career, reaching the minimum seniority requirements later, and receiving the old-age pension five years before men. As a result, they generally receive the old-age pension on retirement, and have thus been hit harder than men by the increase of the minimum requirements. Considering the dependent workers versus the self-employed, the latter category (with an increase of four years in the average retirement age) has been more affected than the former (specifically FPLD workers), which in the same period experienced an increase of two years.

Table 8.2 Effective average retirement age, private sector, various years and schemes

Type of pension		1993			1997			2000			2001		
		M	F	Total	M	F	Total	M	F	Total	M	F	Total
Old-age pension	F.P.L.D.[a]	60.3	55.6	57.6	62.7	58.8	60.5	63.4	59.2	60.9	64.5	60.1	61.5
	C.D.C.M.[b]	65.0	60.2	61.7	65.1	60.3	61.6	65.1	60.3	61.5	65.1	60.2	61.2
	ART.[c]	65.0	60.4	62.8	65.1	60.4	62.7	65.1	60.3	62.7	65.1	60.2	62.5
	COMM.[d]	65.1	60.5	62.3	65.1	60.5	62.4	65.1	60.3	62.1	65.1	60.2	61.9
Seniority pension	F.P.L.D.	54.0	51.4	53.7	56.2	53.9	55.9	56.3	54.4	55.9	55.9	54.8	55.7
	C.D.C.M.	54.2	51.6	53.9	56.6	54.9	56.1	58.8	57.3	58.3	58.5	57.6	58.2
	ART.	56.3	53.1	56.2	57.0	55.0	56.9	59.0	57.6	58.9	59.0	58.0	58.9
	COMM.	56.6	52.9	56.4	57.8	55.8	57.5	59.6	57.7	59.3	59.7	58.1	59.4

Notes:
(a) Private sector employees (*Fondo Pensione Lavoratori Dipendenti*).
(b) Farmers.
(c) Craftspeople.
(d) Traders.

Source: Statistical Appendix to MLSP (2002).

As for the public sector – to which the more stringent rules applying to private sector workers have only recently been extended – statistics show an increase in the average retirement age (in Table 8.3 we concentrate on the state workers). The standardization of the rules between private and public sectors eliminated the very early-retirement phenomenon (so-called 'baby' pensioners) in the public sector and brought public employees' retirement age to the private sector value.

*Table 8.3 Public sector (*Cassa Pensioni Dipendenti Statali*) average effective retirement age, by year and gender*

	Men	Women	Total
<1990	53.4	52.8	53.1
1990	57.0	56.1	56.5
1991	56.5	55.6	56.1
1992	56.6	55.3	55.9
1993	57.9	56.5	57.2
1994	55.0	54.8	54.9
1995	58.2	58.1	58.2
1996	56.7	57.4	57.1
1997	54.5	55.3	54.8
1998	56.8	57.5	57.2
1999	56.2	56.9	56.6
2000	57.6	57.8	57.7
2001	59.5	59.5	59.5
2002	59.9	60.3	60.1

Source: INPDAP (2001).

8.3   A MICRO-ECONOMETRIC ANALYSIS

The picture of the 1990s is thus dominated by two contrasting factors: an unstable normative framework, urging people to exit as soon as possible, and the expectation of lower benefits, due if not to a modification in the formula (which changed very slowly because of the long transition) at least to the downgrading in benefit indexation, from wages to prices, in force since 1992. On the one hand, recourse to 'exit-windows' effectively limited the possibility to retire; on the other, individuals had to revise their expectations and, as a consequence, their plans for retirement.

In order to interpret retirement choices and to understand the likely changes induced by reform, one should estimate a model in a relatively steady period and apply the estimated parameters in order to simulate behaviour in the future, different environment (Heyma, 2001). In this section we present the first step, by performing an econometric study of the individuals' decision. The second step, based on a simulation exercise, is described in section 8.4.

The econometric analysis is performed over the period 1985–91, as it seems reasonable to assume that in those years the pension reforms were not (fully) anticipated. It follows that it can be assumed that in the sample period workers understood the rules determining their pension benefit and on the basis of this knowledge – as well as conditionally to other characteristics known to the workers, such as the earnings career and other demographic features – workers effectively chose when to retire from work and access pension benefits.[14]

The main task of this analysis is the study of the factors determining the individuals' retirement choice; we make use of a sample drawn from the INPS archive to study this choice as a function of money's worth measures and demographic variables.[15]

8.3.1 Money's Worth Measures and Their Changes

Eligibility conditions only define, in econometric terms, 'the individual at risk', who can choose to retire or, conversely, continue working. After having passed the threshold, the worker has to take this decision, possibly by taking into account a set of variables, ranging from the employer's attitude to her health status, from family dimensions to monetary evaluation of the retirement option. In the present work, due to severe limitations in the available dataset, we disregard both the employer's role and worker's personal characteristics, and confine the analysis to *money's worth measures*, limiting the family dimension to the inclusion of survivor benefits in calculation.

We define pension wealth for a worker of age a who will claim her first benefit at age A as the present value of future pension benefits minus the present value of the contributions to the scheme to be paid in before retirement:

$$SSW_a^A = \sum_{i=A}^{T} P_i^A \, \eta_i (1+r)^{-(i-a)} - \sum_{j=a}^{A} c_j \, (1+r)^{-(j-a)}$$

where a is the age of the worker at the time of the computation of pension wealth, P_i^A is the pension benefit to be paid, at the end of each year, to the retired worker from age A as long as she is alive; T is maximum age, c_j is contributions paid at age j, η_i is the probability of being alive at age i, conditional on being alive at age A (assuming that life in the working period is certain).[16] In the period 1985–91 the pension benefits were indexed to wage growth; as indexation was not complete, though, it has been assumed that pensions were increased by a factor equal to 60 per cent of the real wage growth (the latter assumed equal to 1.5 per cent).[17]

As for marginal measures, the *accrual* is defined as the difference between the pension wealth for a worker retiring at age $A + 1$ and the pension wealth for retiring at age A. When the evaluation time coincides with the age of retirement ($a = A$) this is equal to:

$$Accr_A = SSW_A^{A+1} - SSW_A^A$$

In the definition, we assume that labour income and the disutility of work compensate each other, so that the computation takes into account only the variations in the length of retirement, in the pension level and in contributions, all due to the additional year of work. A negative accrual means that the increase in the pension benefit is insufficient to offset the costs of postponement, thus inflicting an implicit tax on the continuation of work. Consequently, we can define a *tax rate* as follows:

$$T_A = \frac{-Accr_A}{\overline{w}_A}$$

that is, minus the ratio of the accrual to labour income. In our computations, we define labour income at age A as an average of the three last wages:

$$\overline{w}_A = \frac{\sum_{i=0}^{2} w_{A-i}}{3}$$

In general terms, the econometric model for the retirement choice should include both overall and marginal money's worth measures. Under the hypothesis that leisure, even in retirement, is a normal good, the former provides a useful proxy to evaluate *income effects*, while the latter captures the *substitution effect*. In this perspective, a 'generous' system – where the generosity is measured in terms of pension wealth – would be characterized, with respect to a less generous system, by a lower average retirement age. The same would be true of a system entailing a high implicit tax rate.

These features (the overall generosity and the deadweight losses) were indeed a hallmark of the Italian DB pension system, while – as already stressed in the first section – the new DC formula will be both fairer and more neutral with respect to the retirement choice. As it stands, however, due to the long transition, the system still is, and will be for some decades, very far from neutral.

8.3.2 Dataset and Sample Selection

We study the retirement decision using a sample of administrative data, drawn from the INPS archive (*estratti conto*), which officially records the complete earnings and contribution histories of all participants, that is employees in the private sector and some categories of self-employed (craftspeople, tradespeople and farmers). The available sample is formed by all individuals born on 5 March – so that the theoretical sample frequency is 1:365 – and reports spells from 1985 to 1998. The archive contains rich information about the earnings histories of the workers covered, and shows when a worker actually retires, as well as the kind of benefit (old-age/seniority, survivor, disability) he is actually receiving. This information, lacking in other administrative samples, makes the '*estratti conto*' archive particularly useful when studying the retirement decision.

As typical with administrative data, demographic information is, on the other hand, less rich: the sample records the date and the province of birth of the worker, and gender. No information about the family status is available, nor about the education level of the worker.

We include in our analysis all private sector employees; self-employed workers and individuals in other minor schemes are conversely excluded. As mentioned above, the sample selected for the analysis covers the years 1985 to 1991.[18]

In order to compute individual pension wealth and money's worth measures, an ad hoc methodology has been developed; this procedure, described in the next two sub-sections, allows pensionable earnings and the number of working years for each individual in the sample to be computed.

Pensionable earnings
In order to build pensionable earnings (that is the average of the last five years of earnings) all the workers in the sample for whom earnings are observed for at least two years between 1985 and 1991 have been selected.[19] For a fraction of individuals, earnings can be actually observed for five years, meaning that pensionable earnings are effectively observed. For the others, it is necessary to reconstruct past earnings: it is then assumed that past earnings are equal to current earnings minus the average wage growth in the intervening period.[20]

As the change in pension wealth deriving from postponing retirement for one year (accrual) is also a variable of interest, it is necessary to make some assumption about how individuals forecast their future salary – in case they decide to remain active for a further year. To this end, we assume that the statistical process underlying individual wages is a random walk process, so that individuals' forecast for next year wage is equal to their current wage.

Number of working years

In order to study individuals' retirement choice it is crucial to select a sample of individuals who actually can, given current legislation, retire and access pension benefits. Therefore, the definition of the 'sample at risk' depends on the pension legislation active in the period of interest. In the years 1985–91, legislation for private sector employees allowed workers to claim old-age pension benefits at the statutory retirement age (60 years for men, 55 for women) provided the worker had contributed to the scheme for at least 15 years. In addition, workers who had contributed to the scheme for at least 35 years could claim the benefit (seniority pension) irrespective of their age.

In the INPS archive the number of years a worker has contributed before 1985 (that is, tenure in the pension scheme at 1985) is not reported; it follows that this information, crucial both to define the sample at risk and to compute pension wealth, has to be reconstructed using alternative data sources.

The procedure implemented to impute tenure at 1985 to each worker in the sample makes use of the average age of entry in the labour market computed – for each cohort, gender and occupation – on the basis of the Bank of Italy survey (Survey of Households' Income and Wealth, SHIW). Each individual in the sample is assigned his group-specific age of entry and, assuming a continuous career until 1985, his tenure in the pension scheme at 1985 is computed. From 1985 onwards, the actual increase in tenure is observed for each worker in the sample. If the observed behaviour of the worker is in contrast to his imputed tenure – for example because he receives unemployment allowance when, according to imputed tenure, he could claim an old-age benefit – imputed tenure at 1985 is corrected, following the procedure described in Box 8.1.

Selected sample

After selection, the sample used in the econometric analysis consists of 1802 males and 467 females. As a number of workers defer retirement (after having met the requirements to claim a pension benefit), there are in total 5023 observations for males and 1015 for females.

Figure 8.5 shows the observed hazard rates computed for the selected sample, separately for men and women. Spikes at legal retirement age (55 years for women, 60 years for men) can be observed. In addition, there is a spike at 65 for men. It should also be noted that in the sample there are no women claiming pension benefits before age 55 (that is, no seniority pensions are observed). This feature of the data emphasizes the fact that for women the 35-year tenure required to claim seniority pensions was indeed binding; on the other hand, women could – and did – claim the old-age benefit five years younger than men.

BOX 8.1 IMPUTING TENURE IN THE PENSION SCHEME AT 1985

A three-step procedure is used to impute tenure in the pension scheme which makes use both of the information available in the INPS archive and of the average age at entry in the labour market computed – for each cohort, gender and occupation – using the Bank of Italy survey.

1) The procedure starts by imputing a tenure at 1985 for each worker in the INPS archive. Tenure is computed according to group-specific average age at entry in the labour market for each individual, where groups are defined by cohort, gender and occupation (white/blue collar). Average age at entry is computed using the Bank of Italy survey. At this stage, individuals are assumed to have continuously contributed to the pension scheme until 1985. For example, a blue-collar male, born in 1935 and observed in the INPS archive for the first time in 1985 is attributed a tenure at 1985 equal to: 1985 – (1935 + age at entry), where age at entry is the average age at entry for the group this individual belongs to.

2) Since 1985 it is possible to impute tenure in the pension scheme on the basis of the observed behaviour of each worker. In other words, each individual is followed through time until she retires and tenure is increased on the basis of the actual spells the worker contributes to the scheme (that is, spells in which the individual works, receives contribution-covered unemployment benefits, pays in voluntary contributions). At this stage it is possible to define individuals at risk – that is workers who have the right to claim a pension benefit. For each worker, only observations (years) in which she is actually at risk will be included in the analysis of the determinants of retirement.

3) In the final step, imputed tenure at 1985 is corrected by observing the behaviour of those individuals who were defined at risk in the previous step. In particular, if for an individual who can claim a pension benefit (according to tenure computed in step 2) spells of unemployment are observed, tenure is reduced; after this reduction the worker enters the sample at risk only after being employed again (or after having met the age requirement for the old-age benefit).

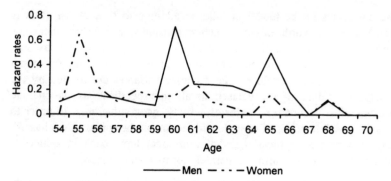

Figure 8.5 Hazard rates, men and women

8.3.3 The Econometric Model

The econometric model is specified as a discrete time duration model. This specification seems appropriate in the light of the data used in the analysis (panel, with yearly observations) and of the 'definitive choice' characterizing retirement in the Italian legislation, which did not allow any possibility to work after retirement.

The rationale in this model is to study how much time workers delay retirement after they are eligible, according to the law, to claim pension benefits. Individual information in the sample has been organized to yield yearly observations: each year, at 31 December, each eligible worker decides whether to retire and to claim the benefit in the subsequent year or to remain active in the labour market (see Box 8.2 for a detailed exposition of the timing).

The econometric specification chosen is a discrete-time, proportional hazard rate with a logistic distribution, where the hazard for individual i at time j is:

$$h_j(X_{ij}) = \frac{1}{1 + \exp(-f(d) - X'_{ij}\beta)} \qquad (8.1)$$

where X_{ij} is a set of covariates, β are the coefficients of interest and the function $f(d)$ captures how the hazard rate depends on duration d (that is, the time the eligible individual spends on the labour market).

The function $f(d)$ can be specified in various different ways: for example it could be specified as the logarithm of duration (and in this case the model is a discrete version of the continuous-time Weibull model), as a polynomy in duration or as a non-parametric specification, which introduces dummy variables for each time at risk.[21]

The covariates in the model include, in addition to time at risk (that is duration), money's worth measures such as pension wealth (which measures the overall financial incentive to retire) and the accrual or the tax rate alternatively (which measure the marginal incentive).[22] In addition, the model includes demographic variables, whose choice variables are limited by the administrative nature of the dataset; in all the specifications we include cohort dummies, occupation, sector of activity, geographic area. In order to capture the possible effect of unexplained factors on the spikes in the hazard, dummy variables at 'typical' ages of retirement have been introduced.[23] Finally, estimates are performed separately for men and women.

BOX 8.2 TIMING

In order to organize the data into yearly observations, the following assumptions have been made:

1) In each calendar year, workers who are active for less than three months are registered as unemployed.

2) Pension benefits claimed in the first half of the year are registered as claimed on 1 January of the same year; pension benefits claimed in the second half of the year are registered as claimed on 1 January of the subsequent year.

   Timing: Every year, on 31 December each worker decides whether she prefers to retire and claim the pension benefit or to continue to work in the subsequent year. Contribution or benefit payments take place each year at 31 December. Workers are defined at risk if they have accumulated 35 years of contribution by 31 December, or they will meet the age requirement on 5 March of the subsequent year (as this is the requirement for eligibility for the old-age benefit, in addition to 15 years of contribution). This definition of eligibility follows from the fact that the available sample includes all workers born on 5 March. Graphically:

31/12/t		31/12/t+1
35th year of contrib.	5/3/t+1	

In the above example the worker contributes for the 35th year during year t; consequently, this worker can claim the pension benefit at 31 December of year t. If he actually chooses to retire, from 1 January of year t+1 he is retired and will be paid his benefit at 31 December of the year t+1. In addition, a worker who meets the age requirement on 5 March of year t+1 can claim his benefit at 31 December of year t.

8.3.4 Results

Table 8.4 reports averages of the variables used in estimation, computed for the selected sample of workers at the first available observation (after the worker is actually classified as at risk). The table shows average pension wealth, average accrual and average tax rate, computed as described above.

Table 8.4 Sample description: averages at entry in risk sample

	Men	Women
Accrual	−0.103	−0.040
Pension wealth (SSW)	5.665	4.135
Tax rate	0.301	0.280
Replacement rate	0.690	0.710
Wage	0.347	0.251
Age	56.69	55.85
Meet old-age requirement	0.143	1.000
Years of contribution	35.446	33.585
Occupation		
Blue collar	0.840	0.715
White collar	0.160	0.285
Year of birth (cohort)		
Cohort 1: 1921–25	0.031	0.039
Cohort 2: 1926–30	0.292	0.133
Cohort 3: 1931–35	0.498	0.574
Cohort 4: 1936–40	0.179	0.255
Sector of activity		
Energy	0.011	0.002
Mining	0.130	0.045
Metallurgic	0.201	0.084
Textile and clothing	0.168	0.203
Building	0.125	0.013
Commerce	0.110	0.169
Transport	0.044	0.009
Bank and credit	0.045	0.090
Other	0.166	0.385
Geographical area		
North-West	0.411	0.460
North-East	0.204	0.178
Centre	0.225	0.242
South and Islands	0.160	0.120
Number of individuals	1802	467

Note: Monetary variables are expressed in hundred millions lire, base year 1995.

The accrual is negative on average both for men and women, showing an average reduction in pension wealth – deriving from a one-year postponement of retirement – equal to 10.3 million lire (about 5300 euros) for men and to 4 million lire for women (about 2070 euros, at 1995 prices). The tax rate is on average positive and equal to 30 per cent for men and to 28 per cent for women. Pension wealth is on average equal to about 570 million lire for men and to 400 million lire for women: this difference reflects both the lower average wage for women (about 35 million lire for men, 25 for women), which implies lower pensionable earnings, and a number of contribution years lower on average.[24]

The variable *meets old-age requirement* shows the proportion of workers who meet the age requirement to claim an old-age benefit when they enter the sample at risk: this proportion is equal to 14 per cent for men and to 100 per cent for women, as already noted in Figure 8.5. The averages of the dummy variables for occupation, sector of activity, cohort and geographical area show the proportion of workers in each group.

Estimated results are shown in Tables 8.5 to 8.7. In Table 8.5 coefficients of equation (8.1) estimated on the sub-sample for men are reported. The variable registering the duration in the state at risk enters with a logarithmic specification.

In the specifications presented in columns (i) and (iii) the marginal incentive indicator included is the accrual, while in columns (ii) and (iv) the tax rate has been included. Both specifications include pension wealth and the individual variables described above.

The estimates reported in columns (i) and (ii) contain, among the explanatory variables, age dummies at 60 and 65, while estimates in columns (iii) e (iv) omit these variables. In every specification the effect of the marginal incentive indicator, accrual or tax rate, is not significantly different from zero. On the other hand, the pension wealth coefficient is positive and significantly different from zero: pension wealth positively affects the probability of retirement.[25] As for the other variables, being white collar (excluded category: blue collar) lowers the probability of retirement, as does being employed in the Centre or in the South of Italy. Finally, the pseudo R^2 in the specifications with age dummies (columns (i) and (ii)) is substantially higher with respect to the specifications without age dummies: this feature indicates how the variables included in the models (iii) and (iv) are not able to capture the spikes at typical ages in the hazard rate.[26] This reduction of fit is also evident in Figure 8.6, where the predicted hazard rates are shown, for specification (i) and (iii).

Table 8.5 Probability of retirement: men

	(i) Coeff. (*std.err.*)	(ii) Coeff. (*std.err.*)	(iii) Coeff. (*std.err.*)	(iv) Coeff. (*std.err.*)
Accrual	0.338	-	0.226	-
	(0.26)	-	(0.21)	-
Tax rate	-	−0.047	-	−0.046
	-	(0.09)	-	(0.07)
SSW	0.069	0.063	0.016	0.012
	(0.03)	(0.02)	(0.02)	(0.02)
Log (time at risk)	0.916	0.914	1.389	1.388
	(0.09)	(0.09)	(0.10)	(0.10)
Age 60	2.833	2.831	-	-
	(0.12)	(0.12)	-	-
Age 65	1.620	1.604	-	-
	(0.32)	(0.32)	-	-
Cohort 2	−0.418	−0.396	0.390	0.404
	(0.23)	(0.23)	(0.19)	(0.19)
Cohort 3	−0.429	−0.402	0.113	0.129
	(0.23)	(0.23)	(0.20)	(0.20)
Cohort 4	−0.132	−0.100	0.304	0.323
	(0.28)	(0.28)	(0.26)	(0.26)
White collar	−0.264	−0.264	0.098	0.097
	(0.15)	(0.15)	(0.12)	(0.12)
Energy	0.136	0.117	0.134	0.122
	(0.58)	(0.59)	(0.45)	(0.45)
Mining	0.584	0.586	0.345	0.347
	(0.15)	(0.15)	(0.12)	(0.12)
Metallurgic	0.794	0.796	0.498	0.500
	(0.14)	(0.14)	(0.12)	(0.12)
Textile and clothing	0.312	0.307	0.160	0.159
	(0.14)	(0.14)	(0.11)	(0.11)
Building	−0.043	−0.040	0.069	0.071
	(0.13)	(0.13)	(0.12)	(0.12)
Commerce	0.070	0.069	−0.011	−0.011
	(0.15)	(0.15)	(0.12)	(0.12)
Transport	−0.333	−0.328	−0.293	−0.291
	(0.21)	(0.21)	(0.16)	(0.16)
Bank and credit	−0.007	−0.019	0.032	0.024
	(0.21)	(0.20)	(0.18)	(0.17)
North-East	−0.172	−0.170	−0.037	−0.036
	(0.11)	(0.11)	(0.09)	(0.09)
Centre	−0.471	−0.471	−0.300	−0.300
	(0.11)	(0.11)	(0.09)	(0.09)
South and islands	−0.437	−0.436	−0.235	−0.234
	(0.12)	(0.12)	(0.10)	(0.10)
Number of obs.	5023	5023	5023	5023
Pseudo R^2	0.254	0.254	0.103	0.103
Log likelihood	−1948.9	−1949.8	−2343.3	−2343.7

Note: Clustering-adjusted standard errors in parenthesis. Excluded categories: cohort 1, blue collar, sector of activity 'other', region North-West.

Table 8.6 Probability of retirement: women

	(i) Coeff. (*std.err.*)	(ii) Coeff. (*std.err.*)	(iii) Coeff. (*std.err.*)	(iv) Coeff. (*std.err.*)
Accrual	−1.066	-	−1.093	-
	(0.66)	-	*(0.63)*	-
Tax rate	-	0.102	-	0.107
	-	*(0.14)*	-	*(0.13)*
SSW	0.144	0.160	0.148	0.163
	(0.06)	*(0.06)*	*(0.06)*	*(0.05)*
Log (time at risk)	0.723	0.736	−0.899	−0.894
	(0.22)	*(0.23)*	*(0.14)*	*(0.14)*
Age 55	2.961	2.964	-	-
	(0.36)	*(0.36)*	-	-
Cohort 2	0.333	0.295	0.211	0.181
	(0.42)	*(0.43)*	*(0.50)*	*(0.51)*
Cohort 3	0.659	0.606	1.175	1.117
	(0.43)	*(0.44)*	*(0.49)*	*(0.50)*
Cohort 4	0.727	0.599	1.605	1.468
	(0.50)	*(0.50)*	*(0.53)*	*(0.53)*
White collar	−0.348	−0.397	−0.389	−0.439
	(0.20)	*(0.19)*	*(0.20)*	*(0.20)*
Energy	-	-	-	-
	-	-	-	-
Mining	0.296	0.257	0.187	0.153
	(0.46)	*(0.46)*	*(0.41)*	*(0.41)*
Metallurgic	0.684	0.662	0.503	0.484
	(0.39)	*(0.38)*	*(0.34)*	*(0.34)*
Textile and clothing	0.630	0.641	0.648	0.661
	(0.24)	*(0.24)*	*(0.25)*	*(0.25)*
Building	1.471	1.499	1.227	1.255
	(0.73)	*(0.73)*	*(0.92)*	*(0.91)*
Commerce	0.318	0.328	0.299	0.312
	(0.22)	*(0.22)*	*(0.23)*	*(0.23)*
Transport	0.740	0.794	0.602	0.655
	(0.54)	*(0.53)*	*(0.75)*	*(0.75)*
Bank and credit	0.056	0.046	0.074	0.068
	(0.29)	*(0.29)*	*(0.30)*	*(0.30)*
North-East	0.058	0.048	0.198	0.188
	(0.23)	*(0.23)*	*(0.24)*	*(0.24)*
Centre	−0.338	−0.340	−0.320	−0.322
	(0.22)	*(0.22)*	*(0.22)*	*(0.22)*
South and islands	−0.657	−0.663	−0.674	−0.674
	(0.27)	*(0.27)*	*(0.27)*	*(0.27)*
Number of obs.	1011	1011	1011	1011
Pseudo R^2	0.254	0.252	0.177	0.175
Log likelihood	−477.7	−478.7	−526.7	−527.9

Note: Clustering-adjusted standard errors in parenthesis. Excluded categories: cohort 1, blue collar, sector of activity 'other', region North-West.

Table 8.7 Probability of retirement: pension wealth

	Men		Women	
	Coeff. *(std.err.)*	Coeff. *(std.err.)*	Coeff. *(std.err.)*	Coeff. *(std.err.)*
Accrual 1	−0.242	-	3.788	-
	(0.58)	-	*(1.63)*	-
Accrual 2	−0.075	-	−2.122	-
	(0.73)	-	*(1.23)*	-
Accrual 3	1.370	-	−3.186	-
	(0.58)	-	*(1.72)*	-
Accrual 4	0.251	-	−1.358	-
	(0.36)	-	*(0.93)*	-
Tax subsidy 1	-	0.101	-	−0.337
	-	*(0.13)*	-	*(0.21)*
Tax subsidy 2	-	0.030	-	0.491
	-	*(0.19)*	-	*(0.27)*
Tax subsidy 3	-	−0.433	-	0.977
	-	*(0.21)*	-	*(0.48)*
Tax subsidy 4	-	−0.045	-	0.649
	-	*(0.20)*	-	*(0.34)*
SSW 1	0.041	0.034	−0.022	−0.002
	(0.07)	*(0.07)*	*(0.23)*	*(0.24)*
SSW 2	0.077	0.073	0.036	0.037
	(0.06)	*(0.06)*	*(0.15)*	*(0.15)*
SSW 3	0.090	0.085	0.046	0.042
	(0.05)	*(0.05)*	*(0.12)*	*(0.12)*
SSW 4	0.065	0.061	0.061	0.057
	(0.03)	*(0.03)*	*(0.09)*	*(0.09)*
Log (time at risk)	0.913	0.912	0.656	0.683
	(0.09)	*(0.09)*	*(0.23)*	*(0.23)*
Age 55	-	-	2.898	2.917
	-	-	*(0.37)*	*(0.37)*
Age 60	2.848	2.847	-	-
	(0.12)	*(0.12)*	-	-
Age 65	1.613	1.606	-	-
	(0.32)	*(0.32)*	-	-
Number of obs.	5023	5023	1011	1011
Pseudo R^2	0.255	0.255	0.263	0.263
Log likelihood	−1945.4	−1946.4	−471.6	−471.5

Note: Clustering-adjusted standard errors in parenthesis. Excluded categories: cohort 1, blue collar, sector of activity 'other', region North-West. Coefficients for cohort, occupation, sector of activity and regional area dummies not reported.

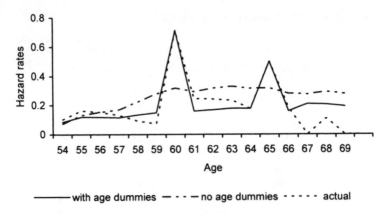

Figure 8.6 Predicted versus actual hazard rates: men

Table 8.6 reports results of similar specifications estimated on the sample of women. In this sample the marginal incentives display the sign predicted by the theory, although they are not precisely estimated (the coefficient relative to the accrual in specification (i) is negative with a p-value equal to 0.11; the tax rate displays a positive coefficient but it is not significantly different from zero). On the other hand, pension wealth still has a positive and significant effect on the probability of retirement, while being a white collar, employed in the Centre-South reduces this probability. The exclusion of the age 55 dummy brings a deep reduction in the pseudo R^2 (although less strong with respect to men). Figure 8.7 reports the predicted hazard rates for models (i) and (iii) in Table 8.6.

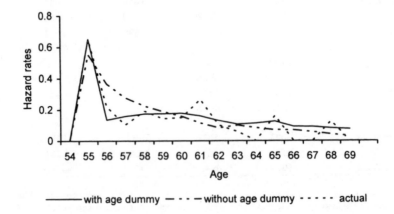

Figure 8.7 Predicted versus actual hazard rates: women

Table 8.7 shows estimates for specifications that allow the coefficients over the marginal financial incentives and the pension wealth to vary across different quartiles.[27]

For example, the variable 'accrual 1' is the accrual for those workers who belong to the first quartile of the pension wealth distribution, while it is equal to zero for all the other workers belonging to different quartiles.

The presented specifications include legal age dummy variables, for both men and women. Results show that in the sample of men the marginal financial indicators – both the accrual and the tax rate, columns (i) and (ii) – have an effect which is not different from zero in every pension wealth quartile; women, on the contrary, display a coefficient which has the opposite sign as predicted by the theory in the first quartile (and it is significantly different from zero), while in the other quartiles the coefficients for both accrual and tax rate have the sign predicted by the theory and are significantly different from zero. On the other hand, the coefficients on pension wealth are not precisely estimated.

8.3.5 Comments

The analysis performed enables us to characterize the individual's retirement choice over the period 1985–91, a period in which pension eligibility and computation rules were known and (perceived as) stable. This exercise, per se interesting, enables us to evaluate the effect of pension reforms, applying the estimated model to different pension rules. Before performing such an exercise, it seems useful to summarize the main results obtained so far.

The estimates of the retirement choice show how pension wealth, which is a global incentive indicator, displays a positive and significantly different from zero effect on the probability to retire in all the specifications. The marginal incentive indicator coefficients (accrual and tax rate) are estimated, in the sample of men, to be of the opposite sign with respect to the theory prediction, although they are never significantly different from zero. On the other hand, estimates performed on the sample of women display an effect of the marginal indicators of the same sign as predicted by the theory, although this is not always precisely estimated. Spikes in the hazard rates, in particular corresponding to legal ages for claiming old-age benefits (age 55 for women, 60 for men), are not adequately captured by the model. This is true in particular in the sample of men, who display two spikes (age 60 and age 65) which are not captured unless age dummies are included in the specification. Two effects seem at work: an effect due to the legal age of retirement, and a sort of rule of thumb (acting as a social norm) applied by some individuals when choosing to retire.

In sum, these estimates suggest that workers tend to retire, conditional on their pension wealth, at typical ages, rather than being sensitive to marginal incentives. This feature renders the evaluation of future reforms in terms of retirement behaviour quite delicate, as only changes in pension wealth and in eligibility requirements, as opposed to changes in marginal effect, will have an effect on retirement. This issue will be extensively discussed in the next section.

Among the other variables that have an influence on the probability of retirement, being a white collar worker or being resident in the Centre-South reduces, *ceteris paribus*, the probability of retirement.

It is also important to recall that the estimated models suffer from some limitations, due to the data source used. In particular, information on individual characteristics which may influence the choice to retire is not available: for example health status or spouse's characteristics are not observed.[28] An additional limitation is the non-observability of tenure in the pension scheme: as described above, an ad hoc procedure (certainly not error-free) has been implemented in order to build tenure at entry in the sample. The assumptions made have an effect not only on the computed pension wealth (and, as a consequence, on the marginal indicators), but also on the sample-at-risk definition. Besides these limitations, the dataset used offers, in addition to very detailed and precise information on the workers' employment periods and wages, the possibility to observe who actually retires and claims a pension benefit.

In the Italian literature on retirement choice, the studies which are closer to the present one are Brugiavini and Peracchi (2001 and 2003), who use INPS archives (O1M) to estimate the probability of exit out of the labour force for older individuals. However, the O1M archives do not show why an individual exits the labour force (to claim a pension benefit, because unemployed or for other reasons). In addition, those archives do not report on tenure in a pension scheme.

Other studies (see in particular Miniaci, 1998; Spataro, 2000a and 2002; Colombino, 2002; and Mastrogiacomo, 2002) use the Bank of Italy sample[29] to estimate retirement choice models. Miniaci (1998) studies the effect of socio-economic and demographic variables on the individual probability to retire: in particular, the education level turns out to be an important determinant of this probability, and workers with a higher level of education tend to retire later.[30] Mastrogiacomo (2002) studies the joint retirement decision for couples and shows how this decision can depend upon family dynamics. It should be borne in mind, however, that all the studies about retirement behaviour conducted upon the Bank of Italy surveys refer to a historical period characterized by an extensive change in the legislation of pensions (that is, the 1990s); interpreting those results therefore requires great caution.

8.3.6 The Effect of a Change in SSW

To evaluate the effect of a change in pension wealth implied by the above estimates, it is of interest to simulate the effect induced by a change in the benefit indexation rule. This kind of reform has actually been implemented in 1992, as part of the pension reform designed in that year. In particular, as already mentioned, in 1992 the indexation of benefits was downgraded from wages to prices. Apart from the fact that this was the only restrictive measure also applied to pensioners, it is plausible that workers 'understood' its bearing in terms of a reduction in pension wealth.

According to our previous estimates, this should have lowered the probability of retirement, which is positively influenced by pension wealth. We have thus estimated the effects of the implied cut on the probability of retirement, trying to separate the consequence of the change in indexation from the others set by the reforms.

To perform this exercise, the same sample used in estimation is employed, together with the parameter estimates of the model including the accrual as marginal indicator, i.e. model (i) in Table 8.5 and Table 8.6 (for men and women respectively). Figures 8.8–8.11 show the average effect of the change in the indexation mechanism on the stock of pension wealth and on the accrual, for men and women. In general, the change in the indexation rule brings a reduction in pension wealth of about 12 per cent at younger ages (54/55 years) and of about 8 per cent at older ages; a 20 per cent increase in the accrual is observed for men aged 54/55, while the increase for women aged 55 is in the order of 30 per cent. Nonetheless, the price-linked accrual is negative or, at most, close to zero.

Table 8.8 shows the predicted hazard rates from the estimated models in Table 8.5 (i) and 8.6 (i) for men and women respectively. The model predicts that the change in the indexation rule lowers the probability of retirement by 0.45 percentage points for men aged 54/55 (that is a 4 per cent reduction in the hazard rate). The reduction in the probability of retirement for men is equal to 0.65 percentage points at age 60, and it becomes lower at higher ages. In the sample for women the effect of the policy is stronger: the hazard rate at age 55 is lowered by 1.8 percentage points, while the reduction is about 1.2 percentage points at 56/60. At higher ages the effect is reduced.

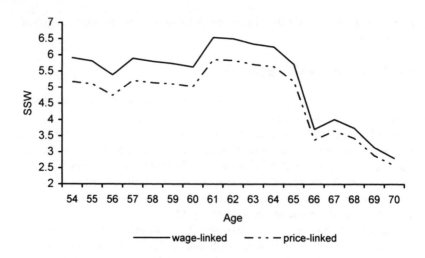

Note: SSW is expressed in hundreds million lire (1995 prices).

Figure 8.8 Effect of change in benefit indexation – men – SSW age profile

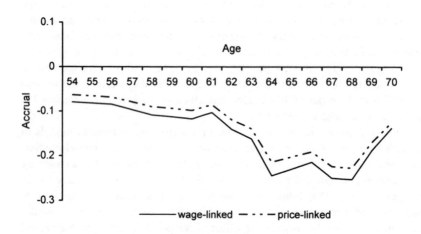

Note: Accrual is expressed in hundreds million lire (1995 prices).

Figure 8.9 Effect of change in benefit indexation – men – accrual age profile

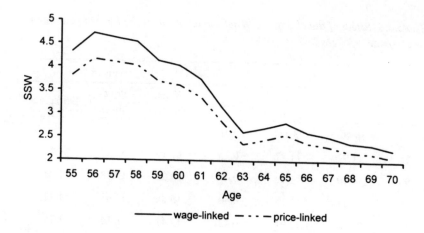

Note: SSW is expressed in hundreds million lire (1995 prices).

Figure 8.10 Effect of change in benefit indexation – women – SSW age profile

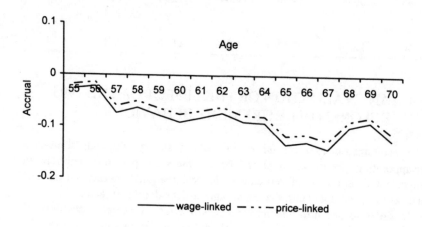

Note: Accrual is expressed in hundreds million lire (1995 prices).

Figure 8.11 Effect of change in benefit indexation – women – accrual age profile

Table 8.8 Effect of the change in benefit indexation on the hazard rate: men and women

	Men			Women		
Age	Wage-linked	Price-linked	Difference	Wage-linked	Price-linked	Difference
54	8.46	8.11	0.35	-	-	-
55	11.92	11.47	0.45	65.19	63.42	1.77
56	11.90	11.49	0.41	13.52	12.48	1.04
57	11.54	11.15	0.40	15.84	14.63	1.22
58	13.34	12.91	0.43	17.41	16.16	1.25
59	14.84	14.38	0.46	17.56	16.38	1.18
60	71.37	70.72	0.64	17.81	16.64	1.17
61	15.92	15.38	0.54	16.06	15.08	0.98
...	...	...	...	...	...	...
65	50.00	49.36	0.64	12.54	11.93	0.61
...	...	...	...	...	...	...
70	22.70	22.52	0.18	11.10	10.71	0.39

8.4   AN EVALUATION OF THE EFFECT OF THE 1995 REFORM ON RETIREMENT BEHAVIOUR

The econometric exercise leaves us with a strong, although somewhat disappointing (from our 'a priori' belief) message: pension wealth is an important determinant of retirement choices; marginal measures (accruals and tax rates) do not count; the 'legal' ages are the dominant factor.

In order to see how the new rules will affect workers' probability of retirement at the various ages, we exploited the parameters derived from the econometric model as inputs in a simulation model. We performed such a simulation exercise both in the transition and in the new NDC regime and – perhaps not too surprisingly – found very limited effects of reforms on retirement probabilities, and thus a very modest increase in the average retirement age.

This rather poor performance may have its roots in the main limitations of our simulation strategy. First, as our dataset did not include information on personal (such as health status) or family (such as the spouse's occupational status) characteristics, we were forced to exclude from the analysis important non-financial variables and family considerations, and to restrict it to money's worth measures. Moreover, given the estimates obtained by the econometric model, we had to concentrate on Social Security wealth, excluding the marginal measures (in particular the tax rate), which had proved largely insignificant. Finally, we inevitably dragged into future scenarios the powerful role of the age dummies in explaining retirement in the reference period. If all these are important limitations, the last one points to a possible 'regime change' in retirement behaviour since in the future NDC regime the 'normal' ages would give way to the principle of flexible retirement (with flexibility corresponding to an actuarially equivalent variation in the pension benefit). Consequently, one should not expect 'typical' retirement ages, but possibly a more uniform distribution, at least in the age band between 57 (the EEA) and 65 (the upper limit for the revision of the transformation coefficients). Of course, how workers will react to the loss of reference points is a question beyond the scope of this work, on which only conjectures are possible.

The simulation had to solve three main problems: the need to control for the growth-induced increase in wealth of successive generations; how to deal with the parameters capturing the spikes at the ages 55, 60 and 65; how to account for any change in behaviour due to the progressive disappearance of the 'implicit taxes' on continuing work, given that, according to our estimation, these losses did not count in the period when they were present and high.

We based the simulation on a set of representative workers identified by a few characteristics, such as gender, cohort (from 1945 to 1980), occupation (white and blue collars), sector of employment (industry, manufacturing, services, other), geographical area (North-East, North-West, Centre, South and islands of Italy) and income percentile (25th, 50th and 75th). The high level of disaggregation and the consequent high number of individuals we distinguished should make the set of representative agents a good substitute of the sample used in the econometric exercise.[31]

We worked through three steps: the estimation of the individual lifetime earnings profile; the computation of the Social Security wealth and, finally, of the hazard rates.

We estimated wage profiles on a sub-sample of workers selected from the INPS administrative archive performing three quantile regressions (the median worker and the 25th and the 75th percentile), separately for men and women.[32] We assumed continuous working careers, starting at age 22 for every individual: the first assumption implies an overestimation of seniority; the second should somehow counterbalance this upward bias, by imposing a later entry into the labour market, with respect to what descriptive statistics show.[33]

We then used a simulation model[34] to compute the Social Security wealth at retirement for the set of representative individuals and for every possible retirement age.[35] We chose a model specification with dummies at age 60 and 65 for men and at age 55 for women. In this way, we implicitly assumed the hazard structure of retirement as defined only by preferences; in other words, we assumed these ages to represent 'rules of thumb' or 'socially accepted' ages.[36] As a consequence, our analysis excludes the impact on retirement behaviour of the elimination of the normal retirement age as well as of the changes in minimum requirements to access the pension.[37]

A particular problem we faced for women is that retirement at age 55, the legal retirement age in the pre-reform period, is no longer accessible. We were thus forced to move forward the relative spike and – according to our hypothesis on the nature of the hazard structure, interpreted as a preference for retiring at the EEA – we fixed it at age 57.

We computed simulations in two different scenarios, accommodating the two main factors determining the changes in retirement patterns in our model: the change in pension rules and the growth-induced changes in pension wealth. The first scenario allows for cohort-specific wage effects, and thus the comparison among cohorts captures the changes in both legislation and growth; the second applies instead the wage profile estimated for the 1945 cohort to all subsequent generations, and therefore isolates the effects of pension reforms.

We computed the hazard rate and the cumulative density function for each representative individual for each possible retirement age between ages 57 and 70, as well as the average retirement age.

Results (not shown but available on demand) show a very limited impact of the reform. In the first scenario and for the lowest earnings quartile we find a slight reduction in the hazard rates from the older to the younger cohorts at age 57, and a (small) increase at ages 60 and 65. These effects are somewhat stronger for higher quartiles and in the second scenario. The general pattern in the hazard rate is driven by the different shape of the individuals' age-profiles of social security wealth under the DB system with respect to the new NDC system, as shown in the following Figure 8.12. In the figure we show that the SSW age profile for a representative individual in the DB system (cohort 1950) is lower, up to age 60, than that of an individual in the NDC system (cohort 1975). At later ages, as the NDC system accounts for the reduction in the life expectancy at retirement while the DB does not, the reverse holds.[38]

When analysing the differences in representative workers (according to gender, occupation and geographical area) we found that the main result – the limited impact of the reform on both the hazard rates and the average retirement age – is robust across groups.

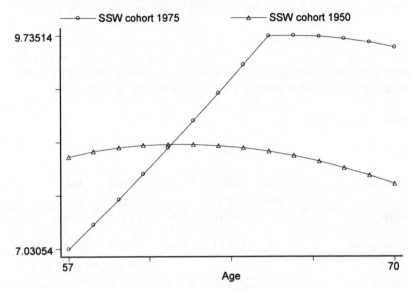

Note: SSW in hundred millions lire 2000. Scenario 2 (GPD rate of growth = 0). Representative individual: male, North-East, industry.

Figure 8.12 Age profile of Social Security wealth for two representative cohorts: 1950 (DB system) and 1975 (NDC system)

Retirement patterns across groups are, of course, the result of two determinants: the estimated parameters and the relative level of Social Security wealth. For example, from our estimates we know that conditional on pension wealth, white collar workers retire later than blue collars (with an odds ratio equal to 0.67, as reported in Table 8.9), while, conditional on other characteristics, a higher pension wealth encourages earlier retirement. Although white collar workers have an average pension wealth higher than blue collars, we computed that white collars retire later than blue collars.

As for the overall effect of other characteristics on the hazard, we find remarkable differences between areas: workers in the South retire later than in the Centre and much later than in the North;[39] disaggregating by gender, this difference is emphasized in the case of women. Hence, a relevant part of the geographical difference in retirement patterns does not come from the (big) differences in the SSW, but is differently motivated. Characteristics of the labour market peculiar to the South, such as more discontinuous careers – not captured by differences in the simulated SSW – translate into differences in the exits and in the retirement age: workers in the more industrialized North commonly exploit seniority pensions, while workers in the South generally leave their job at old-age eligibility, and consequently later.

As for the sector of activity, men in industry and women in manufacturing retire much earlier than the others: for men in industry the hazard rate at age 60 is equal to 79 per cent, while it is 65–68 per cent in the other sectors. For women in manufacturing, the hazard rate at age 60 is equal to 87 per cent, while it is 72 per cent in industry and 63 per cent in the service sector.

Table 8.9 Odds ratios

Coefficient	Males			Females		
	Odds ratio	Std. Err.	z	Odds ratio	Std. Err.	z
SSW	1.0951	0.0281	3.54	1.1759	0.05991	3.23
Time-at-risk	2.2782	0.2044	9.18	1.9520	0.4621	3.02
Age 55	-	-	-	20.8731	6.9457	9.13
Age 60	16.9874	2.1127	22.77	-	-	-
Age 65	6.8743	2.2193	5.97	-	-	-
White collar	0.6686	0.1030	−2.61	0.5990	0.1086	−2.83
Industry	1.8119	0.2008	5.36	1.3379	0.2881	1.35
Manufacturing	1.1124	0.1503	0.79	3.7272	2.6764	1.83
Other	1.0480	0.1361	0.36	0.7540	0.1466	−1.45
North-East	0.8891	0.1019	−1.03	1.0017	0.2179	0.01
Centre	0.6214	0.0669	−4.42	0.7274	0.1549	−1.49
South	0.5850	0.0749	−4.19	0.5351	0.1371	−2.44

Note: Reference individual is blue collar, services, North-West.

Gender is the relevant dimension when considering the average retirement age, women retiring roughly two years before men. Comparisons across occupations and areas reveal smaller variations, amounting at most to one year.

Comparisons of our results with those obtained by others is not straightforward. Brugiavini and Peracchi (2003) use a model with a linear age trend and compare four different regimes (pre-reform, Amato, Dini and a modified Dini scenario). They find an increase in the median retirement age – from the Amato to the Dini regimes – equal to two years for men (from age

58 to 60) and to one year for women (from age 57 to 58). Spataro (2000b) finds a reduction in the hazard rates for men, but his results display a high sensitivity to his hypotheses.

8.5 CONCLUSIONS

Irrespective of its limitations, the analysis lends itself to a numbers of considerations.

Retirement decisions of Italian workers appear strongly influenced by the institutional framework. We can distinguish a stable (pre-reform, that is pre-1992) period and a more unstable one (essentially the 1990s, characterized by intense reform).

In the first period, we find that money's worth measures are an important determinant of retirement, although the empirical performance of the model shows discrepancies with respect to the expectations which can be derived from an intertemporal optimization approach. In particular, our econometric results highlight the important role of Social Security wealth, as an indicator of the standard of living which the prospective retiree expects to be able to maintain in retirement. The irrelevance of marginal effects – that is of implicit taxes – on the other hand, points to two possible explanations: a) the attraction of 'round ages' or the social relevance of certain typical ages, as shown by the spikes, to which workers seem to conform more than responding to the incentive structure; b) the difficulties, particularly for some traditionally weak segments of the labour market (women, low paid workers), of exits at the earliest eligible ages, determined by the very low level of the accrued pension benefit.

In the second period, given that the reform adopted a gradual approach rather than a 'cold shower' strategy, uncertainty about possible future restrictions seems to dominate behaviour, causing – as an anticipation effect – a much larger recourse to early retirement.

As for the future, our simulation is rather robust in showing that, if workers' attitudes will not change, the mere modification in the pension rules (that is the replacement of the previous generous DB system with the actuarially fair DC method) will not by itself bring about the increase in the average retirement age which is called for by the ageing process.

It may perhaps be added, as a final remark, that the adoption of the principle of flexible retirement – as a counterpart to the principle of actuarial fairness in benefit determination – would inevitably reduce the importance of the institutional framework and influence workers' behaviour towards a closer adherence to the option value model of retirement, but also allow due space to family considerations. However, the substitution of the easy-to-apply 'rules of thumb' of the past (for example retiring at 60 with a replacement ratio of, say, 70 or 80 per cent) with a new decision framework will take time and require extensive information. It also will require a more widespread 'culture of decision making', which in its turn, will call for a resolute educational effort.

8.6   POSTSCRIPT: 2008 AND AFTER

As mentioned in the introduction, a new bill has been approved by Parliament in 2004, enabling the government to enact another reform, specifically targeted on two objectives: the development of pension funds and the increase in the average retirement age. To this latter end, new eligibility rules have been introduced, according to a timetable which envisages an initial period (up to 2007) of mere incentives to induce workers eligible for a seniority pension to continue working, followed from 2008 onwards by a compulsory increase of retirement ages, up to 60 for women and 65 for men.[40]

While these provisions are inspired by the right objectives, it may be also argued that they are hardly consistent with the NDC basic philosophy. On the one hand, it is very doubtful that the incentives to postpone retirement, operating until 2007, will be successful (see Marano and Sestito, this volume); on the other, the increase in retirement age is unnecessarily discontinuous and rather rough. Moreover, it represents somewhat a retreat from the principle of flexible retirement, given that it re-establishes a 'legal retirement age', that is an age before which benefits are not payable and after which the continuation of work is effectively penalized, given that the conversion factors are kept constant. In practice, it appears that only women will enjoy a choice period, from age 60 to age 65, with automatic adjustment of the conversion factors. For men, barring new changes, the mandatory age will be 65.

To sum up: the government's intervention, in so far as it drastically reduces the flexibility introduced by the 1995 reform is clearly due to a lack of confidence in the possibility of effectively raising, under the previous framework, the average retirement age. The foregoing analysis proves that this attitude is well grounded. But it is natural to ask whether a similar result could have been obtained by a milder, or at least a more gradual, intervention. One may conclude that reforms are not irreversible and that the Italian Social Security system might perhaps be the object, in the future, of further adjustments.

NOTES

* We gratefully acknowledge financial support from the Italian Ministry of Labour and Welfare. We thank Onorato Castellino, Pier Marco Ferraresi, Paolo Sestito and Tryggvi Þór Herbertsson for useful comments and discussions.
1. Both during transition and in the new regime, the payroll tax rate for employees will be between 32 per cent and 33 per cent of gross earnings, a very high level by any international standard.
2. They survive in the transition towards the new NDC system, although based on stricter combinations of age and seniority.
3. For seniority pensions (those above the dotted line), the graph indicates an age parameter which is not to be intended as a further legal requirement, but only as additional information (a statistical indication?) which assumes two different starting ages: 15 (1) or 20 (2), and uninterrupted careers. For old-age pensions (below the dotted line) the corresponding seniority is a legal requirement.
4. See for example Castellino (1995).
5. Actuarial equity is, however, incomplete, for example because of the difference between the payroll tax effectively paid by the workers and the one used in the computation of the benefit.
6. 'Seniority pensions' are maintained in the new system, but subject to a 40-year working career; very likely, they will be ineffective, given the low probability for workers aged less than 57 (particularly if women) of having accrued such a seniority.
7. The small sample size does not allow us to compute separate statistics for dependent workers and for the self-employed. Given that there were in the past some differences in retirement rules – for example to get old-age benefits – caution in the interpretation of the results is required. See section 2.2 for a description of the data.
8. The introduction of the 'exit windows' was officially formalized in 1995. With the 2004 bill, Parliament has reduced their number from four to two per year.
9. The minimum age for old-age benefit has never been lower than 55 and even this age has only been relevant for women.
10. Of course this statement ignores the aberrant anomalies of norms for public employees, who could retire, particularly if women, at young ages such as in their early forties, and at very favourable terms.
11. This 'guesstimate' derives from the following reasoning. Between 1991 and 1992 no change was introduced in the eligibility conditions; at the same time, a hot debate on the urgent need of a reform was going on, suggesting as plausible the hypothesis that everybody who was entitled effectively retired, in the expectation of the impending cuts. As a consequence, supposing that all eligible workers retired, the exit rate up to age 54 for men observed in 1992 can be used to approximate the number of eligible workers (men) at that age also in 1991.
12. Women continuing working after the age of 60 are likely to be collocated at the tails of the income distributions, being either in the upper part or at the bottom of the income scale.
13. The Parliamentary Committee (Commissione Brambilla) – set up to evaluate the efficacy of the law n. 335/95 in the period 1996–2000 – quantified the saving obtained by the intervention on the seniority pensions, and highlighted the increase in the average retirement age for this kind of pension. See Commissione Brambilla (2001).
14. In Italy, the two decisions are almost invariably one and the same thing (an exception are workers experiencing an unemployment spell just before retirement, something that was rather uncommon because of the various mobility programmes directed at the older workers).
15. A similar exercise is performed for example by Brugiavini and Peracchi (2003) and by Spataro (2002) (see section 3.5).
16. To simplify the exposition, the formulae refer to a single individual, while calculations are tailored on a household, with the wife three years younger than the husband, which means taking into account joint survival probabilities (ISTAT 1996 mortality tables) and survivor benefits (60 per cent of the direct pension benefit).

17. We are grateful to Rocco Aprile, of the Ragioneria Generale dello Stato, who suggested this point.
18. The first available year is 1985, while 1991 is the year before the start of the pension system reform process. Therefore it is assumed that in 1991 workers did not anticipate the reforms of 1992 and subsequent years – an assumption that seems reasonable when considering that the 1992 reform was approved by Parliament right after the financial crises that hit Italy in the summer of 1992. In addition, the descriptive analysis presented above does not show any change in individual retirement behaviour before 1992 (see section 8.1.1).
19. However, workers retiring in 1985 – for whom only one year of salary is observed – are not excluded from the sample.
20. Assumed to be 1.5 per cent a year (in real terms).
21. A discrete time duration model can be estimated, after having organized the data as described in the text, as a logit model with dependent variable given by the (0/1) indicator of the decision to retire and with time at risk among the independent variables. This is the strategy used in this chapter.
22. As there have not been changes in the pension legislation during the years considered in the analysis, and therefore all the individuals share the same pension computation formula, the pension wealth coefficient is identified through the variation – in time and between individuals – of the wage and of the tenure in the pension scheme. Indeed, the individual wage has not been included among the covariates, because of its strong correlation with pension wealth.
23. We also experimented with a number of indicators of the firms' and the labour market conditions, but, probably because this kind of information is only available at city or regional level, and not at the firm level, we did not obtain significant effects from these variables.
24. Men younger than 60 (legal age of retirement) are in the sample at risk because they accumulated at least 35 years of tenure in the pension scheme; consequently, they can claim a seniority benefit. On the other hand, women aged 55 (legal age for retirement) can claim an old-age benefit even if they have a shorter tenure (at least equal to 15 years).
25. Estimates have also been performed including in the accrual computation (and in the tax rate numerator) the wage the worker would earn if he decides to work for an additional year (therefore assuming that he does not prefer leisure to work). Results, available on request, are very similar to those presented in the text.
26. The model inability to capture the spikes in the hazard at age 60 and 65 may depend on some individuals choosing to retire on the basis of some sort of rule of thumb. In addition, it may be a consequence of the exclusion of some relevant variables (that is variables which are relevant for the decision but are not observed by the econometrician).
27. As individuals are observed for several periods, average SSW has been computed for each individual, and then used to define the quartiles.
28. If the excluded variables are orthogonal to the included covariates, however, estimates are consistent.
29. Survey of Households' Income and Wealth.
30. In our estimates, this effect is captured by the occupation: white collar workers, who should have (on average) a higher education level than blue collars, have, other things being constant, a lower probability to retire.
31. We didn't follow an in-sample approach because there has been too marked a change in the rules – particularly in the minimum requirements to obtain benefits – from workers retired in the 1980s to those retiring in the future to make the comparison plausible. In lots of cases we would have had somehow to recover the information about earnings lacking in the data. Another option is to create a hypothetical population taking retirement decisions in the future, by means of a dynamic microsimulation model. We didn't undertake this approach because of the uncertainty about the characteristics of the population in the long time horizon and because of the complexity of the stochastic processes implementation.
32. The logarithm of wage was regressed on a third degree polynomial in age and on a set of dummies for cohort, sector, occupation and geographic area.

33. Averages by gender, cohort and occupation computed exploiting the Bank of Italy survey (SHIW) show values ranging from age 18 to age 21. Career discontinuities are therefore supposed to be more frequent in the first part of the working life and 'summarized' by a later starting age.
34. We used the CeRP simulation model described in Fornero and Castellino (2001).
35. We apply to everyone the minimum requirements established by the law of 1995 for the steady state exits.
36. For a different specification see Brugiavini and Peracchi (2003), who assume a hazard structure defined only by Social Security rules and thus choose a model without age spikes, and linear in age.
37. Variations in retirement behaviour due to changes in minimum requirements are excluded from the analysis also because of the hypotheses on the age of entry into the labour market combined with the continuity of the working career. The variable time-at-risk evaluated at age 57 is, under our assumptions, equal to one both in the past (because seniority is equal to 35) and in the future (because 57 will be the lowest age available for retirement). The effect would thus have been captured assuming a starting age different from 22 (combined with the hypothesis of the continuity), in order to have different values for the time-at-risk variable for different cohorts at each given age. For example, if we assume the worker starts to work at 18 and has a continuous career, at age 57 he will have 39 years of seniority. The time-at-risk variable in this case would be equal to 4 in the DB system and to 1 in the NDC system, thus capturing the change in the requirements. Given the labour market present and expected situation, we do not consider these age/seniority combinations really representative of the mean worker, and we prefer to exclude this kind of effect from our analysis.
38. It is worth considering a couple of additional points: as for the shape of the 1975 (NDC) cohort, it is also apparent that individuals retiring after age 65 do not benefit from an increase in the annuity factor. In addition, as the estimated age profiles at these ages are almost constant, it follows that the shape of the 1950 (DB) cohort is determined by two counterbalancing effects: the annual 2 per cent increase in the pension amount (due to the DB pension formula), and the decreasing life expectancy at retirement.
39. The CdF at age 60 of a male (white collar, industry, median income, second scenario) is about 80 per cent in the North, 73 per cent in the Centre and 70 per cent in the South.
40. The new framework is quite cumbersome – also because it relies on an experimental period, after which the rules could further be changed – with a minute prescription as to the age/seniority combinations. From 2008 onwards, the old-age limit will be 65 for men and 60 for women (instead of 57). The seniority pension (a temporary heritage from the pre-1992 era) will require 35 years of seniority and at least 60 years of age (2008–2009), then 61 and perhaps even more.

REFERENCES

Brugiavini, A. and F. Peracchi (2001), 'Micro Modeling of Retirement Behavior in Italy', Departmental Working Papers, 147, CEIS, Tor Vergata University.

Brugiavini, A. and F. Peracchi (2003) 'Social Security Wealth and Retirement Decisions in Italy', *Labour*, **17**(August), 79–114.

Castellino, O. (1995), 'Redistribution Between and Within Generations in the Italian Social Security System', *Ricerche Economiche*, **49**, 317–27.

Colombino, U. (2002) 'A Simple Intertemporal Model of Retirement Estimated on Italian Cross-section Data', mimeo.

Commissione Brambilla (2001), *Verifica del sistema previdenziale ai sensi della legge 335/95 e successivi provvedimenti, nell'ottica della competitività, dello sviluppo e dell'equità*, final report by the Ministry Commission set up to evaluate the 1995 pension reform.

Contini, B. and E. Fornero (eds) (2002), 'Scelte Lavorative e di Pensionamento degli Anziani in Italia', research report by CeRP, LABORatorio R. Revelli and R&P Ricerche e Progetti for the Ministry of Labour and Social Policies.

European Commission (2003), *Joint Report by the Commission and the Council on Adequate and Sustainable Pensions.*

European Commission (2004), 'Communication from the Commission to the Council, the European Parliament, The European Economic and Social Committee and the Committee of the Regions: Increasing the employment of older workers and delaying the exit from the labour market', COM (2004) 146.

Fornero, E. and O. Castellino (eds), (2001), 'La Riforma del Sistema Previdenziale Italiano', Bologna: Il Mulino.

Heyma, A. (2001), *Dynamic Models of Labour Force Retirement*, Tinbergen Institute Research Series, University of Amsterdam.

INPDAP (2001), *Andamento della Spesa Pensionistica nell'Anno 2000.*

Marano, A. and P. Sestito (2005), 'Retirement Age Rules and Pension Reforms in Italy', Chapter 7 in this volume.

Mastrogiacomo, M. (2002) 'Dual Retirement in Italy and Expectations', CeRP Working Paper no. 20/02.

Miniaci, R. (1998) 'Microeconometric Analysis of the Retirement Decision in Italy', OECD, Economics Department Working Paper n. 205.

MLSP (Ministry of Labour and Social Policies) (2002), *Report on National Strategies for Future Pension Systems, Italy.*

Spataro, L. (2000a) 'Le Scelte di Pensionamento in Italia: un'Applicazione (ed Estensione) del Modello di "Option Value"', *Studi Economici*, **72**, 25–54.

Spataro, L. (2000b), 'Analisi degli Incentivi al Pensionamento Anticipato del Sistema Previdenziale Italiano Dopo le Riforme degli Anni Novanta', Dipartimento si Scienze Economiche, Università di Pisa, Collana Studi e Ricerca, 66.

Spataro, L. (2002) 'New Tools in Micromodeling Retirement Decisions: Overview and Applications to the Italian Case', CeRP Working Paper n. 28/02.

9. Income expectations and outcomes at mandatory retirement in the Netherlands*

Mauro Mastrogiacomo

9.1 INTRODUCTION

According to the life-cycle model (LCM) in its stripped down form, people experience at retirement a relevant (and anticipated) drop in income. Different studies (Banks et al., 1998; Bernheim et al., 2001; Haider and Stephens Jr., 2004) have found that this also implies a drop in consumption, and they question the validity of the standard life-cycle model with consumption smoothing. However, the fact that individuals are not observed smoothing consumption over the life-cycle does not necessarily imply a rejection of the implications of the standard model. Banks et al. (1998) do not consider that retirement may take place at different points in time. Haider and Stephens Jr. (2004) find that, for those who are able to anticipate retirement, the observed drop in consumption is 40 percent smaller than in other studies. Indeed, if retirement is not expected, there is no reason to think that consumption should be smoothed at the pre-retirement level. However, anticipating the date of retirement is only one part of the requirements that rational individuals need to fulfill in the LCM. Are individuals able to anticipate the income fall upon retirement?

In the Netherlands at least, mandatory retirement is perfectly anticipated since it is allowed at age 65. We will show that at that age many also expect a drop in income. This means that relative to the study of Haider and Stephens Jr. (2004) we do not only have a sample of individuals who not only know exactly when they will enter social security,[1] but who also expect their income to drop at retirement. This means that we could be in a perfect setting to check the validity of the LCM, at least for the selected sample of those who anticipate their future. Nevertheless to fit the LCM the expected income drop at retirement should also be realized. We find that this is not the case in the Netherlands, since most retirees do not experience their income changes after retirement as a worsening of their income as expected. We therefore do not return in this study to the post-retirement consumption puzzle, but investigate the mismatch between income expectations and realizations at mandatory retirement. Why do income expectations drop if the realized changes are systematically better than expected?

There are a number of reasons that may answer this question. Shocks not explicitly inherent in the replacement rate of social security may disturb the individual upon mandatory retirement (Disney and Tanner, 1999). Indeed there is no reason to expect a good prediction of the future if new information comes in at retirement (Banks et al., 1998), though this is not specifically related to it (health shock, death of a household member, change of marital status, and so on). A second explanation put forward could be that individuals are intrinsically pessimistic about the future (Das, 1998), and that this is mostly the case at mandatory retirement, when individuals feel that they are entering a new non-revertible phase of their life. A third explanation is that the retirement system in the Netherlands grants very high replacement rates (Lindeboom, 1999), maybe even better than expected. A final explanation is more technical and concerns the ordered nature of the income expectations and realizations question used in this study. Individuals are only allowed to report a categorical, therefore discrete, answer, and this may affect the results. We will show that all these explanations help to answer our question, and we will try to discuss how important these are. The LCM implies perfect foresight of the future and requires that the income drop at retirement should not only be expected but realized, and that the realization should be of the same magnitude as expected. We do not observe this in our data and therefore suspect that in the Netherlands, generally speaking, the preconditions of the LCM only apply to a selected group of individuals. Unfortunately we are not aware of any dataset including all the necessary information (expectations and realizations about retirement date, income and consumption) to test these implications.

Most authors have focused specifically on consumption expectations, rather than income (see Ameriks et al., 2002; Hurd and Rohwedder, 2003). However, evidence from the Netherlands shows that the two definitions have similar patterns, and some authors point to the 'excess sensitivity of consumption to income' (see Lusardi, 1996; Kalwij, 2003). Therefore we feel confident in comparing our results to those of the consumption literature. Ameriks et al. (2002) show that many working households do expect a considerable fall in consumption when they retire. Unfortunately they only examine a cross-section and their respondents are only selected among highly educated academics. They divide the sample into two groups: currently employed and currently retired. Those who are already retired report, in line with our findings, significantly smaller falls in consumption as compared to those expected by respondents who are still in work. More recently Hurd and Rohwedder (2003) have also analyzed a similar cross-section and report different results. They find that the predictions expressed by the future retirees do not differ from the realizations reported by the current retirees. Because of the nature of their data, they cannot control for the future outcomes of those currently employed. However, they defend the LCM in the sense that the consumption drop is framed in the anticipations of the respondents.

Their results indicate that the assumptions underlying the standard life-cycle model cannot be rejected since individuals are able to anticipate the drop in consumption at retirement. This means that an observed drop in consumption is not per se inconsistent with the LCM. We also show that at mandatory retirement an income drop is expected; however, the inconsistency appears when we look at subjectively reported income realizations, which are systematically larger than expectations. Please note that this does not mean that income does not drop, but that it was expected to be (qualitatively) lower than realized. The conclusions of Ameriks et al. (2002) are here in general supported, however, the results also support the view expressed by Hurd and Rohwedder (2003) that it is not the unanticipated inadequacy of resources that surprises individuals. The results of Ameriks et al. (2002) attribute the gap between expectations and realizations to participation in the stock market, indicating that much of the gap is a result of unexpected stock market appreciation. In our study we show that in the Netherlands the occurrence of unexpected health, family or labor market related shocks and, especially, the intrinsically overly pessimistic attitude of respondents (at mandatory retirement) may determine lower expectations. These do not comply with realizations because the income drop at mandatory retirement is not as large as expected, also because of the generosity of the Dutch pension system.

This analysis is relevant for a number of reasons. First if individuals are not able to anticipate the income drop at retirement they might not be saving enough for their old age. It could be interesting to identify what groups, if any, do not actually form rational expectations around retirement. Second, access to better information about the future income after retirement may for instance influence expectations. Since individuals could save more during their working life this may provide new motivation to prolong elderly labor market participation. Indeed a difference between expectations and realizations is per se an indicator of inaccurate planning activity, or it is due to a shock that has not been foreseen. It does not support the assumption of anticipative behavior that is at the basis of the LCM with expected utility.

The study is organized as follows. The next section describes the data and concepts. Section 9.3 shows the descriptive analysis with the main findings. First there is a dip in expectations at age 64 (about income at age 65) that is not supported by realizations, second there is a substantial distance between expectations and realizations around early retirement (ER) age. Section 9.4 presents the econometric model. Section 9.5 shows the results of the two models relative to two dependent variables: expectations, in the first model, and the gap between expectations and realizations in the second. There the unjustified pessimism of respondents, mostly if highly educated, will be underlined. Section 9.6 will summarize the main results and conclusions. In addition two appendices are included. The first will follow the methodology of Das et al. (1999), for the comparison between reported expectations and realizations. Their findings are here supported. The results of the non-parametric tests on predictions and realized changes (in the first appendix) suggest that individuals do not systematically report a location of their individual subjective distribution of expectations if not for the case in which they predict no change (which is the most likely outcome). Any other prediction is systematically inaccurate. This may depend on macro shocks (as will be tested later on) but it is plausible to suspect that over the long period analyzed these will not point in the same direction. The second appendix will also clarify the construction of the financial incentive variables. Before doing that it is necessary to sketch some institutional details.

9.1.1 Mandatory Retirement in the Netherlands

Why should income expectations drop at the age of mandatory retirement? What does it mean for an employee in the Netherlands to turn 65?

The concept of mandatory retirement is different in the Netherlands relative to other western countries. At age 65 Dutch employees can be legally discharged, without explicit permission from the labor office, and enter social security. At the same time all citizens become eligible for an old-age pension (AOW) that is the first pillar of the pension system. This does not mean that at age 65 employees must stop work. However, it is common practice to retire at that time. Actually at that age most employees have already retired, using firm-specific early retirement plans (Mastrogiacomo et al., 2004).

The level of the AOW benefits is independent of tenure, experience or other incomes, but does depend on household composition. In principle, every individual older than 65 receives an AOW benefit equal to 50 percent of the minimum wage. This rule implies that a couple, of which both head and spouse are older than 65, receives a social security (SS) benefit equal to the minimum wage. A single-person household is entitled to a supplement of 20 percent of the minimum wage so that such a household receives 70 percent of the minimum wage. In the 1990s there were special rules for couples of which only one of the household members is older than 65. In any case, they were entitled to an AOW benefit of a single individual. Moreover, such a household received a supplementary AOW benefit which was negatively related to the earnings of the younger (<65) spouse: if the earnings of the younger spouse were high, the household was not entitled to a supplementary benefit. The maximum supplementary AOW benefit is equal to 50 percent of the minimum wage. We have explicitly taken into account the AOW rules in the computation of the residual lifetime resources.

At age 65 most employees also receive a funded occupational pension, which constitutes the second pillar of the pension system. In general, if the employer offers a pension scheme, participation in such a scheme is compulsory. Although there is great variety in pension schemes, the vast majority of the occupational pensions are of the defined benefit type. In most cases benefits are determined on the basis of final pay. Most schemes aim at a benefit level such that the sum of before-tax AOW benefits and before tax occupational pension benefits is equal to 70 percent of the final wage, also before taxes.[2] This replacement rate is reached if one works for 40 years within the same pension fund (implying an annual accrual rate of 1.75 percent). The replacement rates of the Dutch pension system are therefore among the highest in Europe (Andrietti, 1999).

The pension system described above provides income streams from age 65 onwards. However, on average only about 20 percent of the males aged between 60–64 are still at work. Generally it is believed that the strong incentive effects of employer-provided early retirement schemes may be responsible for this. In the 1980s and 1990s, the larger share of the employers (about 80 percent) provided the so-called VUT or early retirement (ER) schemes. The ER schemes, which were generally financed on a pay-as-you-go basis, were characterized by their easy access and generous benefits levels.[3] Eligibility for the ER schemes was typically at the age of 60 or 61 and usually required ten years of tenure with the same employer. Furthermore, while in retirement, one often keeps accumulating pension rights, though possibly at a lower rate than if one were working. Kapteyn and de Vos (1997) and Lindeboom (1999) have shown that these schemes provide strong incentives to retire, at the very moment that individuals become eligible for these schemes. More specifically, once eligible, delayed retirement does not lead to higher early retirement benefit replacement rates. Consequently, implicit tax rates of these schemes become very high at the very moment that an individual qualifies for benefits.

Yet, prior to the age of eligibility for ER, a substantial number of the elderly have already left the labor force. This pattern can be explained by the Dutch social insurance system. It provides, among other things, unemployment insurance (UI) benefits and disability insurance (DI) benefits. Unemployment insurance benefits are provided to protect for loss of income due to involuntary unemployment. Benefit levels are 70 percent of last earned wages.[4] The benefit entitlement period for the earnings-related UI benefit depends on an individual's work history, but can be at most five years. After exhaustion of UI benefit entitlement, benefits are reduced to social assistance (SA) benefits, which are 70 percent of the minimum wage. Special regulations for the elderly, aged 57.5 years and above, allow them to remain on the earnings-related UI benefit up to the official age of retirement (65 years). DI schemes are offered as a safety net for those who are physically or mentally too impaired to obtain gainful employment. DI benefits are a function of last earned gross wage and the minimum wage. At the age of 58 a DI benefit recipient is provided with an earnings-related DI benefit (70 percent of gross wage) up to the official age of retirement. At earlier ages, earnings-related DI benefit is provided for a maximum entitlement period that depends on age. After exhaustion of earnings-related DI benefits, subsequent benefits are a function of the last earned wage and the minimum wage. All these specifics of the Dutch welfare system, before and after age 65, are incorporated into the computation of the individual residual lifetime resources employed for the estimation of the main model (see section 9.4).

9.2   DATA AND CONCEPTS

This study tries to test whether income expectations deteriorate around retirement, and whether their evolution is mirrored into reported realizations. We do not present consumption in the analysis (which is not reported in the data) but look directly at income expectations as the dependent variable, as well as the realizations of these expectations one period ahead. We also address a methodological issue, analyzing whether our results may depend on the very nature of the question posed in the survey. Since the results of this analysis (reported in Appendix 9.A) are only conclusive for one category, we will also attempt to model reported expectations and their deviations from realizations, in order to test how these relate to observable characteristics, and whether available information was taken into account when forming these expectations. Since large deviations are also observed at the ER age, which is uncertain, we bring this uncertainty in the model using a financial indicator that takes into account any possible future early retirement date.

Expectations and individual characteristics are observed in the Social Economic Panel Data (SEP). This survey is administered by Statistics Netherlands (CBS) and contains approximately 5 000 households per year. In structure and contents this panel survey is similar to the German Social

Economic Panel (GSOEP) and the American PSID. The aim of the SEP is to provide a description of the most important elements of individual and household welfare and to monitor changes in these elements over time.[5]

The sample includes non-self-employed respondents aged 50 to 70 who are in the survey in the period 1986 to 1993 for at least three years.[6] The sample is composed of 5 215 observations. This amounts to 1970 individuals participating in the survey three to ten times; the sample selection is reported in Table 9.1. One other sample is used in the form of a repeated cross-section with 17 093 observations in the period 1990 to 1998. This is only used for the income analysis.[7]

Table 9.1 Selection of the sample

Data selection		
Reason for removal	Observations dropped	Observations left
Dimension of the repeated cross-section		23 662
Out of age bracket	5 561	18 101
Attrition	9 053	9 048
3 years rotating panel		9 048 (7 259 excluding year 1990)
Self-employed	597	8 451
Year of birth time inconsistent	6	8 445
Missing income information	2 555	5 890
Missing other relevant information	675	5 215

Source: SEP, own computations.

The questions elicited in the SEP subjective income expectations and realizations refer both to household income and financial situation. Answers to these questions are highly correlated.[8] The former (household income) is used which should be more closely related to the consumption data used in the other studies that we have described. The question about expectations is 'How do you think the income of your household will develop in the next 12 months?'. It is answered by choosing one of the five ordered categories listed from 1 to 5: significantly worsen, somewhat worsen, remain the same, somewhat improve, significantly improve.[9] The question about realizations has the same five ordered categories as possible answers and is formulated as follows: 'How has your income developed in the last 12 months?'. The answers to these two questions will be directly compared in Appendix 9.A in order to question whether individuals form accurate, rational predictions.[10]

The covariates that may have an influence on these two subjective responses are: time effects, taste shifters, retirement indicators, shocks and financial indicators.

Time effects will control for macro shocks common to all individuals over time. Taste shifters will include the usual exogenous regressors, like education and family size.

Early retirement dummies will detect the exact timing of retirement for those observed shifting into retirement. The diffusion of ER has increased over time, and social security benefits are no longer the first retirement provisions that individuals receive. In order to identify the potential early retirees, different definitions of (partial) retirement are used. This is necessary since there is no clear cut definition of ER in the survey. In any of them retirement is identified by a transition to the current state. This means that respondents becoming retired in the year of observation (year t) are identified. Any definition used does not explicitly refer to complete retirement. This is due to the registration in the SEP of the labor participation status. This question refers to the main activity of the respondent, and those answering that work is not their main activity do keep a residual participation in the labor market. The labor participation question is an excellent tool to identify (partial) retirement. Using the amount of weekly working hours allows a second definition of partial retirement as the status of those individuals for whom participation drops at least with 25 percent of their normal schedule relative to the panel observation in $t - 1$. Also an income dependent definition of partial retirement is used. Looking at income sources an individual is defined as retiring in panel wave t if he or she declares in $t +$ 1 an income for period t that is composed by 50 percent of retirement income, provided that the individual was working in period $t - 1$. A fourth definition will mark the shift into old-age pension (AOW). In contrast to the previous definitions, this is straightforward to identify since individuals enter the program when they turn 65.

A variable for labor market related 'shocks' is derived from a question asked to those who stopped working within the last year. The question is: 'Why did you stop working?'. A range of 12 possible answers is given and in this study the ones that are used are: illness of the respondent; illness of the partner or another family member; respondent was fired; company became bankrupt. Since the definition of retirement is based on the answer to different questions, labor market related shocks are not strictly a subset of each retirement indicator. Changes in the family composition will also be included. We assume these changes to be unanticipated.

The financial indicator summarizes the future income profile of the individual (including both her labor income and her expected pension stream till age 70) with an uncertain future date of early retirement (if she is not already early retired). This is the 'present discounted value' term. This variable will be introduced in the estimation to test whether individuals expecting higher residual lifetime resources form higher expectations over the next year, and whether this indicator 'explains' the mismatch with realizations. Appendix 9.B provides some details about the construction of this variable. Indeed some information relative to ER age and ER replacement rates is missing from the SEP but essential for the computation of this variable. This is because future pension streams will depend on the future retirement date. This issue will be addressed using an auxiliary data set, the CERRA (Center for Research on Retirement and Aging), which allows the imputation of the future age of eligibility to ER.[11] This is a two-wave panel with extensive information concerning the pension arrangements of Dutch employees, and was conducted in 1993 and 1995. Information concerning replacement rates and ER eligibility age is well registered and will be implemented in the PDV computation that will include all lifetime sources of income for the individual.

9.3   DESCRIPTIVE ANALYSIS

Figure 9.1 shows that individuals around retirement do experience an income drop.

The figure reports the log total income on the vertical axis. Income is here defined as the sum of labor income, occasional salary and other incomes (such as pensions). The figure plots different cohorts over time (the average year of birth is given). For the two cohorts in which respondents are around ER age (age 61), the income drop is sharp. However, once we separate the different cohorts, not much age effect is evident. Around age 65 the income drop is lower. This indicates that the social security system is able to offer very high replacement rates. The vertical distance among the segments indicates that younger cohorts have higher earnings when they reach a certain age.

Following Table 9.2 using labor income (wage plus occasional salary) returns results that are consistent with qualitative realizations. However, when we use total income (that also includes benefits) we see that those reporting a realized decrease do actually realize an increase of 900 guilders. Therefore, labor income is consistent with the subjective question about realization of household income, while the sum of labor incomes and benefits is not entirely. Results are no different if we introduce household income as the sum of the total income of the two main income earners.[12] The magnitude of the changes is, however, small since the figures are in gross terms. This (at first sight puzzling) table indicates that if individuals report a realized labor income loss, this has indeed taken place. The qualitative question they are asked does not indeed specify all income components (see previous section). However, different income protection programs (unemployment and disability insurance in particular) are generous enough to allow those experiencing a reduction in their labor income, not to fall back in terms of total resources. These programs only apply before one enters social security.

Figure 9.2 plots the main finding of this analysis: the evolution of expectations and realizations over age. The only evident drop in expectations occurs when individuals are about to qualify for the AOW (age 65). Around the age of ER the distance between expectations and realizations also increases, but then it is not due to a drop in expectations, but to a peak in realizations (which also indicates that at ER the pension benefit is more generous than expected).

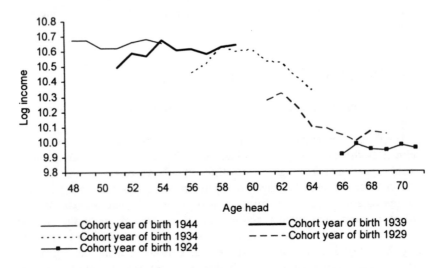

Notes:
This figure is based on repeated cross-sections to increase the dimension of the sample. Income includes all sorts of labor and non-labor income items (such as pensions). Observations = 17 093.

Source: SEP, own computations.

Figure 9.1 Log income drop around (early) retirement age

Table 9.2 Qualitative and quantitative income realizations

Realized category (c)	Value corresponding to the category	Labor income variation	Total income variation	Observations
Big increase	5	1 857	3 451	157
Increase	4	1 255	1 752	1 145
Equal	3	38	266	4364
Decrease	2	−491	900	1 101
Big decrease	1	−1 174	−744	492
Observations				7 259

Notes:
Respondents are selected when participating in the survey for three consecutive years. Income variations between adjacent years are reported in Dutch guilders (f). 1 euro = f 2.2. Base year 1990. Panel period 1984–93. The variation between year 1989 and 1990 is excluded from this analysis because the definition of labor income changes in 1989. Total income includes both labor incomes and benefits.

Source: SEP, own computations.

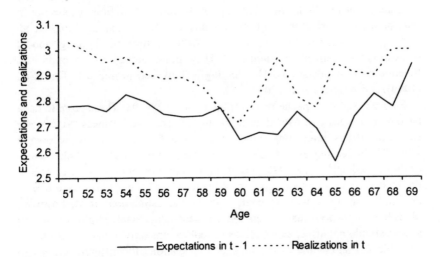

Notes:
Age is fixed and for each age period *t* − 1 expectations are related to period *t* realizations. The figure is based on the 3 years panel. Expectations and realizations are increasingly ordered from 1 to 5.

Source: SEP, own computations.

Figure 9.2 Income expectations and realizations over age

The overall picture that we derive is that realizations are better than expectations, and that this is definitely the case around the entitlement to the AOW. However, both are always below three, that is the value indicating no change, and expectations also decline over age. Both at the age of mandatory and early retirement individuals report an income drop qualitatively less severe than expected. Therefore, the basic intuition of the LCM that individuals expect and experience an income drop at retirement is here supported. However, the magnitude of the drop is not properly anticipated (Gustman and Steinmeier, 2001), and at mandatory retirement this cannot be blamed on the uncertainty about the retirement date. Though it may seem inappropriate to compare income expectations and realizations with studies that use consumption data, Kalwij (2003) shows that the two definitions do not differ substantially in the SEP data, affected by 'excess sensitivity of consumption to income' (see also Lusardi, 1996). This is due to the high level of compulsory saving in the Netherlands that does not require high additional personal savings (Alessie and Kapteyn, 2001) and makes income almost a proxy for consumption. However, since individuals are not able to anticipate properly the magnitude of the income drop, this may partly justify the close relation between income and consumption. We are hence confident in relating our results to this consumption literature. Our findings are not in line, at least in principle, with the already quoted finding of Banks et al. (1998), that estimating consumption with a forward looking model overestimates realized consumption. They point indeed to an optimistic functioning of expectations. This finding is, however, in line with Das et al. (1999), and Ameriks et al. (2002).[13]

Figure 9.3 plots expectations over the period 1984–93. These seem to have become more positive over time following the positive business cycle at the end of the 1980s. Interesting is the pattern around the economic slowdown in 1991–93. Increasing expectations follow the positive business cycle pattern of the second half of the 1990s, but these are not present in the figure because the related realizations are missing. Whether macro shocks do play a role or not in the analysis will be dealt with in the estimation. It is, however, plausible to suspect that, given the ten-year-long panel employed, macro shocks should not affect expectations or realizations only in one direction.

Table 9.3 shows the distribution of expectations for different groups of respondents. It shows that the population of non-retirees[14] is less 'pessimistic' than those partially retiring or entering social security. The sum of those expecting a decrease or a big decrease in their income is about 27 percent for the non-retirees while it is up to 20 percent larger for the retiring individuals. This indicates again that not only around age 65, but also around ER, expectations are lower.

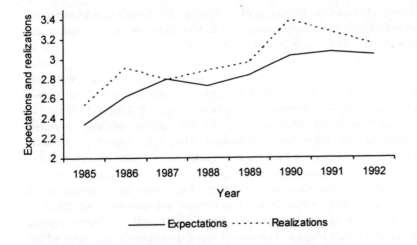

Notes:
This figure is based on the 3 years panel. Expectations and realizations are increasingly ordered from 1 to 5.

Source: SEP, own computations.

Figure 9.3 Income expectations and realizations over time

Table 9.3 Expectations of household income around retirement: different definitions

Expected category	Self reported definition	Working hours	Income definition	Old-age pensioners	Non-retirees
Big increase	0%	0%	0%	0%	0%
Increase	7%	10%	11%	7%	7%
Equal	47%	54%	60%	51%	66%
Decrease	37%	28%	27%	32%	24%
Big decrease	9%	8%	2%	10%	3%
Observations	274	195	227	309	4 417

Notes:
The table is based on the 3 years panel. The total number of observations is 5 215. However, some individuals become early retired according to more than one definition, therefore the number of point observations in this table is larger. Non-retirees are those individuals who do not qualify for any of the four retirement definitions considered in the table.

Source: SEP, own computations.

Table 9.4 shows the frequency of realizations in *t* given expectations in *t* – 1. If individuals were fully rational predictors, experiencing no unexpected events, we should observe the bold diagonal of this table with figures close to 100 percent. This is indeed not the case. Accurate forecasts are only done by individuals expecting no change in their income (largest group), while we also see that improvements occur for those who did not expect them. We extend this analysis in Appendix 9.A, where we show that individuals tend to report the most likely outcome among the five options available (therefore the mode of their subjective distribution), while other reporting behaviors (for example reporting the median) are rejected by our tests. However, this is true only for those predicting no change in their income (largest group) and not for the other four categories. The percentages show that individuals can be overly pessimistic almost as much as they are too optimistic. Nevertheless a sizable fraction of respondents does expect a drop, while a minority expects an increase in their income. This means that the marginal distribution of the outcomes again indicates pessimism of the respondents.

Table 9.4 Income expectations in t – *1 over* t *and realizations in* t

	Income expectations in *t* – 1 over *t*					
Income Realization in *t*	Big increase	Increase	Equal	Decrease	Big decrease	Obs.
Big increase	**0%**	8%	2%	1%	1%	109
Increase	13%	**39%**	15%	8%	3%	739
Equal	50%	41%	**69%**	52%	32%	3 195
Decrease	13%	7%	11%	**27%**	26%	801
Big decrease	25%	4%	4%	12%	**39%**	371
Observations	8	342	3 335	1 336	194	5 215

Notes:
The table is based on the 3 years panel. The total number of observations is 5 215. The table compares the matching, at the individual level, between expectations in *t* – 1 and realizations in *t*.

Source: SEP, own computations.

The descriptive analysis suggests so far that the explanations we have put forward in the introduction (for example generosity of the pension system, excessive pessimism, nature of the question) are all correlated with the observed pattern of income expectations and realizations. A simultaneous consideration of these effects requires the use of a modeling approach that also allows observed shocks and residual lifetime resources to be introduced in the analysis.

9.4 ECONOMETRIC MODEL

In the models, $y_{i,t}$ denotes in turn the categorized answer to the question about expectations and the difference between expectations and realizations.[15] As in a standard ordered response model the dependent variable is related to the underlying latent variable $y_{i,t}^*$ in the following way:

$$y_{i,t} = j \quad \text{if} \quad (m_{j-1} < y_{i,t}^* \le m_j) \qquad j = 1, \ldots, 5 \qquad (9.1)$$

The boundaries $-\infty = m_0 < m_1 < \ldots < m_4 < m_5 = \infty$ are constant across individuals and will be estimated.

The underlying latent variable is modeled by the equation:

$$y_{i,t}^* = \beta_0' x_{i,t} + \lambda_t + \tilde{\alpha}_i + u_{i,t} \quad i = 1, \ldots, N \quad t = 1, \ldots, T$$

where $x_{i,t}$ is a vector of taste shifters reflecting, for example, education, gender and family composition. It will also include shocks and the financial indicator. Time effects λ_t are included to allow for macro shocks, common to all respondents and not varying with $x_{i,t}$. The parameter $\tilde{\alpha}_i$ is an individual specific (random) effect indicating unobserved heterogeneity across individuals.

The white noise, which is the individual time specific error term $u_{i,t}$, is normally distributed and independent of the regressors $x_{i,t}$ and of the individual effect $\tilde{\alpha}_i$ (of which we estimate the variance through simulated maximum likelihood). The latter is treated as a random effect. We allow for an underlying correlation in Mundlak form. This means that the relation between $\tilde{\alpha}_i$ and $x_{i,t}$ is specified as $\tilde{\alpha}_i = \alpha_i + \beta_1' \bar{x}_i$. In $\bar{x}_i$ only those variables expected to be correlated with $\tilde{\alpha}_i$ are included.

9.5 RESULTS

Results are shown in Tables 9.5 and 9.6. Four models are described. The first two have expectations in t as a dependent variable. In the left panel the first model (model 1) does not include the interactions between eligibility to mandatory retirement and education. The second, model 2, in the right panel, does.[16]

The last two models in Table 9.6 show results for model 3 and model 4. The dependent variable is the gap between expectations in $t - 1$ and realizations in t; also, model 3 does not include the interactions between eligibility to mandatory retirement and education.

9.5.1 Expectations Model

This section describes Table 9.5, which is composed of the first two models (one for each column) with estimates and t-values. It refers to the model with categorized expectations in t as dependent variable.

For the estimates in Table 9.5 we had to shift from the analysis of the expectations in $t - 1$, carried out so far, to expectations in t, since we can identify shocks only between years $t - 1$ and t.[17] In addition most comments on the model results will not specify whether we refer to model 1 and model 2 since these are virtually identical, with the exception of the results for eligibility to mandatory retirement.

The first interesting result concerns the time effects. The hypothesis of absence of macro shocks is here rejected. The time effects are, jointly, significantly different from zero, with a $\chi^2_{7;0.05} = 251$ (far exceeding the critical value of 14). The time coefficients are all positive. This means that over time expectations improved, relative to the excluded year 1985.

The coefficients for the taste shifters are generally significant. Highly educated individuals have higher expectations relative to elementary educated respondents (which are the reference case). The educational dummies are assumed to be uncorrelated to the individual effect (for older individuals these are constant over time).

The coefficients for the timing of individual retirement are all negative. This was expected since the descriptive analysis main findings had shown dips in expectations associated to the time of ER and AOW. Of this set of indicators only the ones capturing occurrence of mandatory retirement and ER with income definition are significantly different from zero. This points to the notion that around mandatory retirement, and when an income drop is evident, individuals have lower expectations about the future developments of their household income. This enforces the empirical findings in section 9.3 in the sense that it establishes a causal relation, *ceteris paribus*, between mandatory retirement and the evolution of expectations. The model results indicate also which groups, around retirement, become more pessimistic. Among the dummies that identify mandatory retirement for the different education levels the reference group is mandatory retirement for elementary education. The higher education levels alone indicate a positive relation to expectations. This is not the case any more when education interacts with the individuals turning 65 (model 2). Higher educated respondents have lower expectations when they become eligible for AOW. This is in line with the results of other studies (Ameriks et al., 2002).

Table 9.5 Expectation model. Multivariate analysis

Ordered probit results	Model 1 Expectations in *t* first model		Model 2 Expectations in *t* second model	
	Estimates	*t*-value	Estimates	*t*-value
Time effects				
Year *t* is 1986	0.34	5.63	0.34	5.60
Year *t* is 1987	0.29	5.36	0.29	5.39
Year *t* is 1988	0.50	8.43	0.51	8.47
Year *t* is 1989	0.93	14.59	0.93	14.59
Year *t* is 1990	0.74	9.14	0.74	9.05
Year *t* is 1991	0.77	9.13	0.76	9.04
Year *t* is 1992	0.76	9.67	0.75	9.56
Taste shifters				
Males	−0.05	−1.30	−0.05	−1.36
Family size	0.11	1.69	0.10	1.65
Lower vocational education	0.11	2.17	0.10	2.09
Intermediate vocational education	0.23	5.03	0.25	5.20
Higher education	0.18	3.01	0.22	3.70
Retirement dummies and interaction dummies				
Retiring (self-defined) between *t*−1 and *t*	−0.16	−1.73	−0.16	−1.77
Retiring (schedule) between *t* − 1 and *t*	0.06	0.58	0.06	0.55
Retiring (income) between *t* − 1 and *t*	−0.19	−2.31	−0.18	−2.27
Turning 65 in *t*	−0.33	−4.29	−0.23	−2.41
Mandatory retirement for lower vocational education			0.09	0.45
Mandatory retirement for intermediate vocational education			−0.21	−1.16
Mandatory retirement for higher education			−0.99	−3.80
Change of status and financial indicators				
Labor market related shock between *t* − 1 and *t*	−0.45	−2.27	−0.45	−2.27
Becomes single between *t* − 1 and *t*	−0.19	−1.03	−0.18	−1.02
Gets married between *t* − 1 and *t*	−0.06	−0.23	−0.06	−0.23
Family gets bigger between *t* − 1 and *t*	0.07	0.42	0.07	0.42
Family gets smaller between *t* − 1 and *t*	0.13	1.87	0.13	1.82
First difference of the PDV of earnings/105	0.04	0.14	0.0003	0.0011

Table 9.5 (continued)

Ordered probit results	Model 1 Expectations in *t* first model		Model 2 Expectations in *t* second model	
	Estimates	*t*-value	Estimates	*t*-value
Potentially endogenous variables				
Mean family size	−0.08	−1.15	−0.08	−1.12
Mean of the first difference of the PDV of earnings/105	0.80	2.27	0.85	2.40
$m1$	−1.57	−16.15	−1.58	−16.16
$m2$	−0.37	−3.98	−0.37	−3.97
$m3$	1.90	19.76	1.91	19.78
$m4$	3.48	25.34	3.49	25.35
$\sigma^2 \alpha$	0.13	0.65	0.12	0.60
Log likelihood	−4 397.86		−4 389.84	
Observations	5 215			

Note: Excluded variables: Year 1985, Elementary education.

The coefficient associated with labor market 'shocks' is, as expected, negative and significant. It indicates that those experiencing events like their employer becoming bankrupt or a health shock that prevents them from work, have lower expectations about the future. All the changes in family composition and marital status that are listed do not turn out to be significant with the exception of a reduction in family size.

The first difference of the present discounted value of future earnings and benefits up to age 70 (over 10^5 guilders) is introduced as the financial indicator for residual lifetime resources. A positive sign is expected. This is because individuals with a more generous pension treatment or with high expected future income, should report more positive expectations. The coefficient is, however, insignificant. It also incorporates the future uncertain date of early retirement, which is a key element in determining the expected future retirement benefit. The variance of the individual effect is also insignificant; however, endogenous individual effects arise when looking at some exogenous characteristics, like residual lifetime resources. This is a plausible result: the individual effect picks up some time invariant characteristics such as inclination toward the future, which might well be positively and significantly correlated to larger residual resources. Including (non-capital) income as a regressor did not improve the results; the relative coefficient was not significant and is not presented in this analysis.

9.5.2   Gap Between Expectations and Realizations

Table 9.6 reports the results for the model in which the difference between expectations in $t - 1$ and realizations in t is the dependent variable. It is organized in a similar way to the table with the expectations model results. Including the PDV of future earnings returned a coefficient that was insignificant, indicating no systematic relationship between the dependent variable and the future resources available to the respondents. In the table we have chosen two specifications of the model that do not include this term. Before describing the main results it is necessary to explain how the estimates should be interpreted. A positive sign is associated with higher values of the dependent variable. When the dependent variable increases this means that expectations exceed realizations: individuals are overly optimistic. When the dependent variable is lower it means that realizations exceed expectations: the respondent is overly pessimistic.

In models 3 and 4 (which we describe together) time effects are not always significant, nor do they tend to go in the same direction. No taste shifters turned out significant.

The introduction of the interaction between mandatory retirement and the different education levels does not affect the impact of the retirement indicators. When estimating the model without these interactions again the coefficient relative to age 65 indicates an overly pessimistic attitude of respondents, but it is not significant. The interaction of this indicator with education does not show any significant effect either.

The indicators that identify changes of status are generally not significantly different from zero, with the exception of those experiencing widowhood or divorce. This indicates that a failure to state expectations that will comply with realizations does not depend on labor market related shocks, nor on the occurrence of unexpected changes concerning family size. The coefficient associated with those becoming single (because of divorce or widowhood) is significant. This indicates that those experiencing such an event had been too optimistic. In short after divorce or widowhood individuals report realizations that are lower than the expectations reported before the occurrence of such an event, as it might be expected. Family size, as a time invariant potentially endogenous covariate, is not significant.

A comparison of the two models reveals the following:

- At mandatory retirement expectations deteriorate. Such fears are unjustified in the sense that they do not come true. The following year the realizations of income situation are better than expected. This is particularly evident for higher educated individuals becoming eligible for the old-age pension.

Table 9.6 Gap between expectations and realizations. Multivariate analysis

Ordered probit results	Model 3		Model 4	
	Expectations in $t-1$ and realizations in t		Expectations in $t-1$ and realizations in t	
	Estimates	t-value	Estimates	t-value
Time effects				
Year t is 1986	−0.11	−2.01	−0.11	−2.00
Year t is 1987	0.28	5.45	0.28	5.46
Year t is 1988	0.06	1.08	0.06	1.08
Year t is 1989	0.12	2.16	0.12	2.16
Year t is 1990	−0.19	−2.62	−0.19	−2.60
Year t is 1991	−0.01	−0.09	−0.01	−0.11
Year t is 1992	0.06	0.80	0.06	0.79
Taste shifters				
Males	0.01	0.20	0.01	0.20
Family size	0.003	0.05	0.002	0.03
Lower vocational education	0.003	0.08	0.01	0.28
Intermediate vocational education	0.03	0.75	0.03	0.78
Higher education	−0.01	−0.16	0.001	0.02
Retirement dummies and interaction dummies				
Retiring (self-defined) between $t-1$ and t	0.33	3.97	0.33	3.97
Retiring (schedule) between $t-1$ and t	0.20	2.07	0.20	2.07
Retiring (income) between $t-1$ and t	0.11	1.49	0.11	1.46
Turning 65 in t	−0.06	−1.02	−0.02	−0.26
Mandatory retirement for lower vocational education			−0.16	−0.89
Mandatory retirement for intermediate vocational education			−0.01	−0.04
Mandatory retirement for higher education			−0.17	−0.74
Change of status and financial indicators				
Labor market related shocks between $t-1$ and t	−0.07	−0.37	−0.07	−0.37
Becomes single between $t-1$ and t	0.69	4.17	0.69	4.17
Gets married between $t-1$ and t	0.06	0.24	0.07	0.27
Family gets bigger between $t-1$ and t	0.04	0.23	0.03	0.22
Family gets smaller between $t-1$ and t	−0.0004	−0.01	−0.0003	−0.0044

Table 9.6 (continued)

Ordered probit results	Model 3 Expectations in $t-1$ and realizations in t		Model 4 Expectations in $t-1$ and realizations in t	
	Estimates	*t*-value	Estimates	*t*-value
Potentially endogenous variables				
Mean family size	−0.02	−0.38	−0.02	−0.37
*m*1	−1.61	−18.44	−1.60	−18.40
*m*2	−0.50	−5.91	−0.49	−5.87
*m*3	1.08	12.76	1.08	12.78
*m*4	1.96	21.95	1.96	21.97
$\sigma^2\alpha$	0.08	0.44	0.08	0.43
Log likelihood	−6 140.82		−6 140.2	
Observations	5 215			

Note: Excluded variables: Year 1985, Elementary education.

- Changes of status, such as stopping with work for illness do play a significant role in the evolution of expectations. Becoming single instead is significantly correlated with the gap with realizations. Their effect is consistent with their expected effect. Eligibility to mandatory retirement appears to be a significant determinant of the drop in expectations at age 64.
- It is not clear what determines the mismatch between expectations and realizations before mandatory retirement. One interpretation could be that many early-retirement-events could be unplanned, however, when we bring uncertainty about early retirement in the financial indicator, this does not turn out to be significant. More simply the mismatch could be due to financial shocks that are not picked up by our indicators. Indeed shocks do affect income expectations, but because of the high level of income protection and income maintenance programs in the Netherlands, these may not affect realizations. The only observable shock that positively and significantly affects the gap is widowhood.

9.5.3 Decomposition

Given the above, we feel confident to use the estimation results of models 1 and 2 to perform some simulations. The aim is to decompose the observed drop in expectations of individuals eligible for the old-age pension as determined by two different effects. The first effect is determined by all individual characteristics, the second exclusively by eligibility for mandatory retirement (e). In order to identify these two effects an Oaxaca-like decomposition is computed.

In order to isolate the effect of eligibility, which enters the model with some indicators (d_e), the following steps are followed. First the estimates in the left panel of Table 9.5 are used to predict the mean value of expectations (y) for those who are not eligible ($E(y_{e=0}|d_e = 0)$) separately from those who are eligible ($E(y_{e=1}|d_e = 1)$). For this second group, which is aged 64 in $t - 1$, a second prediction is computed, that is the same as the previous one, but dropping the eligibility indicator ($E(y_{e=1}|d_e = 0)$)

In this way the overall effect $E(y_{e=0}|d_e = 0) - E(y_{e=1}|d_e = 1)$ is decomposed in two effects:

$$\underbrace{[E(y_{e=0}\mid d_e =0) - E(y_{e=1}\mid d_e =0)]}_{\text{characteristics}} - \underbrace{[E(y_{e=1}\mid d_e =1) - E(y_{e=1}\mid d_e =0)]}_{\text{eligibility}} (9.2)$$

where the second term of (9.2) identifies the effect of the eligibility indicators on average expectations, since these are the only parameters to differ between the two predicted values.

In the observed data, expectations drop at age 64 from approximately 2.76 to 2.57. The result of the decomposition indicates that individual characteristics account for an average drop of 0.09, while eligibility indicators do account for the remaining drop of 0.11. This means that 55 percent of the drop in expectations is attributable to an eligibility effect while the remaining 45 percent may be attributed to all other remaining characteristics, including early retirement indicators, shocks and residual lifetime resources.

9.6   SUMMARY AND CONCLUSIONS

A drop in expectations about next year's income is observed at age 64. Such an expected drop is in line with the standard life-cycle model hypothesis, which predicts a drop in earnings after retirement, but its magnitude is not mirrored in the observed outcomes. Even after controlling for observable characteristics and for the residual lifetime resources available to individuals, the drop is still evident. This shows that individuals become overly pessimistic at the age of eligibility for the old-age pension. Also around the early retirement age the gap between expectations and realizations increases, and the descriptive evidence shows that this may be due to the generosity of the retirement system. This study exploits the Social Economic Panel Data to investigate whether individuals fear a shock in their income around retirement and whether their fears are justified. Tracking individuals over time allows for a direct comparison between expectations about the next year and the realizations the year after, following the methodology of Das et al. (1999). Rational individuals, loosely speaking, should be able to predict with accuracy their future if macro or micro shocks do not disturb their environment. This is directly tested in this study and we find that different factors may determine the mismatch between expectations and realizations. Thanks to the panel nature of the data several definitions of micro shocks are introduced and these turn out to be significant determinants of the mismatch. Also time effects turned out to be significant. Neither the uncertainty about the date of early retirement, which enters the model through a financial indicator, nor the amount of residual lifetime resources, seem to affect the evolution of expectations significantly, nor the mismatch between the two. Two types of random effect panel data models are estimated, both for expectations and for the gap with realizations.

The empirical results can be summarized as follows:

- The covariates introduced produce, in general, plausible estimation results.
- Individuals do fear an income shock at mandatory retirement but their fears are partly unjustified. Such fears are mostly evident for the higher educated. The high level of income protection for employees in the Netherlands could well be responsible for the better-than-expected realizations.
- Measuring the effect of all observed characteristics on expectations attributes to 'eligibility for old-age pensions' a large effect in determining the expectations drop at age 64. This means that individuals around (mandatory) retirement are overly pessimistic and attach more weight to prospective bad events than to good events.

The results of this study are in line with several studies that make use of directly reported expectations and realizations. In particular the findings of Ameriks et al. (2002), are here confirmed and enforced by the exploitation of the panel, the inclusion of an individual effect, the inclusion of different definitions of retirement status and micro shocks. The idea that individuals may be surprised by the inadequacy of resources, and therefore experience a sudden and unexpected shock in income or need to decumulate their wealth, does not find direct support in this study. It seems plausible to conclude that 'at mandatory retirement' it is eligibility in itself that drives the drop in expectations and therefore the mismatch with realizations. According to the descriptive statistics, for 'before mandatory retirement' the mismatch could be due to the high level of income protection in the Netherlands.

9.A APPENDIX: EXPECTED VERSUS REALIZED WEALTH CHANGES

If no shocks takes place, according to Das and van Soest (2001), individuals are perfectly rational if they report a location of their individual subjective distribution that coincides with the one relative to the distribution of the realization.

In this appendix we study whether such location could be interpreted as the mode or the mean of their individual subjective distribution. As in Table 9.4, some insight could be gained by comparing predictions with self-reported outcomes. But such comparison is not straightforward since there is no reason to expect that the distribution of expectations across the population is the same as the distribution of the actual variable. Even when realizations and predictions coincide, the two variables are not comparable. While the outcome is based on the distribution of the actual variable, expectations reflect some location of the individual subjective distribution (mode, mean and so on). One could try to study such locations by considering different models generating best predictions of the prospective realizations. One could think of respondents minimizing a loss function. Respondents could for instance refer to the modal category or to some quantile of the subjective distribution. In the first case, when confronted with the five ordered categories of the question, respondents could report the mode of their subjective distribution. In the second, for instance, they could instead report the median.

The data contain questions eliciting expectations of outcome y = income; where respondents may choose among ordered categories. Let $f(y|s)$ be the subjective probability density of outcome y given information s. Respondents choose one of the K categories $C_1,..., C_K$ of the form $C_k = (m_{k-1}, m_k]$ with $-\infty = m_0 < m_1 < ... < m_{k-1} < m_K = \infty$. The threshold values m_k are subjectively determined and ordered models may be used to estimate their values. The answer to the expectation question is denoted by p. The minimization of some loss function will return p (see formula 9.3). If the respondents answer the question having in mind the most likely outcome they will report the mode of their subjective distribution. This means that they report the category $p = \arg\max_k P\{y \in C_k | s\}$. This corresponds to minimizing, with respect to k, the expected loss function: $E\{1(y \notin C_k)|s\}$. Here the behavior of an individual forming some point expectations p^* and choosing the category p that contains p^* is treated. The general form of the problem is minimizing the expected loss for some loss function L:

$$p^* = \arg\min_{\pi} \int_{-\infty}^{\infty} L(y - \pi) f(y|s)dy \qquad (9.3)$$

$$p = k \quad \text{iff} \quad p^* \in C_k.$$

If respondents interpret the question as eliciting the median of $f(y|s)$ the relative loss function will be $L(u) = |u|$ while for the category containing the mean the loss function will be $L(u) = u^2$.

If individual expectations are rational the categorized answer to the question about expectations and to the question about realizations should mirror a location from the same distribution. This location could be for instance the mode or the median of such individual distribution. By comparing expectations and outcomes the following tests are performed to show that what individuals report is not one of those locations.

9.A.1 Modal Category

Following Das and van Soest (1997), we formalize the modal category assumption for individual i, given the available information x_i, as:

$$P\{c_i = k | x_i, p_i = k\} \geq P\{c_i = j | x_i, p_i = k\}, \quad j = 1,..., K \qquad (9.4)$$

Where c_i is the realized category and k is the predicted category. For those individuals with $p_i = k$ most outcomes will be located in category k. Realizations, in the best-case scenario, are based upon drawings from the same distribution leading to probabilities (9.4). We can use observations of c_i to see whether (9.4) holds. Define for notational convenience $P_j \equiv P\{c_i = j | x_i, p_i = k\}$.[18] Let $\hat{P}_j$ be the sample equivalent of P_j.[18] Under the hypothesis of the independence of realizations, frequencies of income situation can be used to estimate the probabilities in (9.4). Assuming x_i = year of observation Table 9.A1 reports the frequencies.

Table 9.A1 shows that only for the case $k = 3$ the modal category assumption could be used as a model generating expectations. For $k = 1$, for instance, this is only true in years 1984–85, 1987–88, 1988–89 and 1989–90. Globally only 15 cases out of 40 behave according to the modal category assumption, suggesting its irrelevance.[19] However, since most observations report $k = 3$ the model is a good predictor for that category (Bernheim, 1987).

9.A.2 Median Category

If the survey responses correspond to a category that contains a point prediction that minimizes a loss function, it is natural to interpret p_i as containing the α-quantile of the respondent's subjective distribution of y_i. For

Country Experiences

Table 9.A1 Modal category

Estimates of $P\{c_i = c \mid p_i = k\}$

	Year	$c = 1$	$c = 2$	$c = 3$	$c = 4$	$c = 5$	Obs
$k = 1$	84–85	**49%**	25%	25%	1%	0%	72
Strong	85–86	29%	20%	40%	9%	3%	35
decrease	86–87	20%	43%	37%	0%	0%	30
	87–88	**42%**	38%	21%	0%	0%	24
	88–89	**50%**	13%	38%	0%	0%	16
	89–90	**43%**	0%	43%	0%	14%	7
	90–91	33%	0%	67%	0%	0%	3
	91–92	29%	14%	43%	14%	0%	7
$k = 2$	84–85	16%	30%	46%	7%	6%	443
Decrease	85–86	6%	22%	61%	10%	1%	240
	86–87	13%	39%	43%	6%	0%	204
	87–88	7%	22%	64%	7%	1%	209
	88–89	17%	19%	54%	9%	1%	147
	89–90	8%	15%	42%	27%	8%	26
	90–91	12%	18%	47%	24%	0%	17
	91–92	8%	36%	42%	14%	0%	50
$k = 3$	84–85	5%	22%	**63%**	9%	1%	318
No change	85–86	4%	11%	**68%**	15%	3%	381
	86–87	4%	16%	**68%**	10%	1%	746
	87–88	3%	7%	**81%**	5%	3%	526
	88–89	3%	5%	**79%**	12%	1%	697
	89–90	2%	7%	**50%**	38%	4%	226
	90–91	3%	7%	**58%**	30%	2%	215
	91–92	4%	9%	**54%**	30%	3%	226
$k = 4$	84–85	0%	23%	55%	14%	9%	22
Increase	85–86	5%	2%	60%	31%	2%	42
	86–87	2%	6%	55%	27%	10%	49
	87–88	9%	9%	57%	26%	0%	35
	88–89	6%	0%	42%	**45%**	6%	31
	89–90	0%	2%	18%	**71%**	9%	45
	90–91	2%	7%	29%	**41%**	20%	41
	91–92	6%	9%	31%	**44%**	9%	77
$k = 5$	84–85	0%	100%	0%	0%	0%	1
Big increase	85–86	100%	0%	0%	0%	0%	2
	87–88	0%	0%	100%	0%	0%	1
	88–89	0%	0%	100%	0%	0%	2
	89–90	0%	0%	0%	100%	0%	1
	91–92	0%	0%	100%	0%	0%	1
Observations							5215

Notes:
k = predicted category, c = realized category. In the table $c_i = c \mid p_i = k$ only for the bold figures. Respondents are selected when participating in the survey for two consecutive years.

Source: SEP, own computations.

$\alpha = 0.5$ the category is the one containing the median. If p_i^* is the α-quantile (corresponding, for convenience, to the cumulative probability α) then in the best case scenario it must be:

$$P\{y_i - p_i^* \leq 0 \mid x_i\} = \alpha$$

Since we observe the category c_i, we focus on the case with $c_i = k$. Then:

$$P\{c_i \leq k-1 \mid s_i, p_i = k\} < \alpha \leq P\{c_i \leq k \mid s_i, p_i = k\}$$

that implies the following inequalities:

$$P\{c_i > k \mid x_i, p_i = k\} \leq 1 - \alpha \qquad (9.5)$$

$$P\{c_i < k \mid x_i, p_i = k\} < \alpha \qquad (9.6)$$

To fit in the best case scenario the α-quantile of c_i must fall in category k, given that $p_i = k$; with no more than $100\alpha\%$ of realized values in lower categories and no more than $100(1-\alpha)\%$ in higher categories. A test for (9.5) and (9.6) is reported in Table 9.A2 using the data of Table 9.A1 and is based upon:

$$\sqrt{n}\left(\sum_{j=k+1}^{K} \hat{P}_j - \sum_{j=k+1}^{K} P_j \right) \xrightarrow{\ \prime\ } N\left(0, \left(1 - \sum_{j=k+1}^{K} P_j\right) * \sum_{j=k+1}^{K} P_j \right).$$

where n is the number of observations and x_i is only composed by year of observation. In the table the value of $\alpha = 0.5$ should be included in the confidence intervals in order to conclude that individuals are reporting a median as a point expectation.

This test uses the ordering of the categories. This suggests that the assumptions required for the modal category case were less stringent. For the case of $\alpha = 0.5$ we see that (9.5) and (9.6) for all k do not imply that (9.4) holds for all k and j, and vice versa. It is true though that for the extreme values of the k categories the inequalities (9.5) and (9.6) will hold.[20] Such a test imposes the condition that an absolute majority should fall into a certain category, rather than a relative majority as in the modal case. In this sense the median category assumption is more restrictive and it does not come as a surprise that the results are poor in terms of predictive capacity.

It seems plausible to conclude that individuals report the most likely outcome when answering the expectations question, and that this is the case especially for those predicting no change in their income situation.

Table 9.A2 Median category

90% confidence intervals

		$p\{c_i < k \mid p_i = k\}$		$p\{c_i > k \mid p_i = k\}$		
	Year	lower	upper	lower	upper	Obs
$k = 1$	84–85			**0.42**	**0.61**	72
Strong decrease	85–86			0.59	0.84	35
	86–87			0.68	0.92	30
	87–88			**0.42**	**0.75**	24
	88–89			**0.29**	**0.71**	16
	89–90			**0.26**	**0.88**	7
	90–91			**0.22**	1	3
	91–92			**0.43**	1	7
$k = 2$ Decrease	84–85	0.13	0.19	**0.50**	**0.57**	443
	85–86	0.04	0.09	0.67	0.77	240
	86–87	0.09	0.17	**0.43**	**0.54**	204
	87–88	0.04	0.10	0.67	0.77	209
	88–89	0.12	0.22	0.57	0.70	147
	89–90	0.00	0.16	0.63	0.91	26
	90–91	0.00	0.25	0.52	0.89	17
	91–92	0.02	0.14	**0.44**	**0.68**	50
$k = 3$	84–85	0.23	0.31	0.07	0.13	318
No change	85–86	0.12	0.18	0.14	0.21	381
	86–87	0.18	0.23	0.09	0.13	746
	87–88	0.08	0.13	0.06	0.10	526
	88–89	0.07	0.10	0.11	0.15	697
	89–90	0.06	0.12	0.36	0.47	226
	90–91	0.06	0.13	0.27	0.38	215
	91–92	0.10	0.17	0.28	0.38	226
$k = 4$ Increase	84–85	0.63	0.92	−0.01	0.19	22
	85–86	0.55	0.79	−0.01	0.06	42
	86–87	0.52	0.75	0.03	0.17	49
	87–88	0.62	0.86	0.00	0.00	35
	88–89	**0.34**	**0.63**	−0.01	0.14	31
	89–90	0.10	0.30	0.02	0.16	45
	90–91	**0.26**	**0.52**	0.09	0.30	41
	91–92	**0.37**	**0.56**	0.04	0.14	77
$k = 5$	84–85	1	1			1
Big Increase	85–86	1	1			2
	87–88	1	1			1
	88–89	1	1			2
	89–90	1	1			1
	91–92	1	1			1
Observations						5 215

Notes:
k = predicted category, c = realized category. Only the bold figures fall within the confidence interval. Respondents are selected when participating in the survey for two consecutive years.

Source: SEP, own computations.

9.B   APPENDIX: IMPUTATION OF PDV VARIABLE

The present discounted value of future incomes and benefits is included as a RHS variable in the ordered probit model described in section 9.4. This variable is derived under several assumptions concerning both the behavior of individuals towards the pension system and the evolution of their income profile until age 69.

9.B.1   Opting out at Early Retirement

Previous research demonstrates that the institutional and financial incentives related to ER are so favorable in the Netherlands that the vast majority of individuals who are eligible for ER do actually opt out as soon as they become eligible (see for example Lindeboom, 1999). Unfortunately, in the SEP the ER entitlement age is not observed. That is why we use an auxiliary data set, the CERRA, to estimate the probability distribution of eligibility.

A logit model and an ordered logit model are estimated, for the availability of an ER scheme and the age of eligibility given entitlement, respectively (see Table 9.A3). As explanatory variables we include some individual background variables, a dummy variable for public sector and experience. The choice of the RHS variables is motivated by convenience and based on the consideration of the most common entitlement rules to ER schemes. Next, the parameters' estimates are used to compute the probability distribution of the expected ER age for individuals in the SEP. This distribution is used to compute part of the present discounted value of working up to the age of ER eligibility, retiring early at that age and receiving ER benefit until age 64 and old-age pension plus occupational pension from age 65 to 69. Namely knowing the probability of retirement at a certain age identifies the (fraction of) the future income that will be used for the computation of the occupational pension after age 65.[21] We report the model results for eligibility in Table 9.A3.[22]

9.B.2   Income Profiles

Income profiles are generated according to the following auto regressive fixed effect panel data model.[23] The estimator for the fixed effect model is derived from

$$y_{it} = \alpha + x_{it}\beta + v_i + \varepsilon_{it} \qquad i = 1,...N; \qquad t = 1,...,T_i,$$

where $\varepsilon_{it} = \rho\varepsilon_{i,t-1} + \eta_{it}$ and $|\rho|<1$ and η_{it} is i.i.d. with zero mean and variance σ_n^2 while v_i are fixed parameters that can be correlated to x_{it} if those vary over time. Table 9.A4 contains the results of the fixed effect model for total earnings in t and $t-1$.[24]

Table 9.A3 Eligibility model

	Eligibility	Eligibility age
Age	0.060	0.031
	(2.26)**	(1.61)*
Experience	−0.060	0.005
	(8.28)***	(0.90)
Married	0.158	−0.113
	(0.33)	(0.44)
Divorced	−0.071	−0.080
	(0.13)	(0.25)
Single	0.660	−0.195
	(1.06)	(0.46)
Sector		2.271
		(17.02)***
Constant	−3.527	
	(2.31)**	
Observations	987	1240
Pseudo R^2	0.07	0.09
Log likelihood	−502.80	−1 742.44

Notes:
The reference case for marital status is widow. For sector it is private sector. *T*-values within brackets. Level of significance: *=10%, **=5%, ***=1%.

Source: CERRA, own computations.

Table 9.A4 Non-capital income model

	Total income in t	Total income in $t-1$
Non-capital income in t	−0.045	
	−(2.96)***	
Age in t	1 599.866	
	(4.83)***	
Age square in t	6.050	
	(1.60)	
Non-capital income in $t-1$		−0.094
		−(6.39)***
Age in $t-1$		−684.795
		(2.71)***
Age square in $t-1$		30.826
		(8.36)***
Constant	−67 311.886	−17 536.867
	−(8.97)***	−(5.01)***
Observations	4 836	5 202
Number of groups	1 341	1 420
Log likelihood	−53 757.26	−57 789.98
ρ	0.16	0.31

Note: *T*-values within brackets. Level of significance: *=10%, **=5%, ***=1%.

Source: SEP, own computations.

9.B.3 Implementation of ER Age in the Present Discounted Value

As stated above the SEP does not show eligibility age of ER schemes in the private sector, but the probability distribution of it. We may observe an individual working at age 57. For this individual we have imputed a probability distribution for e (year of eligibility) in the SEP. This associates a probability of becoming eligible to any age between 55 and 64. We will treat this individual as if he was not eligible at age 55 and 56. So the probability of becoming eligible at age 57 will be conditioned on the sum of the probabilities at age 55 and 56. In the remainder of this appendix we will show how to integrate out of the pension formula the unknown ER eligibility age using its distribution. Define the random variable e_t as the year in which someone becomes eligible for ER, y as non-capital income and l as labor participation.

The *present discounted value (PDV) of continued work* will result from the sum of the PDV of non-capital income till age 64 (y_t), as derived in Table 9.A4, plus the PDV of pension (P). This last item, the pension benefit from age 65 on, is the sum of old-age pension (AOW) plus occupational pension. Eligibility probabilities only matter for the computation of the occupational pension (that depends on experience (ten), last salary (w), and the franchise (fra)). This means that for any individual the following will hold:

$$PDV\,(y_t + P \,|\, l_0 = 1) =$$

$$\sum_{t=\tau}^{R} y_t + \sum_{t=R}^{T} \{AOW + \Pr(e_t \le t \,|\, e_t > \tau) * [\min(40, ten + t - \tau) * 1.75\% * (w_t - fra)]\}.$$

where R = first year of the old-age pension (age 65), τ is the current period and T is the terminal period. Evidently both the franchise and the AOW are kept to the current level and the discount rate is 0 (does not appear in the formula).

NOTES

* I thank Rob Alessie, Bas van der Klaauw and Maarten Lindeboom for commenting on previous versions of this study. In addition I also thank the participants of the conference 'Improving Social Security Programs' held at Maryland University on 12 September 2003 and the participants of the CeRP conference, 16 September 2003. Part of this research was developed when affiliated at the Vrije Universiteit of Amsterdam and Tinbergen Institute.

This study is based on the Social Economic Panel Data (SEP) administrated by Statistics Netherlands. The views expressed in this study are of the author and do not necessarily reflect the views of Statistics Netherlands.

1. In this study we use the terms 'social security' and 'mandatory retirement' as substitutes. In section 9.2 we will show that both definitions have a different meaning relative, for instance, to the American one.
2. After tax, the replacement rate is substantially higher because early retirees do not pay social insurance premiums.
3. Because of their generosity, from the mid-1990s onwards many employers (pension funds) have replaced the VUT schemes by so-called flexible early retirement schemes. These schemes are more actuarially fair than the VUT schemes and only apply for younger employees (born after 1946). For older employees (born before 1947) the VUT schemes still apply.
4. There is a maximum benefit level. In 1996 this was 25 816 euros.
5. As such this survey is not specifically designed to cover retirement issues per se. The SEP is representative of the Dutch population, but it excludes individuals living in special institutions like nursing homes. Statistics Netherlands applied a two-stage sampling procedure. Firstly, municipalities are drawn with probability depending on the number of inhabitants (big cities are drawn with certainty). Next, addresses are selected randomly. All households present at the selected address are interviewed, up to a maximum of three households. Over the years 1984 to 1989, households were interviewed twice a year. Since 1990 the survey has been held annually.
6. The self-employed are dropped because of the impossibility to compute their future pension benefits. The three years panel is necessary because of the lag of the income questions, which refer to earnings in the previous year.
7. Income is registered in the SEP differently across the 1980s and the 1990s, therefore the income analysis only includes the waves available for the 1990s though these do not exactly correspond to the period studied in the remainder of this chapter.
8. Seventy-five percent of the respondents report exactly the same answer to both questions while 22 percent report adjacent category (computations available on request). This indicates that individuals report the same concept while answering both questions, or that they have difficulties in separating the two concepts.
9. 'Don't know' answers are accepted but not used in this analysis.
10. Responses to questions on expectations are not straightforward in interpreting where individuals are asked to report point expectations. Previous literature has argued that individuals will not necessarily make a prediction that corresponds to a mathematical 'expectation'. This is tested more extensively in Appendix 9.A.
11. We will impute the probability distribution of ER age by means of an ordered model. This is because we observe common and comparable characteristics in the CERRA and in the SEP but the ER age is only reported in the CERRA.
12. However, partners have a low participation in this age group (see Alessie et al., 2004). This makes the income information other than that of the main income earner, very sporadic and not always reliable. Therefore we present results based on individual data.
13. In Appendix 9.A this result will be considered in more detail, by comparing expectations and realizations directly. The distributions of the two variables will be compared. This allows non-parametric tests to be performed that investigate which location of the individual subjective distribution (mode or median), if any, is reported when answering the question about expectations.
14. Those who are not retiring according to any retirement definition.
15. Expectations are ordered from 1 to 5 where 1 is very poor and 5 very good. The dependent variable in the second model is expectations in $t - 1$ minus realizations in t of household income. The original nine possible categories (from -4 to 4 including zero) have been reduced to five by grouping the values $-4, -3, -2$ and $2, 3, 4$. The variable is then re-coded from 1 to 5 where 1 stands for 'expectations a lot lower than realizations', 2 stands for 'expectations somewhat lower than realizations', 3 stands for 'expectations equal to realizations', 4 stands for 'expectations somewhat higher than realizations', 5 stands for 'expectations a lot higher than realizations'. Which means that the higher the dependent variable the more unjustifiably optimistic the respondent.

16. This approach is similar to a 'difference in difference approach'. This means that extra regressors are included which are the product of the educational dummies and the indicator for mandatory retirement eligibility age.
17. We want shocks to precede the reporting of expectations. However, the pattern of this variable over age is identical to the one in Figure 9.2. However, some attrition is present between waves $t - 1$ and t. Hence the different number of point observations. We return to expectations in $t - 1$ in Table 9.6.
18. That is the number of observations with $c = j$ and $p_i = k$ and the given value of x_i.
19. We have also estimated Table 9.A1 conditional on several covariates of x_i such as gender and education. The results are confirmed.
20. Namely for $k = 1$, that is the first category, (9.5) implies (9.4), while for the last category $k = K = 5$, (9.6) implies (9.4).
21. Another option could be to predict only labor earnings. This, however, would be problematic for those who already partially entered an ER scheme and have a low labor income and a positive pension income.
22. Eligibility is derived from the answer to the question: 'Does the company you work for now have an ER scheme?'. Eligibility age is derived from the question: 'What is the minimum age to enter the ER scheme offered by your company?'
23. The model is specified only for predictions and is not meant to be an income model with causality relations.
24. This is done to allow the computation, for each panel wave, of the first difference of the PDV which is used in the estimation.

REFERENCES

Alessie, R. and A. Kapteyn (2001), 'Savings and Pensions in the Netherlands', *Ricerche Economiche*, **55**(1), pp. 61–82.

Alessie, R., M. Lindeboom and M. Mastrogiacomo (2004), 'Retirement Behaviour of Dutch Elderly Households, Diversity in Retirement Patterns across the Different Household Types', *Journal of Applied Econometrics*, special issue; forthcoming in J. Rust, N. DattaGupta and B. J. Christensen (eds), *The Econometrics of Social Insurance*, John Wiley and Sons.

Ameriks, J., A. Caplin and J. Leahy (2002), 'Retirement Consumption: Insights from a Survey', NBER working papers, 8375.

Andrietti, V. (1999), 'La Previdenza Complementare nell'Unione Europea', Fondazione Giacomo Brodolini.

Banks, J., R. Blundell and S. Tanner (1998), 'Is There a Retirement-Savings Puzzle?', *American Economic Review*, **88**(4), pp. 769–88.

Bernheim, B. D. (1987), 'The Timing of Retirement: A Comparison of Expectations and Realizations', NBER working papers, 2291.

Bernheim, B. D., J. Skinner and S. Weinberg (2001), 'What Accounts for the Variation in Retirement Wealth Among US Households?', *American Economic Review*, **91**(4), pp. 832–57.

Chan, S. and A. H. Stevens (2001), 'Retirement Incentives and Expectations', NBER working papers, 8082.

Coile, C. and J. Gruber (2000), 'Social Security Incentives for Retirement', NBER working papers, 7651.

Das, M. (1998), 'On Income Expectations and Other Subjective Data, A Microeconometric Analysis', Ph.D. Thesis, Tilburg University, Tilburg, The Netherlands.

Das, M., J. Dominitz and A. van Soest (1999), 'Comparing Predictions and Outcomes: Theory and Application to Income Changes', *Journal of the American Statistical Association*, **94**, pp. 75–85.

Das, M. and A. van Soest (1997), 'Expected and Realized Income Changes: Evidence from the Dutch Social Economic Panel', *Journal of Economic Behaviour and Organization*, **32**, pp. 137–54.

Das, M. and A. van Soest (1999), 'A Panel Data Model for Subjective Information on Household Income Growth', *Journal of Economic Behaviour and Organization*, **40**, pp. 409–26.

Das, M. and A. van Soest (2001), 'Expected Versus Realized Income Changes: A Test of The Rational Expectation Hypothesis', Discussion Paper, 105, Tilburg University, Center for Economic Research.

Disney, R. and S. Tanner (1999), 'What Can We Learn from Retirement Expectations Data', IFS working paper, W99–11.

Dominitz, J., J. Heinz and C. F. Manski (2002), 'Social Security Expectations and Retirement Saving Decisions', NBER working papers, 8718.

Gustman, A. L. and T. L. Steinmeier (2001), ' Imperfect Knowledge Retirement and Savings', NBER working papers, 8046.

Haider, S. J. and M. Stephens Jr. (2004), 'Is There a Retirement Consumption Puzzle? Evidence Using Subjective Retirement Expectations', NBER working papers, 10257.

Hurd, M. D. and S. Rohwedder (2003), 'The Retirement–Consumption Puzzle: Anticipated and Actual Declines in Spending at Retirement', NBER working papers, 9586.

Kalwij, A. (2003), 'Consumption and Income Around the Time of Births', mimeo.

Kapteyn, A. and K. de Vos (1997), 'Social Security and Retirement in the Netherlands', NBER working papers, 6135.

Lindeboom, M. (1999), 'Het Arbeidsmarktgedrag van Oudere Werknemers', VU Boekhandel Uitgeverij Amsterdam.

Lusardi, A. (1996), 'Permanent Income, Current Income and Consumption: Evidence from Two Panel Datasets', *Journal of Business and Economic Statistics*, **14**(1), pp. 81–90.

Lusardi, A. (2000), 'Explaining Why So Many People Do Not Save', Working paper of the University of Chicago, Harris School of Public Policy.

Mastrogiacomo, M., R. Alessie and M. Lindeboom (2004): 'Retirement Behaviour of Dutch Elderly Households', *Journal of Applied Econometrics*, Special Issue: 'The Econometrics of Social Insurance', ed. by J. Rust, N. DattaGupta, and B. J. Christensen. John Wiley and Sons Ltd, **19**, pp. 777–93.

Index